For Willia

with adv

Rochester April 5 2019

Dorinda Outram.

FOUR FOOLS IN THE AGE OF REASON

Studies in Early Modern German History

H. C. Erik Midelfort, Editor

DORINDA OUTRAM

FOUR FOOLS

IN THE

AGE

OF

REASON

*Laughter, Cruelty, and Power
in Early Modern Germany*

UNIVERSITY OF VIRGINIA PRESS
Charlottesville and London

University of Virginia Press
© 2019 by the Rector and Visitors of the University of Virginia
All rights reserved
Printed in the United States of America on acid-free paper

First published 2019

1 3 5 7 9 8 6 4 2

Library of Congress Cataloging-in-Publication

Names: Outram, Dorinda, author.
Title: Four fools in the age of reason : laughter, cruelty, and power
in early modern Germany / Dorinda Outram.
Description: Charlottesville : University of Virginia Press, 2019. | Series: Studies
in early modern German history | Includes bibliographical references and index.
Identifiers: LCCN 2018046953 | ISBN 9780813942018 (cloth : alk. paper) |
ISBN 9780813942025 (e-book)
Subjects: LCSH: Fools and jesters—German—History—18th century. | Germany—
Court and courtiers—History—18th century. | Germany—Court and courtiers—
Biography. | Gundling, Jacob Paul, Freiherr von, 1673–1731. | Morgenstern, Salomon
Jakob, 1706–1785. | Fröhlich, Joseph, 1694–1757. | Prosch, Peter, 1744–1804. |
Germany—Social life and customs—18th century.
Classification: LCC GT3670.5.G4 O87 2019 | DDC 792.702/809—dc23

LC record available at https://lccn.loc.gov/2018046953

Cover art: Fool's Cap Map of the World. (Ashmolean Museum)

You have to find a way to put the extremes together, not necessarily by diminishing the extremity of each one, but to form the art of transition. . . . You have to keep the extremes but find the link, always find the link, so that there is an organic whole.

   —Daniel Barenboim to Edward Said, 2004

Contents

Acknowledgments

Individual authorship is a polite fantasy. Many people have contributed to the making of this book over a long period of time, often more than they were aware of. First of all must come Martin Gierl, who would not let me dedicate this book to him. Without him this book would not exist. It was he who read an earlier version of chapter 1 and told me I had not an article but a book. His steadfast support sustained through difficult times. The hospitality that he and Michaela Hohkamp extended in Berlin and Göttingen did much to reassure me of the joys of writing, reading, and simply talking history. I would also like to acknowledge the support given to this project by H. C. Erik Midelfort, who accepted a letter and a packet of typescript nearly out of the blue, and by Beth Plummer, who advised me to send the letter and the packet. Bill Bell, Ritchie Robertson, and Jürgen Schlumbohm sustained my spirits, and, last but not least, Hans Bödeker provided, at a difficult time, constant intellectual stimulation, mixed with kindness and humor. Anthony LaVopa asked questions. Answering them greatly improved this book.

It is rare to express fondness for an institution, but I will do so now: the Herzog August Bibliothek in Wolfenbüttel showed itself a wise, kind, and humane institution in its daily dealings with scholars, and on special occasions that I will not detail here. Its magnificent holdings were a constant support and delight during a project that often required obscure materials. Jill Bepler, leader of the Fellowship program at the library, maintains an extraordinary mixture of moral sensibility and practical efficaciousness. Frau Gerlinde Strauss dealt with the numerous problems that arose during my two stays at the library in 2015 and 2014 with efficiency moderated with *Schwung*. The reading room of the library became a home away from home, and it was there that I began to understand something of the life of fools. And historians.

At the Lichtenberg-Kolleg of the University of Göttingen, I was given four uninterrupted months in the fall and winter of 2016 to put the finishing touches to this book. Whether this confidence was well placed is for the reader to judge. Martin van Gelderen and Dominik Hünniger's leadership in both practical and intellectual matters is a treat to behold. Seminars and reading groups create an intellectual community. In spite of Göttingen's weather, many friendships were formed here

At the Staatliches Museum in Dresden, which contains the so-called Grünes Gewolbe, I was astounded by the generosity of curator Dirk Weber, who offered to show me the two extraordinary figures of Joseph Fröhlich that are reproduced in these pages and to do so at a time when the museum was closed to the general public.

I would also like to thank my Department Chair, Professor Matthew Lenoe, for supporting my requests for leave in 2015 and 2016, and the University of Rochester for granting them.

FOUR FOOLS IN THE AGE OF REASON

Introduction

Numerus Stultorum Infinitus Est

The fool does not necessarily inhabit a beautiful or romantic world.
—Enid Welsford, *The Fool: His Social and Literary History* (1935)

This is a book about fools in the Age of Reason, that time running from the end of the seventeenth century to the French Revolution, which began in 1789. It is mostly concerned with fools and fooling at princely courts in Austria and the German states, with sidelights on England, France, and Russia. It tries to understand the nature of these courts through a reconceptualization of fooling, and it puts that fooling against some of the central concerns of the Enlightenment. It examines the life of four famous fools—Peter Prosch (1744–1804), Salomon Jacob Morgenstern (1708–1785), Joseph Fröhlich (1694–1757), and Jacob Paul Gundling (1673–1731), as case studies of the way humor—often black humor—was used as a way of making human community, controlling human waywardness, and strengthening power. Cruelty and the exploitation of the weak by the strong were integral to this humor and will give rise to some difficult moments for readers. This book also carries along with it some thoughts sparked by the writing of history in general, and of a book about fools in particular. It ends with the story of how I, as a fool, came to write this book about fools, a story that contains both cruelty and joy.

This is the first time that these four fools have been studied together, and rescued, I hope, from their half-lives as literary and historical curiosities. It is also the first time that their lives as fools have been examined in the context of Enlightenment, court, and power. Their discoveries about the Enlightenment form the fabric of this book.

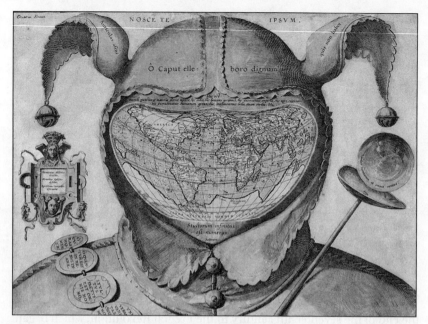

Fool's Cap Map of the World. Dating from the 1590s, the map shows the traditional attributes of the fool: cap, bells, and mirror. The picture also shows Latin mottos, such as "Nosce te ipsum" (Know thyself) and "Numerus stultorum infinitus est" (The number of fools is infinite). (Ashmolean Museum)

Even that most gloomy book of the Bible, Ecclesiastes, reassures us, first of all, that the number of fools is infinite (1:15). I am therefore a fool (doubly, for it is also true that anyone who writes about fools must be a fool too), and you too are a fool, dear reader. This book enrolls us all in the company of the foolish, and allows us, as fools in the present, to understand other fools in the past. I make no apology for enrolling myself as a character in this book.

In what voice will we speak about our discoveries? Surely, a quiet one. For this will not be a history built around "controversies," where historians lose their tempers, raise their voices, and parade their expertise until it almost dies on a forced march.[1] It will also, on the other hand, not make claims, even in a quiet voice, to detached clarity. Historians have often presumed that we can see the past more clearly, can look down upon the fair field of folk, when at a distance, and that distance is a prerequisite for the writing of history.[2] I do not believe that. It is a statement that smacks of hubris. How can any human creature lay claim to detachment?

Four Fools in the Age of Reason

What are we studying when we study the history of fools and foolishness? We are studying the lives and work of experts in foolishness, professional entertainers who were by turns buffoons, jesters, and poets, who worked using a combination of crude physical humor and pointed repartee, at large and small courts all over Germany, from the end of the seventeenth to the end of the eighteenth century. These were not the creatures dressed in cap and bells of the medieval and Renaissance periods. They were not the Fool in *King Lear*. Yet they were still called fools and called themselves fools and had some of the functions of fools, such as giving counsel to rulers.

Laughter was their weapon and tool. Yet as I worked on this book it became clear to me that although laughter was what fools elicited, and what they wielded, fools were, on another level, embodiments: embodiments of contradiction. They were, often in the same person, humble and companions of princes, foolish and wise, buffoons and poets, public and private, archaic and modern, scholars and practical jokers, honored and dishonored. These contradictions stand at the stress points in the culture at large, stress points about the definition of status and the meaning of power. This is the historical value of studying fools. We learn about the pleasures and dangers of laughter in a way that is sobering because laughter is not simple. The pleasures and dangers of laughter are also the pleasures and dangers of power.

Or: do we have perhaps to undergo a rebuke to foolishness and face the fact that we might be studying what the German Jewish philosopher Walter Benjamin (1892–1940) called the "rubbish-heap of history"[3]—in other words, the things that no one else thinks worthwhile to study: the jokes that can no longer be understood, the crafts that are no longer practiced, and the roles that are no longer played? For we have to account for the fact that especially in the twentieth and twenty-first centuries, few if any professional historians have occupied themselves with fools. Perhaps the role of fool seems so utterly over and done with that it is not even quaint anymore and seems to be without legacy for the present. It may be that not only is the particular humor of fooling incomprehensible to us now but that it is embedded in now lost relationships of power and emotion. Or it may be that the story of fooling has simply been written out.

Yet other historians have picked over other rubbish heaps. History written from the perspective of the New Historicism movement of the 1980s, in books such as Natalie Zemon Davis's *The Return of Martin Guerre*, Robert

Darnton's *The Great Cat Massacre and Other Episodes in French Cultural History,* and Stephen Greenblatt's *Renaissance Self-Fashioning from More to Shakespeare* are distant from the "big history" of wars, price curves, the conquest of continents, and the making of scientific revolutions. They speak instead of peasants and apprentices, struggles over land, the inner workings of marriage, manners, mistaken identity, and cruel rituals involving cats. New Historicism would seem ideally suited for the study of fools. So why has this not happened? Why has no recent historian (except this fool) pulled a fool from historical oblivion?

What follows in answer to this question is speculation. First, fools probably seem more distant from us than do peasants and apprentices, each of whom have modern representatives. Fools, on the other hand, are surely a dead end, surely the very type of *Abfall.* No one is a fool now as these fools were, and no amount of drawing parallels between historical fools, who had the ruler and his court as audience, and television satirists, who have a mass public as theirs, will alter this fact. Studying fools perhaps also seems unlikely to help the historian draw a moral for the present or fulfill any sort of critical function. This is one challenge. It is also not surprising that no historian now wants to get close to that obscure, palpitating, nexus between humility and power that was the life of the fool. The study of the fool, as history writing swings back toward the grand narrative, seems to be so remote, so specialized, so *over,* as to be unlikely to illuminate the great patterns. (This, however, says something about the way in which professional historians designate something as specialized, when in fact there is no topic that does not illuminate some other one.) And, surely most important, historians have feared the contamination of foolishness. She who writes about fools must surely be one. For all these reasons, historians have been loath to be identified with the study of the *Abfall* that is the fool and foolishness. It is also the case that our culture sits atop many "suppressed narratives," histories that have not merely been written out of the record but for which there is now no human personality or group ready and able to receive them. It is the objective of this book to show that the study of the fool is the study not of the rubbish heap of history but of the gold mine of contradiction.

Fools and fooling attracted their first historians in the very age of their disappearance, just as the field notes of the anthropologist mark the end of the authentic life of the tribe. The great *Geschichte der Hofnarren* (History of court fools) was written by Karl Friedrich Flögel (1729–1788) and post-humously published in 1789, a year that has often been designated as the opening of the modern era.[4] This 510-page work of mingled heroic compilation, humane analysis, and vivid writing not only resumes most other contemporary writing about fools but also covers fools from most countries and all eras. It can reasonably be said to have influenced every subsequent history of fools and fooling, including this one. (Flögel does not write about any fool still living in 1789, a pity since one of the great fools, Peter Prosch (see chapter 4), was then still alive and working). So influential was Flögel's work that new, updated and enlarged editions were published in the nineteenth century, and one as late as 1914. Flögel's work even influenced the Danish philosopher Søren Kierkegaard (1813–1855). In this century, there is even a paperback edition.

Flögel's interests were not confined to fools but ranged widely within the realm of the comic. *Geschichte der Hofnarren,* however, has stayed in print longer than any of the other works that Flögel conceived as its companions.[5] It is worth noting that Flögel was writing during the Enlightenment, an age deeply concerned with the construction of a "science of man," the encyclopedic bringing together of all knowledge about mankind. He may well have seen the mapping of humor as part of that construction, and the ability to laugh as part of the human spirit.

Who was Flögel? Biographical details are hard to discover. But we know that he was born in the small Silesian market town of Jauer in eastern Germany in 1729, went through the ravages of First Silesian War, and died in 1788 in the larger Silesian town of Liegnitz. As a small child, he was fascinated by the municipal fool in Jauer. He acquired more formal education at the Maria-Magdalena Gymnasium in the provincial capital at Breslau, and later at the University of Halle, where he read theology with the famous scholar Siegmund Jakob Baumgarten (1706–1757). From 1761 he taught in the Maria-Magdalena Gymnasium, becoming its prorector. In 1766, he published a German translation of Alexander Gerard's *Enquiry into Taste.* In 1773 he became superintendent of schools for his birthplace and in the following year was appointed as professor of philosophy at the Ritterakademie zu Liegnitz, an institution founded by Frederick William I of Prussia as a university for the aristocracy.

Flögel's life looks like that of a more successful than average provincial intellectual. He was clearly not a man to have used words without attending to their meaning. So what does he mean by calling the book for which he is best known a "history" (*Geschichte*)? Flögel was someone well aware of the past. He believed that the past was different from the present. In his *Geschichte der komischen Litteratur* (1784), he wrote that every writer carries "the sign of their time on their forehead."[6] Yet at the end of the eighteenth century, the terms to describe writing about the past were still in flux. It was long time, for example, before Johann Heinrich Zedler's authoritative *Universal-Lexikon* replaced the term *Historie* with *Geschichte,* and by 1775 Johann Christoph Adelung's *Wörterbuch* was still having to argue that history was "true," that is, not fabricated, and that it could form a coherent whole.[7]

Let us turn to the influential writings on history of Flögel's Halle teacher Baumgarten to find where the meaning of "history" was being worked out.[8] Baumgarten (1706–1757) had argued, against the Halle philosopher Christian Wolff, that the same methods were to be applied to sacred and to secular history; and that history could produce certain knowledge—an important argument when presuppositions about history's lack of certainty drove much of the contemporary critique against it. In other words, in Baumgarten's account, history could be worth writing.

Coherence was important. History to Baumgarten was not a dry recitation of facts or events but rather a "comprehensible and lively presentation" formed by "an appropriate narrative coherence." Such an account was innately pleasurable because it was "in accord with the wise purposes of the creator of human nature." Even the use of anecdotes in history was supported by Baumgarten's observation that revelation consisted "mainly of stories." Baumgarten thought the advantage of biography was that the individual's life, rather than abstract concepts, provided coherence. Yet coherence also required authenticated evidence. Documents had to be conned with a critical eye for forgery, eyewitness accounts had to be scrutinized for reliability, and the character and number of witnesses ascertained. Later reports had to be compared with earlier ones. The above phrases could stand in as a description of the methodology of the *Geschichte der Hofnarren*. Flögel wrote mightily as a historian and used "stories" or anecdotes throughout his work, all of which were gathered around individuals who provided coherence to his account of the history of court fools in all times and (most) places.

Baumgarten's work on history had grown more urgent around the time that Flögel was his student. He knew that Deists and freethinkers had made history their most effective weapon against Christianity. He was convinced that freethinking and atheism could be dispelled by systematic historical knowledge. Knowledge of history was salutary to belief, providing proof of revelation and providence. From the late 1730s, Baumgarten recognized history as an alternative form of authority capable of raising questions about dogma, or, for that matter, the received interpretation of Scripture. He thus dismantled the barrier between history and dogma to fashion a moderate version of history that relativized neither revelation nor belief.

Critical history was thus foundational for true Protestant belief. And it could also be pressed into the service of the fools' history. Baumgarten's own writings showed abundant information on the practices, customs, sciences, and agriculture of peoples around the world in the same way that Flögel's book looked at the history and practices of fools and foolishness in many diverse peoples. In turn, this agenda linked the histories of fools to the grand Enlightenment project of the "science of man," the gathering together of knowledge concerning mankind from the medical to the geographical to the historical.[9] This is the force field within which Flögel constructed his *Geschichte der Hofnarren*. What looks like the history of a frivolous subject turns out to have deep roots in the historiography that arose from the religious conflicts of the sixteenth and seventeenth centuries in Europe and left it still searching for certainty and moderation in the eighteenth .

How are we therefore to evaluate Flögel's value as a historical source? An important question, since Flögel's book has constituted a mine of information for all subsequent writers on the topic, including this one. We can say that the earlier sections of the book, which cover the activity of fools in the ancient world, are characterized by an extraordinary density of sources, a density so great that one wonders how they were obtained in Jauer, or even in Liegnitz. As we approach the period in which we are interested, the attributions grow thinner, and he relies heavily on contemporary sources, whose authors were witness to the events they describe. Such sources could include the waspish Prussian satirist David Fassmann (1685-1744). Fassmann, a well-known writer who had briefly held the office of newspaper reader at the Prussian court, had written a hostile biography of his predecessor, Jacob Paul Gundling, who had been treated by monarch and court alike as a fool. Flögel is well aware of Fassmann's prejudice against Gundling and controls for it in his own discussion of the text. Techniques of documentary criticism were thus not unknown to him. He also writes in the latter part of the book about people who were well known and had only recently died. Too great a deviation from the truth about them would immediately call forth a host of contrary living witnesses. Flögel also summarized the major contemporary works on fools by other writers, such as Jean-Baptiste Lucotte Du Tilliot, and thus positioned himself as a storehouse of fool-lore. He also kept up with the travel literature. For the Russian court fools of Peter the Great and Empress Anna, for example, he used the recently published eyewitness accounts of the Russian court in F. C. Weber's *Das veränderte Ruszland*.[10] In chapter 6, the discussion of the tomb of the Pomeranian fool Claus Hintze, he seems to be giving the result either of his own or his informant's firsthand observation.[11]

Flögel's was the most influential text on the history of fools from the late eighteenth century to the First World War. Nearly 150 years later another text, published in 1935 and reprinted in 1962, took over its position in the English-speaking world.[12] Enid Welsford delighted in recounting how her publisher commissioned the work on fools, telling her that she was the ideal person to write on the subject, that is, a truly foolish historian. One bows to another. Though the 1935 book represented the culmination of her thinking about fools, much material about them can be found in the pages of her earlier book, the classic *The Court Masque* (1927), in which she sees the masque—theater combined with singing and formal dancing—as connected to the survival of folklore and ritual from the preliterate past—a theme that will be explored in chapter 3 of this book, devoted to the Saxon fool Joseph Fröhlich. Welsford describes the masque as "strangely like those pantomimic ritual dances of which we hear so much from the students of comparative religion."[13] Here, she acknowledges the influence of her friend and colleague, the classicist and anthropologist Jane Harrison (1850–1928), and two experts on world oral literatures, her friends Nora Kershaw (1891–1972) and Hector Monro Chadwick (1870–1947), to whom Kershaw was married. For Welsford, anthropology, literature, and history were closely allied.

Welsford lived all her adult life in the intellectual hothouse of interwar Newnham College, Cambridge, at that period open only to women.[14] Beginning as a scholar of Old English and Norse, in 1918, shortly after the death of her brother Geoffrey in the First World War, she changed her field of interest to later periods of literature, became a Fellow of Newnham in 1921, and was University Lecturer in English from 1928 to 1959. A staunch and committed Anglican, she was no friend to the modern world. Intrinsic to her work is a strong sense of nostalgia, which makes it in sense and style very different from Flögel's work, on which she is still reliant for content. She heeds the call of I. A. Richards's new style of literary criticism, pointing out that Richards in his *Science and Poetry* describes "a difficult and dangerous mental situation created by the contemporary dominance of the scientific outlook and the disappearance of religion which he assumes to be inevitable and complete. He hopes that we may be saved by poetry, if poetry can be cut loose from 'beliefs,' a term which for him includes far more than religious dogmas."[15] To her, in other words, her own day was one where sacred things were already beginning to vanish, and memory signified loss. Her social and religious concerns and her deep nostalgia came together to inform the 1935 book on fools. She did not, however, possess a rosy view of the world of the fool. "There is no need for sentimental regret," she writes of the passing of the fool. Yet, in commenting on the current age, in the context of an analysis of Erasmus's classic 1511 *In Praise of Folly*, she writes:

> To the child of the Renaissance man was essentially great, and nothing except his own inertia need hinder steady progress in scientific knowledge and complete attainment of earthly happiness. To the medieval thinker, man was essentially vain, and it was only when he knew himself for the fool that he was, that he could become the lowly recipient of Divine Wisdom. Erasmus stood between two worlds and saw his vision of Folly. He was on the losing side. Now in our turn we begin to feel heretical misgivings as we listen to the "high astounding terms," of our scientific humanists, who for all their enlightenment cannot show us how to provide all workers with work to do, or comforts to enjoy, or an adequate motive for living peaceably together in a stable social order.

This nostalgia makes Welsford very different from Flögel, who saw his fools rather more as part of a carnival of the comic, and who assumed that laughter was deeply rooted in human nature. Nostalgia, as a critical tool that contrasts the lost past with the unsatisfactory present, plays little role in his history.

Welsford's nostalgic idealization of the social and poetic fabric of the Shakespearean past is noteworthy. After a brilliant analysis of Lear and his Fool, she writes:

Shakespeare was indebted to his contemporaries as well as to his ancestors. In his day, kings and fools were no mere historically ancient institutions, invested with an ill-defined glamor; they were still part of the practical structure of contemporary society and the intellectual structure of a living religion. The king was revered as the anointed representative of the Divine Government of the world, the fool was laughed at as a popular entertainer, and moralized over as an embodiment of the Christian paradox. Therefore when Shakespeare decided to communicate his reflections on the human tragedy he could make use of figures who were already partially stylized, and invested with symbolic significance in everyday life . . . he could produce profoundly serious art without any of the self-conscious aestheticism which is such an unhappy result of the present divorce between men of the world and members of the intelligentsia; and also of the fact that the all-pervasive worship of money and science together is rapidly depriving our institutions of all religious and poetic value.[16]

Welsford, however, is well capable of seeing that

the Fool does not necessarily inhabit a beautiful or romantic world; on the contrary, the world may be very well adapted to his nature, which is often greedy, grasping, dirty and heartless. . . . The fool's trade was too often a brutal one. His history is in many respects a striking illustration of human callousness. Yet that is not the whole truth of the matter. It is not quite clear that the change of mental climate which was so fatal to the fool is proving in the long run altogether wholesome to ourselves. [For] . . . who is to laugh at us and remind us of mortal inadequacy? Who is to present our humanists and dictators with the Cap and Bells? A good many things have been said and done in the last century and in our own day to attract the Evil Eye; perhaps a little more nonsense and self-mockery might have brought us better luck.[17]

Welsford's work has enjoyed high popularity from the 1930s to the present day. It has also influenced several stage productions. Accounting for its success is not difficult. As well as the interestingly told histories of fools and the exegesis of *King Lear,* her nostalgia may well have chimed in with the mood of the postslump 1930s, and then of the 1960s, the time of imperial divestment, which left Britain unsure of its international role for the first time since the mid-eighteenth century. But however well-known Welsford's work, it probably made it more difficult to write a history of fools. The relentless coupling of court fool and nostalgia made the book popular and timely, but it did not lead to, for example, an analysis of the courts themselves. Welsford was, rather, seeking the authentic, and in nostalgia for the fool she finds that fictional domain.[18]

Beatrice Otto's book *Fools Are Everywhere* is mentioned here because it is the most recent full-length treatment in the English language of the court fool. The book overwhelms the reader in a deluge of often unrelated anecdotes about fools around the globe. For Otto, the fool and fooling are universal. She has, she writes, a passion for the court jester:

> I argue that he is very much a universal character, more or less interchangeable regardless of the time or culture in which he happens to cavort-the same techniques, the same functions, the same license. . . . The evidence points to his having existed across the globe and across history, in most of the civilizations of the world. . . . [B]y and large he seems to have arisen spontaneously and independently within societies . . . suggesting that he fulfills a deep and widespread social need. The frequency of his occurrence, and the diversity of the cultures he has thrived in, make it hard to see how his universal nature can easily be refuted.[19]

Otto here swallows the Enlightenment ideas of universalism, and notably that of the universal human subject. It was in this vein that the famous Scots philosopher David Hume (1711–1776) remarked that the study of history allows us to "discover the constant and universal principles of human nature."[20] It is the program of this book to regard human nature as, on the contrary, infinitely variable, as far from constant and universal, and to regard its detail as the historian's most precious resource. The struggle between universalism and relativism that this implies was begun in the Enlightenment itself and now plays a key role in current debates over multiculturalism.[21] Are the Chinese fools, for example, with whom Otto spends so much time, to be valued, as she writes, as examples of the same universalism, of the universal tendency among mankind to laugh, and to laugh at the same jokes; or are they to be understood as uniquely Chinese? Otto's anecdotal method seems to absolve her from answering that question and from investigating the specific courts in which they and her other court fools had their being. To investigate each court she mentions would rapidly bring to light their differences and particularities. That the number of fools is infinite does not mean that one cannot make claims about fools that relate to specific times, places, and people. To challenge the assumption of universal human history, and a universal human penchant for laughter, would involve writing an entirely different history of fools than that produced by Otto, a history that would critique the Enlightenment rather than accepting its values. It is my hope to do exactly this, in spite of the fact that I—paradoxically—make no exemption for myself to the universality of foolishness. The universality of mankind's foolishness is the only universality to which I will cling. I want, in the end, to make claims about fools that relate to the specific times of the European Enlightenment, to local places and individual people, and that do not take for granted the universality of humor, or of specific forms of it. To look at the history of fools and fooling in specificity rescues it from its current outlier status and enlarges both that history and all the other histories in which it comes into contact.

Flögel, Welsford, and Otto proceed by way of anecdotes, which in Welsford's case, as well as in Otto's, are often drawn from Flögel. Flögel's importance as a source of anecdote cannot be overstated. We may take the example of the fool Claus Hintze (d. 1599) (misspelled "Hinsse" in Otto), fool to Herzog Johann Friedrich of Stettin (d. 1600), whose native village of Buttendorf was renamed Hintzendorf in his honor. Johann Friedrich also granted it freedom in perpetuity from the ducal wolf hunt. The story has its origin in Flögel and passes from Flögel in 1789 to Welsford in 1935 to Otto in 2001.[22]

In maintaining unbroken this chain of anecdote, all our historians are using an important genre. The term "anecdote" has a very long history. It was first used by the seventh-century writer Procopius of Caesarea. Procopius, the author of a "Secret History" of the Byzantine emperors, meant by the term a fact or detail that was unknown to the public.[23] By the eighteenth century that fact or detail was still a private one, but it often became embedded in a longer narrative, in the so-called "secret histories" beloved by the eighteenth century. Otto treats anecdotes as straightforward little stories. But the "little story" often provided a clinching point in a larger history. Often its humor arose from paradox. Not surprisingly, contemporaries were undecided about the value and propriety of anecdotes. Some argued that paradox made anecdote immoral, in the sense of it being difficult to locate the truth in one side or the other.

We can see this played out in the relationship between the famous author, critic, and dictionary maker Dr. Samuel Johnson (1709–1784) and his friend and biographer James Boswell (1740–1795). Boswell's anecdotal *Life of Johnson* stands out in marked contrast to Johnson's own aesthetic doctrine, which approaches the taxonomic. In Johnson's 1759 novella *Rasselas,* for example, the character Imlac remarks: "This business of the poet is to examine, not the individual, but the species; to remark general properties and large appearances."[24] Boswell, on the contrary, portrayed Johnson through an accumulation of anecdotes, the "individual," which were arranged carefully to reveal Johnson's character, a "large appearance." It was not obvious that Boswell would proceed in this way. Anecdotes were regarded by contemporaries as a very minor sort of history. Yet because anecdotes were history, even if minor history, they were valuable because they were well within the realm of the verifiable. In piling up anecdotes Boswell was thus ensuring himself against challenges to his account of his friend's life. It is in this sense, as in others we have previously discussed, that Flögel's *Geschichte der Hofnarren* is a true "history" by the standards of his time. In this history, moreover, the anecdote allows an appeal to a common humanity. The affective power of anecdotes is very strong and serves the additional function of enlisting audience sympathies and keeping them in place over a very long work.

Marcel Henaff has also argued that the anecdote involves what is "circumstantial, trivial, unimportant, and even—if one can say so—what is left to the scrapheap of history."[25] (Yet who is to say what is trivial and what not?) I would argue, however, that anecdotes are not fiction, and certainly not part of the scrapheap; they are history. They report something that actually happened and therefore come into the category of the verifiable, however odd, strange, or "trivial" they may seem. And not only are they in the category of the verifiable, but they almost always reveal something of importance about a grander narrative structure. This book therefore will carry on this tradition. Writing can be seen as bird cage or cathedral, grand narrative or anecdote. This book will veer, unapologetically, from one to another, believing that they are intrinsically entangled.

"In unser aufgeklärten Zeit / Kann meines Lebens Seltenheit vielleicht noch manchem dienen" (In our enlightened time / my peculiar life can perhaps serve many).[26] So run some lines from a much longer poem written by the itinerant fool Peter Prosch (chapter 4). Who better than a fool to take as our companion into the tangled wood of history writing about the Enlightenment, sometimes called the Age of Reason?

But what is Enlightenment? How would we recognize an "enlightened time"? A famous question. In December 1783, the Berlin enlightened journal the *Berlinische Monatsschrift* published an article on marriage reform by an obscure theologian, Johann Friedrich Zöllner. (1753–1804). In a footnote (probably the most important footnote in the history of thought), he asked, "What is Enlightenment? This question, which is almost as important as 'what is truth?' should indeed be answered before one begins enlightening! And still I have never found it answered!" His contemporaries in fact rushed to answer Zöllner with articles in the *Monatsschrift*. So many answered that it soon became obvious that there was no single definition of the Enlightenment. Debate on this question continued for years and spilled over into other journals.

Let's look in more detail at some of the essays that appeared in the *Monatsschrift*. Karl Leonhard Reinhold (1758–1823), for example, gave a very broad definition: "I think that Enlightenment means, in general, the making of rational men out of men who are capable of rationality. The sum total of all the institutions and means that lead to this great end gives the word enlightenment its broadest sphere of meaning." Reinhold saw ordinary people as intrinsically able to become enlightened: "In every cultured nation, which consists of scholars and masses, the means of popular Enlightenment are constantly at hand. . . . For every truth there are channels of communication always present in the minds of the philosopher and the masses. It can happen that the philosopher never finds them or never wants to use them, and that certain truths must therefore remain eternal secrets for the masses; but at least the fault does not lie in the capacity of the masses for reason." In spite of its tribute to the presumptive rationality of the people, therefore, Reinhold still thinks that philosophers should be their guides and educators rather than ordinary people being trusted enough to find their own way to the "eternal secrets" of rationality. Paradoxically, the people are both capable of reasoning and yet have to accept the secrecy adopted by the philosopher.[27]

Within the year, the great Prussian philosopher Immanuel Kant (1726–1804) also submitted an essay to the *Monatsschrift* in answer to Zöllner's question. Published in December 1784, Kant's text has remained the best known of all those submitted, in spite of its many problems and contradictions. For Kant, Enlightenment, in his stirring opening words, is "Man's release from his self-incurred immaturity," by which Kant means the ability to think for oneself without guidance from another. He believed that the free use of reason should be taken as far as possible. He quoted the ancient motto, *Sapere aude!* (Dare to know!), and asserted it as the motto of the Enlightenment.[28]

Yet, as one reads further into the essay, it becomes clear that Kant was well aware that the unbounded development of reason, when carried too far in unlimited questioning, could dissolve the social, religious, and political order into chaos. Kant attempts to solve the problem by declaring: "The public use of man's reason must always be free, and it alone can bring about Enlightenment among men; the private use of reason may be quite often seriously restricted."[29] In what he calls the public sphere, where people are free from the obligations of their calling, subjects are free to write or speak critically. In what he calls the private sphere, subjects have an actual duty to restrain the expression of critical political judgement, in the interest of upholding the ruler's will and lessening the likelihood of a descent into chaos. The curate must not criticize the bishop, the soldier, the superior officer, even if their commands seem absurd. It becomes clear (though this is not elucidated by Kant himself) that the enlightened person is one hopelessly torn between public and private, and is thus without a secure moral center.

In the end, however, Kant sees Enlightenment as paradoxical: "a strange and unexpected tendency in human affairs, so that generally, when it is considered at large, almost everything in it is almost paradoxical. A high degree of civic freedom appears advantageous to the spiritual freedom of a people and yet it places before it insuperable restrictions; a lesser degree of civil freedom, in contrast, creates the room for spiritual freedom to spread to its full capacity."[30] Discussions of Enlightenment by other authors who contributed to the debate in the *Berliner Monatsschrift* could equally be relied on to refer to the making of paradoxical divisions and distinctions (see chapter 5). The Jewish philosopher Moses Mendelssohn (1729–1786), for example, began his contribution to the debate by making an important point about language: "The words enlightenment, culture and education are newcomers to our language. They currently belong only to literary discourse. The masses scarcely understand them." Mendelssohn went on to make distinctions and divisions by dividing "civil Enlightenment," which must adjust itself according to the ranks of society it addresses, from "human enlightenment," which paid heed neither to social distinctions nor to the maintenance of social order.[31] Just as Kant splits humanity into the public and the private, Reinhold separates people and philosopher, providing no bridge between them, so in the same way nothing ensures that these two types of Enlightenment described by Mendelssohn will in fact complement each other. Because of this, paradox also enters in: "Certain truths," Mendelssohn wrote, "that are useful to man as man, can at times be harmful to him as a citizen."[32] The Enlightenment, it would seem, can be defined only by divisions in experience, divisions that created, as Kant was well aware, nothing but paradox.[33]

Debates about Enlightenment were seldom resolved. Helpfully, Kant points to the paradoxical nature of the Enlightenment as one reason for this. Where is truth, in the midst of paradox? For, most of the time, Enlightenment beliefs and Enlightenment thinkers and Enlightenment people did unresolved and unresolvable battle with their opponents. The "enlightened times" seemed for many to constitute an attack on revealed religion, for example. There were others who saw its principles, so high-minded in theory, as coercive in practice. The compulsion inherent in the idea of a universal human subject, to take one example, was quickly spotted by such Enlightenment thinkers as Johann Gottfried Herder (1744–1803), who rejected the idea that there existed a universal human nature somehow unchanged by history, geography, and climate, without, in other words, *Seltenheit* (peculiarity), to quote the fool Peter Prosch. Herder indicted his own time: "The general philosophical, philanthropic tone of our century, which wishes to extend our own idea of virtue and happiness to each distant nation, to even the remotest age of history . . . has taken words for works, Enlightenment for happiness, greater sophistication for virtues, and in this way invented the fiction of the general amelioration of the world."[34]

Other issues also underlay this condemnation of the Enlightenment. There were struggles over religious tolerance as mass religious movements such as Pietism, Moravianism, Hassidism, and Methodism got under way. Philosophers such as John Locke (1632–1704), David Hume, and Kant debated perception and cognition, and the nature of the human person. Political economists, and cameralists in the German lands, debated whether economies could be made prosperous by state intervention, by free trade, or by mercantilist relations between colonies and metropole. Thousands entered into debates on the social importance of education.

More people became more literate, read more books and newspapers, and thus transmitted Enlightenment ideas through society. In many countries in western Europe, the economy prospered, paradoxically, in "enlightened times," by the use of slave labor to cultivate the luxury commodities produced by European colonies in the Caribbean. Until the end of the century, few fought against the institution of slavery while, paradoxically, many proclaimed the dignity of man. These are just some of the major controversies that occupied the men and women of the Enlightenment and that give their time its *"Seltenheit."* We will discover more as this book proceeds, as we see the fools also enmeshed in the paradoxes of the "enlightened times."

Kant guarantees us that paradox is the character of the Enlightenment. It is also the character of the fool.[35] He resumed within himself a life—and a historical memory—that showed him by turns as riddling and truth-telling, scholar and butt, public and private, modern and archaic, entertainer and counsellor, poet and scatological humorist. How does this paradoxical character sit with the well-known opinion of the French philosopher Michel Foucault that the Enlightenment period was characterized by a "taxonomical urge"? Taxonomy, the study of classification, and especially the classification of natural entities like plants, animals, or rocks, or even human races, is not, after all, about paradox. It is, if I may resume more than two centuries of debate in a bold paragraph, about division (species are divided from each other) and definition (in order to make judgment about species allocation, individuals must be defined in virtue of chosen characteristics). Foucault's opinion has itself come under attack, most recently and most fiercely by Jonathan Sheehan and Dror Wahrman, who point out the extent to which taxonomy was unable to deal with the growing problems of describing "life" and its development through time. The great taxonomist Carl Linnaeus, for example, admitted that his famous classification system was only a heuristic model.[36] On the other hand, I think it impossible to deny the sheer amount of energy in the Enlightenment that went into the making of systems of classification. I argue in this book that the Enlightenment took these impulses of division and definition and spread them widely from the zoological garden, herbarium, greenhouse, and anatomy museum, into social and intellectual life. I will be arguing this in chapter 3 on the Dresden *Hofnarr* Joseph Fröhlich, and especially in chapter 5. There, I attempt to account for the end of fooling at the close of the century by using the case study of the increasing attempts by German theater reformers to act taxonomically, by dividing and defining performers and audience into different species. We shall see that inherent in the very notion of the paradoxical fool is a force opposed to taxonomy. Taxonomy at the level of the individual by definition questions paradox. A leopard cannot also have the characteristics of a worm, but a fool can definitely be both powerful and abject. How the end of the fool was bound up with the rise of forces of division and definition in the German theater from the 1730s onward is one of the red threads running though this book.

Before we turn to the first of our fools, let us ask a final question. We have mentioned (often) court fools but have not yet tried to understand the nature of the court in general, or the specific courts in which our fools had their being, that is, the courts of Berlin and Potsdam in Brandenburg-Prussia (for Gundling and Morgenstern), of Dresden in Saxony (for Fröhlich), and for Würzburg, Munich, Vienna, and—from the sublime to the ridiculous— Ellwangen (for Peter Prosch).

Until recently, thinking about the court in general was dominated by the ideas of Norbert Elias (1897–1990). His two best-known works, *Die höfische Gesellschaft* (*The Court Society*) and *Über den Prozess der Civilisation* (*The Civilizing Process*)[37] described the growth of state power and argued that the restraints of court life gradually transmitted themselves to the rest of society, which internalized affect-control and physical restrictions. No one who wished to remain accepted as part of that society would have public outbursts of anger or lust, burp or spit, put hands in a common dish, remain unwashed, or perform bodily functions in public. Elias agrees here with Freud's idea of civilization as originating in the restraint of affect, in his 1930 *Das Unbehagen in der Kultur* (*Civilisation and Its Discontents*). Elias's work, *Die höfische Gesellschaft* (*The Court Society*) was published in 1933, and its continuation, *Über den Prozess der Civilisation* (*The Civilizing Process*) in 1939. They attracted little attention because of the contemporary political situation and were only rediscovered in the English-speaking world when the former was translated and reissued in a revised version in 1969. As Jeroen Duindam has pointed out, the two books are relics of a time in historical scholarship when grand syntheses could still be produced. They remain the only grand synthesis at a high level of generality dealing with the relation between court society and state formation. They also remain the only synthesis that posed the question of the relationship between the structure of individual personality and that of the absolutist court, a question that will be repeatedly considered in these pages.[38]

In the court, the character of the monarch was, as Elias argues, clearly paramount, and its human twists and turns gave the court its characteristic and fundamental instability. But the prince's position and whether he had the ability to institute change depended in turn on the convergence between his character and those of his courtiers. This is an idea that will receive some testing in this book, particularly in the case of Peter Prosch. Yet Elias does not convincingly show that court life did in fact lead to changes in behavior either in the aristocracy or in the rest of society. Duindam has argued that the court nobility, far from being dominated by the court, attempted to an increasing degree to assert its power through the court. He asserts that the upper nobility gradually came to dominate the court and confirm its position as an elite and an example to society. All of the characteristics of life at court as presented by Elias, Duindam argues, can also be seen as instruments of power used by the nobility.[39] I believe this argument to be of limited validity. It is difficult, for example, to apply to the Saxon court of this period, dominated as it was by conflicts between prince and aristocracy. It is also difficult to apply to the court of Brandenburg-Prussia before about 1730, for many of the same reasons. But it does have the advantage of pointing out that monarch and aristocracy were not necessarily cooperating in the making of the centralized state.

Several historians, such as R. J. W. Evans, have pointed also to the protean nature of the court, arguing that the constellation of courtiers around the individual prince was so deeply influenced by his character and by his personal program for the realm that each court differed to a marked degree from every other.[40] This makes it hardly surprising that the extent of the applicability of Elias's theory, based largely on the court of Louis XIV of France (1643–1715), is unclear. In the case of the German courts, it is almost impossible to produce any synthetic view. With more than three hundred sovereign entities in the German-speaking lands, there was no norm but variation. They all, however, seem to have gone through (though at different times) the same evolution, of a gradual distinction between mainly or wholly aristocratic courtiers holding court officers, and those who held offices of state. Slowly, by the end of the eighteenth century, the normal business of government left the court and became separate from it.[41] It was here that "state building" could begin to happen. It could also happen, Elias argues, that when the aristocracy had been "restrained" by court life, it no longer challenged the authority of the prince. But historians such as Rudolf Vierhaus have pointed out, contrary to Elias, that the German princes themselves were scarcely in control of their courts or capable of state making even by the early decades of the eighteenth century.[42] In this flux, extrastate actors such as the fools were able to intervene in court life and stay close to the prince, even intervene in his state making. How they intervened in the vital consequent search by the prince for control over systems of honor will be examined especially in the chapters on Gundling and Morgenstern.

The last decades have seen the emergence of considerable research devoted to the Enlightenment German court, and particularly to those of Saxony and Brandenburg-Prussia.[43] More particularly, Benjamin Marschke has launched a new research project focused on the court of Frederick William I of Brandenburg-Prussia.[44] In that project, the fools are only mentioned once. Marschke often tries to "normalize" the complex character of Frederick William, whose intelligence, propensity for cruelty, piety, hatred of organized learning, and love of black jokes will be explored when we turn to the lives of Gundling and Morgenstern, in the context of Frederick William's struggle for sovereignty in Brandenburg-Prussia.[45] Unlike Marschke, this book regards Frederick William as impossible to normalize. The reader will have to decide on her own reading of these two very different views.

One question must be posed, deriving as it does directly from the project of this book and the events described in it. What made the German courts so apt to be theaters of cruelty? Historians have pointed to the general culture of cruelty that runs through the eighteenth century, making the exploitation of animals, the insane, the blind, the ill, Jews, the deaf, women, children, beggars, anyone weak or vulnerable, usual behavior.[46] Fools fell into the category of the vulnerable. Often from a lower social class and always completely dependent on the prince, they had nowhere to turn to escape cruel japes, physical humor, and insults. Cruelty was a resource. It was a way of leaving a mark upon a person, of expressing the power of a group over an individual. It was, in fact, a symptom of the insecurity vibrating among the courtiers themselves, who were also dependent on the prince and always in competition for his favor, or *Gnade*. To be cruel to a fool was a way of constructing solidarities through identifying and using a necessary outsider. To be cruel to a fool was also a way of asserting superiority in a court dependent on the prince's will. This idea will be discussed throughout this book and will be one of its contributions to the argument not only on the importance of the court fools but also on the nature of the courts they inhabited.

Now, dear foolish Reader, delaying no longer, let us meet the first of our four fools, Jacob Paul Gundling, fool to Frederick William I, King in Prussia.

✦ ONE ✦

Jacob Paul Gundling

The Honor of Historians and Fools

Bey dem Herr ein Hang zum Scherzen zu bemerken war. (The lord
had a noticeable proclivity for joking.)
—Jacob Morgenstern, *Ueber Friedrich Wilhelm I* (1793)

Jacob Paul Gundling had a contradictory life. Born in the late seventeenth
century to a minister's family, he was educated at the Pietist University of
Halle, where his brother Nicolas Hieronymus became a famous jurist. In Berlin he took up posts simultaneously at the Heroldsamt, an office for the verification of aristocratic lineages and armorial bearings, and the Ritterakademie,
an institution for the higher education of the aristocracy, where Gundling
taught history, geography, and languages. We have little information on how
he came to hold court office. But the Heroldsamt was shut down, as was the
Ritterakademie, which must have led to a free-floating period for Gundling
until he was recruited for the court as a newspaper reader and commentator. At the court of Frederick William I, King in Prussia (1688–1740; reigned
1713–40), Gundling was employed as a historian (among other things) and
yet treated as a fool, given absurd titles and yet appointed president of the
Akademie der Wissenschaften (Academy of Sciences) in Berlin, with special reference to the silkworm industry. He had the important role of expli-
cating newspapers to the king and his companions and himself became
the news as he was hustled and bullied and had bad encounters with the
young bears that were allowed to roam the royal palaces. He was the allotted
butt of the dark practical jokes that were vital to the way Frederick William
controlled his court and shaped his elites, and so shame was his everyday
meal. Gundling's shaming fed the sense of humor of the times, which to us

23

Dismar Degen, *A Meeting of the Tabakskollegium*, ca. 1737. A hare, symbol of foolishness, can be discerned sharing the top of the table. Painting by Dismar Degen, around 1737. (bpk-Bildagentur/Preussische Schlösser und Gärten/Castle Koenigs Wusterhausen/Art Resource, NY)

must seem brutal. It also drew together elite groups such as the Tabakskollegium, Frederick William's inner circle, who were involved in the shaming. Even when it looked as though Frederick William was according Gundling high honors, those honors were the very opposite of what they seemed.

Contradiction also lay deep in the character of King Frederick William. Here I accept Theodor Schieder's argument that Frederick William's character permeated not only the character of his son Frederick II but also the structures of Prussia itself.[1] Developing Schieder, I argue that Gundling, court historian and court fool, was shaped by Frederick William, that "bizarre" monarch and, conversely, played a role in shaping Frederick William's court, and thus the elites of Prussia.[2]

How have historians treated Gundling's extraordinary life? It was fascinating enough to contemporaries that even in the absence of direct testimony from Gundling himself, four biographies were written in the eighteenth century. First in time comes the 1729 *Der gelehrte Narr*, by the writer and novelist

Four Fools in the Age of Reason

David Fassmann, Gundling's major rival at court, with whom he once fought a duel.[3] This work was commissioned by Frederick William himself, maybe as a mark of Gundling's declining favor, and has obviously to be treated with care. Nonetheless, its level of detail and its status as an eyewitness account, even a hostile one, have ensured that material from it has entered every subsequent biography, even Martin Sabrow's 2001 revisionist work.[4]

With the second biography, Michael von Loen's 1750 *Der unglückliche Gelehrte am Hof, oder einige Nachrichten von dem . . . Freyherrn von Gundling* (The unhappy scholar at court, or some reports on Freiherr von Gundling),[5] we enter a different world. Von Loen is partially reliant on Fassmann, not only on *Der gelehrte Narr* but also on the funeral oration for Gundling that Frederick William coerced Fassmann into delivering in 1731. He did not, however, pick up Fassmann's hostility to Gundling. On the contrary, von Loen's links with Gundling were close. From 1712 to 1715 he had studied in Halle with Gundling's brother, the well-known jurist Nicolas Hieronymus. He had also spent the winter of 1717–18 at the court at Berlin and thus almost certainly saw Gundling's life at close quarters. In 1742, von Loen published his bestselling moral romance *Der redliche Mann am Hofe* (The upright man at court), a critique of the court life that so fascinated him. A minor noble, and a major figure in the cultural life of mid-eighteenth-century Frankfurt, he was related to Goethe, and the parents of the great writer were married in von Loen's country house. He wrote in his leisure copiously and with humor on many subjects including honor and Gundling.[6] Von Loen's approach to Gundling often has the brightness of an eyewitness account. His evidence was not only drawn from Fassmann but was based on letters sent to von Loen by Gundling himself. The content of these letters unfortunately did not make its way into subsequent accounts of Gundling's life. Von Loen's account also captures the troubling contradictions of Gundling's career, as he describes Gundling's life as "both comic and sad."[7] Von Loen, an acute observer of court life, makes the humane remark that he is puzzled to know how the great ones of the world have the right to mistreat unhappy men who happen to be slightly eccentric, thus making them draw closer to more serious disturbance. For von Loen, the issues raised by Gundling's life were those of defining the legitimacy, power, and honor of the great. This is also the major moral issue raised by their use of jokes.

By the time of Karl Friedrich Flögel's heroic compilation, his 1789 *Geschichte der Hofnarren,* the time for eyewitness accounts had passed, and

Flögel draws on the accounts by von Loen and Fassmann. Flögel had seen the Gundling letters held by von Loen, "die ein ganz ordentliches und gesetztes Wesen anzeigen" (that show an entirely orderly and settled character), but he has little else that is new to add.[8]

At far greater length, Anton Balthazar König discussed Gundling, fooling, and honor in 1795. König was writing at a time when Prussia was involved in the wars of the French Revolution and the partitions of Poland (1772, 1793, and 1795). A new history of the Fatherland was being constructed to suit the times. Some aspects of it were problematic. Historians could neither, on the one hand, leave Frederick William I and his major reforms out nor, on the other hand, integrate his life into the picture the dynasty wished to construct of itself. König wrote in his many books of the honored who had served the dynasty and helped to construct its greatness, and of Gundling, the dishonored, who brought shame upon himself. Anecdotes about Gundling might take away some responsibility from Frederick William's dark jokes, cruel actions, and anti-intellectual attitudes.

The only considerable modern historian to tackle the themes of Gundling's life is Martin Sabrow, a well-known scholar of the history of the Deutsche Demokratische Republik (DDR).[9] He sees the conjunction in Gundling of sense and nonsense, rationality and black jokes, comedy and tragedy. Sabrow tries to smooth out Gundling's life, arguing for example that his time as president of the Berlin Akademie der Wissenschaften was devoted to entirely appropriate enterprises such as silkworm cultivation. He asks if Gundling was really a fool at all. Sabrow's book attempts to minimize Gundling's position as a fool and to emphasize his work as a historian; in other words, Sabrow belongs to the school of historians, which began with König in 1795, that is attempting to produce a modernized Gundling, whose contradictions and fool-dom were less important than his work as a "rational" historian or administrator. I, on the other hand, will argue that Gundling was indeed a fool. He was called so by Frederick William and by other people. His life also fits the criteria for fool-dom established by Flögel in his 1789 *Geschichte der Hofnarren:* the court fool should entertain; tell the truth, and give good advice; restrain the anger of the monarch; and heal illness.[10] In only the last was Gundling deficient.

Yet the polarity of fool or historian was not the only one in which Gundling was involved. This makes it difficult to accept arguments such as Martin Sabrow's that discuss only one polarity (fool versus historian) and not

Four Fools in the Age of Reason

others that were equally present. For Gundling's roles at court were multiple, not singular. Not only was he a historian (and fool), but he was president of the Akademie der Wissenschaften, master of ceremonies, director of the silkworm industry, and, most important, *Zeitungs-Referent,* or court newspaper reader. In Gundling's case, the central drama is that of the conflict between his roles. Who is he? This is an issue that historians have been unable to bring to resolution by the technique of emphasizing one side and downplaying another, arguing for the fool role against that of the historian, or for the historian role against that of the fool, in order to find Gundling's "real" identity. Identity and role have become separated in our own times. For the eighteenth century, particularly for the early eighteenth century, the relationship between the two was tighter.

The term "identity" causes problems when applied to the early eighteenth century. As Dror Wahrman and many others have pointed out, the concept of "having an identity" was a slow-growing one and may have to be replaced in this period by that of the playing of roles.[11] Each person played their role differently, extrapolating from chance and circumstance and social convention. They "filled" their role. Some roles were more honorable than others, but the concept of honor ranged up and down the social scale. Peasants and urban workers who were guild members had honor as much as did aristocrats.[12] As we will see, the story of Gundling is as much a story of a struggle over different conceptions of honor as it is a struggle between the roles of court fool and court historian on which both contemporary and modern historians have focused, thereby enclosing the story of Gundling in an oscillation from which there is no escape. Downplaying one side of a contradiction at the expense of the other misses the point of their coexistence.

Historians have also perhaps been influenced by the ready-made role of the scholar-fool. There existed for scholars since the religious Reformation of the sixteenth century the topos of the learned fool, of the paradoxical person who combines two opposing qualities, just as Gundling has been regarded as doing. The Reformation of the sixteenth century had seen a great shift of the practice of learning from the ruthlessly disendowed monasteries that had carried the burden of learning in the medieval period, into the homes of secular scholars, who were portrayed in the topos as too mesmerized by the delights of scholarship to notice crying children and deceiving wives: as fools.

By the eighteenth century, the figure of the learned fool was long-standing, the subject of an enormous number of publications, joke books, and comedies, even finding a role (Polichinello) in the Commedia del'Arte. The learned man who is a fool (easily inverted to the fool who is a learned man) was distinguished by such qualities as *Hochmut* (arrogance), *Eitelkeit* (vanity), pedantism, the making of lists, and an intolerance of contradiction. Scholars were routinely accused of deception and cheating, *Betrügerei*, arising from common practices such as plagiarism, the advance announcement of articles that then never appeared and of lectures that were never intended to be given.

This topos directly affected Gundling. In 1729 Frederick William I, as a joke, perhaps, suggested to David Fassmann, Gundling's major rival at court, that he should publish a satire on the learned fool.[13] The resulting book's frontispiece shows a learned fool drawn with Gundling's features, dressed in a house robe, slippers, and a long wig. He is sitting at a table with the iconic pen in inkwell in front of him. The paper in front of Gundling is blank. He is raising a stick in ire against a chattering monkey, symbol of foolishness. Seated on the table in front of him, it is wiping its rear on a page torn out of a book that Gundling has open in front of him. The book is held up by a satyr labeled as Silenus, in classical mythology known as the buffoon to the gods. Meanwhile, another satyr offers Gundling a lighted long-stemmed pipe of tobacco, an object connected with the so-called Tabakskollegium, the small informal advisory group to Frederick William that met most evenings with the aid of long pipes of tobacco and mugs of beer. Other spaces in the picture are taken up by images of a hare, another image of foolishness, which is seated on the back of Gundling's chair, combing his overlong wig. Another hare holds a book in the lower left-hand corner, perhaps asserting the foolishness of publication. On the floor, another monkey is measuring a miniature globe with a pair of dividers—since the whole world is the resort of foolishness. Gundling's well-known partiality for drink is illustrated by the beer flask nestled against the leg of his chair.

This illustration so well portrays the topos of the learned fool that the book following it is largely superfluous. So hostile is it to Gundling that its biographical information must be treated with care, although it was drawn upon by Gundling's other contemporary biographers, and even by Sabrow. Flögel is critical of it, while still using some information from Fassmann's book. It shows that the topos of the learned fool was alive and well in the early eighteenth century and that learned men operated in a

der Satyr Silenus

Frontispiece to David Fassmann's satire of Gundling, showing Gundling as a learned fool. (Staats- und Universitätsbibliothek, Göttingen)

paradoxical context where fools and scholars could be found together in the same person.[14]

Yet Gundling's fool-ishness can be gauged not only by his conformity to the stereotype of the learned fool but also by the way he carried out his functions at Frederick William's court and by his relationship with that famously "bizarre" and contradictory monarch. Historians have called Frederick William "puzzling and contradictory," "*eigenwillig und bizzar*," and have noted a "seemingly self-contradictory mix of militarism, frugality, efficiency, asceticism, brutality, organization, work ethic, piety and crudeness."[15] Theodor Schieder points out that while many historians of our own day have seen Frederick William as a reformer, his contemporaries saw him as highly contradictory in character and as subject to wild mood swings that may have been the result of mental illness: "Throughout his life he was unable to moderate his dangerous disposition to violent temper, brutality and misanthropy that made him appear as the very image of an inhuman despot. His propensity to rage as well as regret and melancholy had him blown hither and thither by powerful emotions, and seemed almost incompatible with his immense shrewdness."[16] Martin Sabrow sums up, describing the peculiarly contradictory character of court life under Frederick William.[17]

Frederick William came to the throne in 1713 already determined drastically to reduce the splendid and extremely expensive ceremonial life of the court of his father, Frederick I. He was also determined to carry out what historians call "state building," part of the project of enhancing the power of the particular monarch, and the monarchy as such. To these ends, Frederick William abolished many court offices and sent many aristocratic courtiers away. Instead of the aristocracy, military men, often of nonaristocratic birth, began to dominate the court. Frederick even declined the ceremony of coronation, citing the expense of the splendors of his father's coronation in 1701. His was a thrifty court. As part of the movement to curtail expense, two institutions founded by the king's father, the Ritterakademie, an advanced learning institute for the sons of the aristocracy, and the Heroldsamt, an institution concerned with the verification of aristocratic genealogies, were also closed down. These two institutions were both concerned with the aristocracy, whose relations with the king were to be flash points in the reign.[18] Both institutions had employed Jacob Paul Gundling.

The process by which Gundling was pulled out of unemployment into the position of court *Zeitungs-Referent,* or commentator on newspapers, has never been clear. Sabrow convincingly argues that his unemployment was more apparent than real and bridged by a fact-finding commission from Frederick William. As *Zeitungs-Referent,* Gundling had the task of excerpting and commenting to the Tabakskollegium on the most recent newspapers of the day, papers such as *Die europäische Fama,* which gave news from other courts, and of political and military developments. Gundling's position would have been impossible to bring into being without the contemporary expansion of the European newspaper press. It is also important that the news Gundling relayed came from the standardized written, and not the personal spoken, word. Even Frederick William saw it as important to have a person qualified in history, geography, and law (Gundling's former teaching fields at the Ritterakademie) and competent, as Gundling was, in several languages, in order to gain adequate commentary on the events described in the newspapers. Gundling would excerpt articles from the newspapers, which gave him considerable control over the content actually brought before the Tabakskollegium. It is not recorded whether Gundling took part in the ensuing discussions, but whether he did or did not, he certainly played a great role in setting their agenda. In this sense, Gundling was no fool. The papers themselves had to be as current as possible. Frederick William was seeing the uses of a source of knowledge that was not only standardized but also validated precisely because of its newness.

Andreas Gestrich has, along the same lines, noted how monarchies in the early eighteenth century gained control of the "public sphere" by the use of newspapers and pamphlets.[19] In this sense, Gestrich's book begins a process of turning back historical inquiry to where it was in the nineteenth and early twentieth centuries, to a focus on state and monarchy. This book also aims to turn back to the history of monarchy and state, but seen from the point of view of the fool and his master. State building could be done in many different ways, not just by the reform of the army and civilian government for which Frederick William is well known, but by using his fool.

Nor was Gundling's intervention simply in domestic matters. Frederick William wished to read newspapers from the Netherlands, France, Paris, Frankfurt, Leipzig, Vienna, Breslau, Hamburg, and several other places to try to educate himself in a way that would not only feed his own interests but also profit his exchanges with other princes and his instructions to ambassadors and envoys. Foreign diplomats were often present at the newspaper readings that took place at the evening meetings of the Tabakskollegium. They became, in other words, a theater at which foreigners could be entertained and impressed by the up-to-dateness of the Prussian government.

Salomon Jacob Morgenstern, Gundling's successor (chapter 2), described the work of a *Zeitungs-Referent:* "The *Zeitungs-Referent* [he calls him the *Zeitungs-Erzähler,* the 'newspaper story-teller'] must be there, commentating, until the King or anyone else breaks in. He brings to the fore what men do with reason or with the heart, which brings more or less honor to them. The

King or another of those present, would bring up the history of similar cases, and everyone was free to contribute their own thoughts and opinions."[20]

Frederick William persisted, however, in gradually settling fool-dom on Gundling. Throughout the 1720s Frederick William, in apparent recognition of Gundling in his role as *Zeitungs–Referent,* loaded him with honors. Over protests by aristocrats, the king elevated Gundling to the aristocratic rank of Freiherr, and also gave him titles whose Baroque number, length, and elaboration could scarcely be equaled: *Preussischen Geheimen Kriegs-Kammer-Ober-Appellations-und-Kammergerichts-Raths, Zeremonienmeisters,* and president of the Prussian Akademie der Wissenschaften (in succession to Leibniz). It was even discussed whether he should be tutor to the Crown Prince (this came to nothing), and at the end, he was given responsibility for the new efforts to create a silk industry as part of Frederick William's efforts to revive Prussian agriculture.[21] When Gundling protested at this last office, Frederick William had WURM G (WORM G) embroidered on the back of the Frenchified coat he was commanded to wear. Nor were these titles simply exercises in ridicule. They carried with them the expressly granted right to attend sessions of all these bodies of general oversight that Frederick William had created to help him administer his kingdom in the direction to which he had committed himself on his accession in 1713, and the duty of reporting to Frederick William on their sessions.[22]

The patents for this accumulation of titles were ridiculously long and elaborate. The king explained, for example, that the patents for the post of *Ober-Zeremonienmeister* were "a mark of honor. . . . By Our own intention We raise him to the honorable state of Freiherr in consideration of the manifold and frequent pleasurable, useful and continuous services of Our chief master of ceremonies, Jacob Paul von Gundling, also as a token of Our grace and happiness because of his great capacity for learning and thoroughness of mind exceeding thousands of other very well-known people in Europe in reading and praiseworthy conduct."[23]

As Freiherr, Gundling also had the right to a coat of arms, and the one he was granted carried its heraldic description over many pages. Nor was the shield any less ridiculous than the overlong patents. The Prussian eagle is represented there divided between many quarterings, so that here a leg and here a wing, and here the tail feathers peep out, instead of the black eagle being displayed in full on the shield. Minerva is the shield's supporter. She not only wears the head of Medusa on her breastplate, as usual, but also has a small owl at her feet.[24] The owl belongs to Minerva, patron of learning and wisdom, but is here displaced, as it is nearly always represented as standing on Minerva's shoulder. It is also a bird associated with fools. Frederick William in the heraldic patent, surely ironically, reassures Gundling that it will "show as an example for the learned world the unparalleled Freiherr von Gundeling."[25] The two feet of the eagle are meant "to display that Freiherr von Gundeling has from youth on grabbed the writings of learned people right and left and thereby gained a golden treasury and afterward presented it to the stupendous admiration of the world by public print."[26] Gundling's ridiculous coat of arms was thus an exercise in double reading and dishonor. It shows how Frederick William, by the exercise of royal patronage, had blurred the boundaries not only between fool and historian but also between real aristocracy and a foolish one, and had undermined the one by the use of the other.

This was especially so because fools in this period were seen as carrying out one of the dishonorable trades, trades carried out by such people as skinners, prostitutes, executioners, shepherds, actors, and the illegitimate. These were people who were excluded from public and social life because of their status. Thus the nobility found Frederick William's insistence on Gundling's "aristocratic" status doubly insulting. If Gundling was a fool, then he could not also be an aristocrat at the same time. His foolishness dishonored his coat of arms and new status.

There were other ways in which Frederick William forced fool-dom on Gundling. As master of ceremonies—at a court where there were few ceremonies—Gundling was forced to wear an overelaborate costume in the extravagant French style popular at the court of Frederick William's father, Frederick I. Gundling's enormous wig stretched down beyond his shoulders, his coat had gold buttons and exaggerated sleeves, his stockings were in red silk. To cap it all, Frederick William ordered him to wear at all times an enormous gilded wooden key as a sign of his office as *Kammerherr,* or chamberlain.[27] The costume was part of Frederick William's drive to rid the court in particular, and Prussia in general, of the elaborate and expensive French fashions that had found favor under his father's rule, by making them ridiculous. The key was as exaggerated as the costume and the patents. Anyone who wore Frenchified costume was a fool. It was in wearing this costume that Gundling passed from playing the roles of court historian and newspaper reader to that of the court fool. For the king, too, this transition was important, so important that he had two portraits painted of Gundling, one life-sized in the "French" costume, and another smaller one, showing a scene from the Commedia dell'Arte that portrayed Gundling as Polichinello, the learned fool. These portraits, which are now lost, moved with the king in the court's seasonal peregrinations between Berlin, Wusterhausen, and Potsdam. Gundling and his foolishness clearly meant a great deal to Frederick William.

There are still questions to be asked, however, about the way in which Frederick William heaped titles on Gundling. We notice first of all their sheer number. Why not leave Gundling as simply court historian and *Zeitungs-Referent*? Perhaps it might have been that by making Gundling's titles many and spreading them wide the king hoped to exercise the maximum surveillance over the remaining court nobility and the army officers with whom he was replacing them. By concentrating them in one person, Frederick William could also exercise maximum surveillance and control over that person.

In approaching Gundling, we thus have to remember that the polarity of fool and historian may be no more or less important than the polarity between monarch and fool. And that it may be bound up with Frederick William's often difficult relationship with his aristocracy, who also carried coats of arms reflecting their genealogies, the very coats of arms that Gundling had once had the task of verifying at the Heroldsamt. So well-known was the proud attachment of the Prussian nobility to their coats of arms, with all the genealogical information they contained, that it was even famously parodied in the opening pages of Voltaire's 1759 *Candide,* in which a noble lady refuses to marry her faithful suitor because he does not possess enough quarterings on his family shield.[28] It is difficult to resist the conclusion that Gundling's coat of arms was a practical joke by Frederick William aimed at undermining the aristocracy and their pretentions. As Claus Hinrichs wrote, the king took "the art of heraldry, like ceremonial, as a theme for wit and practical jokes."[29]

Aristocratic honor could easily escape royal power, however. Core values of the Prussian military aristocracy were ambition and honor, *Ehre* and *Ehrgeiz,* each of them disruptive and unpredictable. The most well-known practice that expressed these values was dueling. Royal decrees forbidding dueling were issued in 1688 and 1713, and as well by Frederick William's son, Frederick II, but all to no effect. Dueling over issues of honor, in fact, continued well into the nineteenth century. One of the tasks of the monarchy was thus to provide structures that could contain the disruptive consequences

Four Fools in the Age of Reason

of honor and use it for the service of the state.[30] Thus it was that Gundling's previous appointment in the Heroldsamt, and his ridiculous patent and coat of arms, fell squarely into struggles between king and aristocracy, not only over taxation but also over honor.[31] Frederick William was threatening in the person of the ennobled Gundling, his fool, to represent the aristocracy as fools, as not *satisfaktionsfähig*, as not honorably duel-able. A duel fought by Fassmann and Gundling, the outcome of their bitter rivalry, could only enhance this impression.[32]

But what was honor? This was a concept in flux at the time of Gundling's death in 1731, and afterward. Zedler's *Universal-Lexikon*, the major reference source of the era, pointed out the restless, disruptive nature of honor.[33] The lust after it is "unersättlich" (insatiable), setting itself "immer ein weiter Ziel" (always a fresh goal). It was something monarchs had to control. The alternative was chaos. The French Enlightenment thinker Montesquieu (1689–1755), however, in his famous *De l'esprit des loix* of 1748, argued that honor is the very principle of monarchial rule: "Honor sets all the parts of the body politic in motion, and by its very action connects them; thus each individual advances the public good, while he only thinks of promoting his own interest."[34]

Yet, though Montesquieu's definition is famous, it is not representative. Generally speaking, the century slowly redefined honor into virtue. The English political thinker Thomas Hobbes had already argued in his *Leviathan* of 1651 that the desire for honor, defined for men as martial prowess, easily lead to warfare. Those who hold contrary beliefs, he argued, are themselves fools. Von Loen discussed the question of honor in his 1751 essay "Die närrische Ehre" as a matter of urgency, in a century that saw decades of war. He argued that the honor of the ruler lies in his virtues, not in his martial prowess. Indeed, the ruler might even see it as his duty to hold back from the field of battle, recognizing that his life was more precious to his subjects than precarious military renown. The extraordinary career of Frederick William's contemporary Charles XII of Sweden (1682–1718), who had beggared his country in the exercise of his undoubted military genius, was always held up as a warning example on this side of the debate.

Honor and virtue thus battled with each other. Von Loen came out on the side of virtue. He saw honor as intrinsically hierarchical. But when honor became equated with virtue, then all could aspire to it: "The least man in the world has an idea of honor that urges him to brave deeds: it is based on virtue, on wisdom, on learning, and is a gift of nature or heaven." *Hochmut* (arrogance), on the other hand, is what von Leon calls "*närrische Ehre*," or "fools' honor." Honor and virtue thus slowly became linked.[35] This idea was the great solvent of the connections between honor and privilege.

So far, we have discussed honor in relation to the nobility and to martial prowess. But another social group, the academic elite, was also defining new standards of honor for itself. The old idea of the scholar-fool implicated in David Fassmann's 1729 prolonged, poisonous satire on Gundling—which begins: "You fool! You monkey physiognomy! Face to make everyone laugh! You monkey! You hare! You pedant! You ignorant! You unruly child! You clumsy! You shoe sole!"[36]—was written in a world that had already seen in the previous century the growth of international scientific organizations committed to the maintenance of scholarly standards, such as the Royal Society of London, and had heard of the famous debate between Leibniz and Newton over who was the first to invent calculus. The personal honor of the scholar was much implicated in such issues as priority disputes. It was so because scholars lived with national and international audiences who policed their actions and regarded their profession as an honorable one and subject to the judgment of their peers.

This was a transitional period, the period of Leibniz's lifetime (1646–1716) and of Gundling's (1673–1731), that saw, as many historians have noted, the working out of a "moral economy" of honorable learning, characterized by its disdain for and suspicion of political power.[37] Gundling's historical work would therefore have been seen as suspect. It was produced too close to Frederick William and too often at his personal command. Transparency was also a primary value, in this moral economy, as were the value of authorship and the criminality of plagiarism. This "moral economy" was concerned with establishing honor standards for the life of scholarship, which should be the very opposite of the shame and shaming associated with the charlatanry of the learned fools.

At stake here was not only the honor of the collective "estate" of scholars but also the honor of each individual scholar. Von Loen, whose 1750 portrait of Gundling was heavily drawn upon by König in 1795, remarked even at midcentury that everyone has the capacity to become learned, and thus everyone could potentially join the "estate" of the learned—which was thus no "estate" at all—and partake in the moral economy of its honorableness.[38] Honor was changing into virtue. Learned authority and honor in fact became inextricably intertwined and have remained so. Personal honor meant that scholars, instead of being demeaned in one satire after another as mere learned fools, were becoming secure in their own version of honor. Self-discipline, objectivity, austerity, personal dedication, disdain for corruption and the political life were emerging as the new characteristics of the scholar and defined his personal authority.

It also made a new learning. Instead of the listings beloved by Baroque scholars, sciences of measurement, observation, and documentation were rising to the fore. They demanded the self-discipline of attentiveness in the scholar, which yet again went directly to his personal authority and to the honor that compelled him into accurate reporting of results. Above all, the honor of the scholar allowed expertise and experts to emerge. Frederick William was confronted, for example, with an upcoming generation of juridical academic experts, of whom Gundling's own brother, Halle professor Nicolas Hieronymus, was one. It was a group that would unavoidably breach the ideals of honor of a masculine feudal aristocratic world and yet be one on which Frederick William and other monarchs would depend for their bureaucratic manpower and opinions on history or international law.[39]

These developments in thinking and acting on the honor of the scholar were the more powerful because they were backed up by new institutions, institutions that were standardized and internationalized, and transmitted the ideal of the personal honor of the scholar across Europe and into the New World. The Berlin Akademie der Wissenschaften (of which Gundling became president after Leibniz), the Royal Society of London, the St. Petersburg Academy of Sciences, and the Paris Academy of Sciences were all founded in the same period, between the 1660s and the early eighteenth century.

All this has implications for the history of Gundling. First of all, the new values of scholarship of the first decades of the eighteenth century are strikingly close to those claimed by scholars today. When historians such as Sabrow ask whether Gundling was a *fool or* a historian, the dichotomy projects the now universally accepted values formed in what might be called the "revolution in honor" of the scholar onto Gundling's transitional world. Sabrow assumes that "a historian" has a distinct identity formed by the honor code of the scholar, an identity that cannot be exchanged for another. This may not have been true in the court of Frederick William.

In relation to the modern value system of scholarship, Gundling fails as a historian. In spite of his industry, on which Sabrow rightly remarks, all of his work was produced as what we might now call a "house-historian," close to the very sources of the power that made the moral economy of scholarship so uneasy. His work, such as his biographies of the first two Electors of Brandenburg, also very largely dealt with subjects set by the king. Contemporary reviews of Gundling's works, however, were not unfavorable.[40]

His interest in historical geography, the history of public law and of the Holy Roman Empire, his use of large numbers of original documents (drawn from royal archives), his documentary criticism, his use of critical footnotes, set at the bottom of the page and taking the place of the enormous glosses of Baroque scholars, and his narrative rather than chronical-like style seem to place him well in line with contemporary practice. König, however, saw him in other lights. He gives an ambivalent critical bibliography of Gundling's historical works, which also, strangely for a generally laudatory biography, repeats claims that Gundling had plagiarized from Pufendorf.[41] König's attitude to Gundling's work as a historian is ambiguous. He praises Gundling's *Märkische Geschichte,* on the one hand, and then, on the other, complains that Gundling's books have become very rare, "like all bad books."[42] Most of Gundling's works were published. But his closeness as a historian to royal demands and his dependence on the king for the use of the archive undermined any claims to independence of judgment. He was a "house-historian." In order to make Gundling into a historian as we understand the term, Sabrow has to project the values of modern scholarly honor onto a thoroughly unmodern situation.

Frederick William's disdain for academic knowledge was well-known. As König remarks, for all the branches of learning, the king's policy was "nicht allein in ihrer Ausbreitung zu hindern, sondern auch lächerlich zu Machen" (not only to impede their diffusion, but also to make them ridiculous).[43] He well appreciated the destructive power of laughter. To make his house-historian out to be a fool was the perfect implementation of this policy. It meant that Gundling's personal union of fool, historian, minor nobility, and president of the Berlin Akademie der Wissenschaften, was not, in Frederick William's eyes, the problem it has appeared to modern historians but rather the very reason for Gundling's existence at court. He was, as the king said, "diese närrische Exzellenz" (this foolish excellency).[44]

In his presidency of the Berlin Akademie der Wissenschaften, Gundling explored with difficulty the world of the honorable scholar. He served in this role after Leibniz, the universal genius of the early Enlightenment who had practically become the intellectual guide of the Hohenzollern dynasty due to his correspondence with Frederick William's mother, Electress Sophia Dorothea. Gundling's presidency, whatever his merits as a historian, must have seemed a severe anticlimax to the scholarly world. And the Akademie itself underwent considerable change. It became different from the other academies established in this era, which all tried to embrace many areas of knowledge. For their members, prize competitions, fellowships, organized research programs, and long-standing polymathic traditions kept the range of scholarship broad. As Martin Sabrow points out, it was not so in Berlin. Frederick William demanded the Akademie concentrate on the practical work of silkworm rearing, under the auspices of Gundling's responsibility for the new silk industry. Lost were any claims the Akademie had previously been able to make, as did all other academies, that it represented the full spectrum of knowledge. Those scholars who were already members of the Akademie had the stark choices of withdrawing or working on silkworms. The scholars were working to a ready-made program, as the sole work of the Akademie. And although members of other academies were often asked by governments to research particular problems, this did not absorb all their manpower or threaten their polymathic claims. Sabrow argues that Gundling's organization of the work on the silkworms was solid, but he misses the point that it was part of the academic collapse of the Akademie der Wissenschaften, and of the victory of Frederick William over the major learned institution in Prussia, which was meant to enforce the scholars' new honor code. In appointing an adventurer, the "Baron" von Stein, an aspirant fool, as vice president of the Akademie, Frederick William followed the same procedure of shaming. Von Stein's patent, even more ridiculous than Gundling's, recommends him for his abilities in "antiquities, old and new numismatics, physics and mechanics, botany, hydraulics, pneumatics and statics, and not least in the Cabbala. He can also tell good from evil spirits, knows about the economy and households of the pre-Adamites, history and metaphysics, logic and algebra. Is not obliged to publish anything, except the Prognostications for the year in weather, health and illness, fruitfulness and infertility." And so it continues, another elaborate and destructive joke played on the Akademie by Frederick William. It was not only Gundling but the Akademie itself that the king would try to shame.

Gundling's position with the king fluctuated. Particularly in the early years in court, like the classical fools, he was allowed to say things to the king that others could not: "konnte er auf die leichteste Art vieles sagen, was den höchsten Personen am Hofe nicht erlaubt war" (he could say much in an easy manner that the highest at court were not allowed).[45] In this time, Gundling spent many hours working alone with the king, dealing with confidential matters. He even acquired such power as to be able to help to procure the exile of the famous philosopher Christian Wolff, who, like Gundling's brother, was a professor at the University of Halle. Wolff gave a lecture in which he proclaimed that a heathen Chinese might live as virtuously as a Christian; even worse, he was denounced by academic enemies as a believer in predestination, a belief that the king not only detested in itself but regarded as dangerous for the realm. He demanded Wolff leave the kingdom at short notice. König states that this was at Gundling's suggestion.[46] It is unlikely that König, writing a generally favorable account in 1795, when condemnation of Frederick William's order for Wolff's exile had become almost universal, would have included the story of Gundling's involvement if it had not been true.

Of the four biographies of Gundling, König's is the only one to mention this incident. Why should this be? We find an answer in König's intention. While stating, on the one hand, that his aim was to write a new biography of Gundling using original sources, König admits that he cannot write about Gundling without writing about Frederick William and his "bizarre" character. König, for example, has to admit that Frederick William had young bears running loose in the hunting lodge at Wusterhausen, bears with which Gundling was—as his fool—to do battle. Frederick William had somehow to be included in the story of the dynasty, but his times already seemed remote and barbarous by the 1790s, and the story of his actions could contaminate that of the rest of the dynasty, which wished to found its renown on that of Frederick William's son, Frederick II, "the Great." In particular, the way that scholars like Wolff were treated seemed incomprehensible by 1795, sixty years after Wolff's exile. Having Gundling intervene in the story of the ejection of Christian Wolff from Halle takes away some of the responsibility for this scandal from the monarch, makes Frederick William seem less "bizarre." And also consigns Frederick William to the past. The office of fool was long gone in Prussia by 1795. König confesses how much he prefers "unsern jetzigen Zeiten, wo man dergleichen nicht zu befürchten hat" (our own times, where similar things are not to be feared).[47]

Historians were caught between two conflicting objectives: how to honor Frederick William and yet deal with the fact that the king had lived in a brutal and fantastic world very different from the Berlin of the 1790s, a brutal world in which, in 1730, Frederick William had had Lieutenant Hans Hermann von Katte, the Crown Prince's intimate friend, executed before his eyes for being complicit in the prince's attempted flight to England. To the later eighteenth century, this seemed a scandal so deep it could barely be acknowledged. Frederick William's biographer, Gundling's successor, the fool Morgenstern, omits these incidents completely. Frederick William's cruelty, impossible to imagine by the 1790s, had to be played off by the historian against his importance for the dynasty.

Gundling's movement toward fool status had, in a less marked way, the same quality of scandal. If Gundling had had power at a certain stage of his life at court, Frederick William's gift of offices, paradoxically, started the movement toward fool-dom. A turning point here was Gundling's flight to Halle in 1721. He was brought back under guard and never again attempted to leave the court. It is tempting to bring to bear psychological explanations for his flight, such as the stress between the office of *Zeitungs-Referent* and that of chamberlain, or wearer of foolish clothes, or the stress of his position as president of a sadly declined Akademie der Wissenschaften concerned only with the rearing of silkworms. We have no evidence from Gundling himself on his motivation. Be that as it may, it seems that the failed flight increased his drunkenness, already Gundling's favorite recreation, and thus made him an easy butt for king, courtiers, and Tabakskollegium alike.

Gundling's role as a fool was imposed by Frederick William, who called him his "Narr" on several occasions.[48] Anecdotes about Gundling in his fool's role abound. All of them contain elements of shaming, the very shaming that Norbert Elias identified in a classic text as essential to the smooth functioning of an absolutist court.[49] Frederick William ran a court that, although not totally without splendor, was frugal by comparison with others and lacked the "representative splendor" (to use Elias's phrase) that had held together monarchy and courtiers in more splendid courts. Gundling's shaming may have been crucial to the operation of Frederick William's court, giving cohesion to its disparate members as they together found in Gundling a butt for their humor, and a communal site for their taboo breaking. As Norbert Elias remarks, to be effective, shaming also has to be grounded in the butt's own internalization of the anger and disrespect directed at him. It means that Gundling's personality and the evolution of his role from scholar to fool not only allowed the shaming to happen but that it could shape Frederick William's court. His government depended as much on the incorporation of different individual personality structures as it did on coercion.[50]

So what actually happened to Gundling? The court nobility, pages, and young military officers, for one, delighted in pinning to his back pictures of hares, monkeys, and donkeys, animals associated with fool-dom, and then watching his response to the ensuing mockery. They imitated hares and donkeys in his presence. The court "Moors," or black African servants, played practical jokes on him. Others stole and tore up the notes Gundling needed as *Zeitungs-Referent*. They dressed up a young monkey (adding to our knowledge of the menagerie at Frederick William's palaces) in the same costume that Gundling was forced to wear and began the "joke" in front of Gundling that the monkey was his own child. In the end, he gave in to the shaming and accepted the monkey on his knee, acknowledging an intimate relationship with one of the most frequently used symbols of foolishness and showing that he was, indeed, a fool. Even his biographer König admits that Gundling brought shame upon himself with his own drunkenness.[51] Gundling sometimes appeared incapacitated even at meetings of the Tabaks-kollegium and thus aroused Frederick William's ire. When this happened, the king had him carried to the watch guard of the night and let him sleep off his inebriation on the floor. Sometimes Gundling still retained sufficient wit to cry "*peccavi, peccavi*" (I have sinned) to Frederick William and thereby restrain his anger—as Flögel says, one of the main functions of court fools.

It was in that drunkeness that his vulnerability to shame lay, and that allowed the king to control him. His drunkenness meant that he became the butt of jokes even by members of the Tabakskollegium, who played with his addiction to drink and gained great entertainment thereby. There were other episodes of shaming. At table in the king's hunting lodge at Wusterhausen one day, he put his foot in a mess left by one of the bears and became the butt of uncontrollable laughter from the rest of the court. His tormentors put a bear in his bed to meet him when he came back drunk from a meeting of the Tabakskollegium. His ensuing terror, Morgenstern states, caused the court to regard him as "nicht nur ein Narr, sondern auch poltroon" (not only a fool but also a coward).[52]

In a drunken state one winter evening, Gundling fell through the ice covering the moat at Wusterhausen, attracting many spectators to the windows, who thought the spectacle of his struggles to escape the freezing water "extremely funny." So funny did Frederick William find it that he had a picture painted of the scene, which traveled with him on his journeys between Berlin, Potsdam, and Wusterhausen. In the end Gundling was helped from his life-threatening predicament but not before it was almost too late. Gundling of course tried to seek revenge for this "mobbing." While drunk, he tried to strangle a court servant who had played many practical jokes on him. Complaints from other victims to Frederick William, however, only produced the comment that those who tangled with fools deserved what they got.[53] Frederick William protected Gundling when he wanted to and reserved to himself the right to be angry with Gundling.

Gundling's drinking turned him into a walking contradiction: the man loaded with titles who had no honor. Gundling could not control himself or control the actions and attitudes of others toward him. He was a walking joke who only had to exist at all to be of great amusement to everyone. But it was Frederick William who had the last laugh. At his orders, Gundling, over the brave resistance of the local clergy, was buried in a coffin in the shape of a beer barrel. Frederick William ordered the funeral oration to be given by Gundling's enemy David Fassmann.[54]

Why did Frederick William protect rather than dismiss Gundling, especially when Gundling's chronic drunkenness could make him incompetent in his important post of *Zeitungs-Referent?* He did so precisely because he needed Gundling as a place of contradiction, which meant a place of shame. No one else could serve this role as well as a historian-fool, paradoxically honored and dishonored at the same time. Frederick William thereby demonstrated power. This making of Gundling into a place of paradoxical shame also has implications for the interpretation of Frederick William's court. There has been much controversy about its nature. Recent scholars find that the traditional view that Frederick William stood out from other rulers of his time by his thriftiness, his refusal to continue the representative splendor of his father's court life, build palaces, or regularly hold the ceremonies and festivals through which power and glory were instantiated is misguided. Sabrow and König, as well as Marschke, hold this view. They are historians who have an interest in smoothing out the differences between the early modern and the contemporary, Frederick William and later rulers, historians and fools.

Marschke attempts to argue that this older thesis about Frederick William's court is incorrect.[55] He points to his queen's court held in the new Monbijou Palace in Berlin, which certainly tried to be a "representative court" on the contemporary model, with its fetes and ballets, and argues that Frederick William in fact had not rid the court of his father's splendor. This argument, however, falls down. That the queen's court was more splendid still leaves the character of Frederick William's own court to be explained. So perhaps we are forced back onto older arguments, deep in the historiography of Prussia, as Marschke comments, about the austerity—and the oddness—of Frederick William's court and thus left with the unanswered question of how his court managed to function in the absence of "representative" splendor.

It seems likely that Gundling played an important role here. Norbert Elias, as we have seen, pointed out the importance of shame in the fabric of the court. Gundling was the vulnerable place where shame was located, could be made visible, and was manipulated, and where negativity could thus be moved away from the ruler. As Frederick William said, Don't bring me your quarrels with the fool. In a court that had been profoundly altered by Frederick William, mobbing resulted in tightening group loyalties within the court, such as that of the Tabakskollegium. All this could only benefit Frederick William's control over his court. Gundling's shame and contradictions balanced Frederick William's own notorious contradictions of character. King and fool should be understood as a tightly knit dyad of dominance and humiliation. They show that the instantiation of power (whether we call this "absolutism" or not) relies just as much on the presence of certain character-structures in prince, courtiers, and subjects as it does on blunt force.

Perhaps Frederick William after 1713 had taken the flesh off the early modern court, but he kept the bones. He ran a thrifty court, where one man worked in many roles. In doing so, he had begun to instantiate his famous statement: "I do what I want to do and stabilize my power and put the crown on a rock of bronze."[56] He did so with the aid of contradiction, shaming, and cruelty, with a fool as butt: that is, with the aid of Gundling. If Frederick William once described himself as a "fool for a soldier," he must also be counted a "fool for a fool," and was to describe himself as such in 1737 (see chapter 2). Frederick William's court may have been thriftily reduced from that of his father, but it still retained great importance, alongside all the administrative reforms of the reign, as a place for disciplining and shaping the elite.

How unusual does this make his court? And given the relationship between court and character, how unusual does this make Frederick William? If we take Elias's paradigm, based on the very different court of Louis XIV, then the Berlin court was odd indeed.[57] To have a fool who was also the president of the Akademie der Wissenschaften, who walked the palace halls wearing red silk stockings and a coat with WURM G embroidered on the back, trying to avoid the bears roaming the corridors only to find one had been secreted in his bedchamber, would seem to support Marschke's comment that by the time of Frederick William's reign, the shape of courts had become far more fluid than Elias allowed. Within limits, as Marschke points out, rulers were able to create any form of court they wished and use it to project themselves to their courts and to their domains. But be that as it may, in comparison to the other courts we will encounter in subsequent chapters—Munich, Vienna, Würzburg, Ellwangen, Ansbach, and Dresden—Berlin was bizarre indeed.

Benjamin Marschke has argued that the king's behavior, though often borderline, does not merit the adjectives of *eigenwillig* or "bizarre" that later historians have lavished upon him, some of whom have even seen him as mentally unstable. However, Marschke's attempt to "normalize" (whatever one means by "normal") Frederick William and his court is largely undermined by the account I have just given of his actions toward Gundling. It is also undermined by his execution in 1730 of Hans Hermann von Katte, an act of both extraordinary brutality and political courage, since von Katte's family were among the most respected in his army. This act, consigned to a footnote by Marschke, developed into an international scandal, as did the imprisonment of the Crown Prince, who had tried with von Katte's aid to flee to England to escape Frederick William's mistreatment.[58]

We will see much more of Frederick William in the next chapter. For now, I would argue that much of his character can be understood as that of a joker of a black kind. He liked a joke. He liked to see the practical jokes to which Gundling was subjected by the Tabakskollegium. His own jokes often changed things to his advantage. They were not often appreciated by their butts. This aspect of his personality has not often been explored. But in the following chapter, concerning Gundling's successor, Salomon Jacob Morgenstern, it will be seen to be very much at work.[59]

TWO

Salomon Jacob Morgenstern

Newspapers, Professors, and Playing the Fool

Es ist ja nur rein erlaubter Spass und Scherz! (It is only good clean fun
and jokes!)
—Frederick William I, King in Prussia

On an autumn evening in 1737, Salomon Jacob Morgenstern, professor of
history and geography at the University of Halle, sat in a carriage with Frederick William. Their conversation opened a bond between them, and Frederick William offered him the post of court *Zeitungs-Referent,* or newspaper
reader, formerly held by Jacob Gundling. That same year, Morgenstern,
dressed in a blue gown embroidered in silver with the fools' symbol of the
hare, conducted a famous debate on reason and folly with the professors of
the Prussian University far to the east of Berlin, at Frankfurt-an-der-Oder.

Who was Morgenstern, and how had he come into Frederick William's
orbit? A poverty-stricken scholar, he sought to better his position by seeking
a post in Russia, as did many in the German lands in that period who were
educated beyond the capacity of their states to employ them. He duly wrote
a book in Latin on the public law of the Russian Empire, for which compli-
ment the Empress Elizabeth awarded him a hundred roubles, to be collected
from the Russian embassy in Berlin. On his way there, he was stopped by
the town guard in Potsdam. When the commanding officer heard of Morgenstern's academic status and then took in his unusual appearance, he had
him brought to Frederick William. An unusual appearance was a prerequisite for a fool, and the court was without one. If the fool could be a scholar
as well and replicate Gundling's composite nature, so much the better. So
that was how Morgenstern, who only just missed dwarfish stature and was

distinguished by a large beaked nose, flowing black hair, and green eyes, was told to climb into the carriage and meet the king, who almost immediately engaged him as reader to the Tabakskollegium.[1]

Why did Frederick William engage him, and engage him so quickly? These acts of very quick commitment are commonplace in the accounts of acts of patronage in this period and are constitutive of patronage relations over the whole field of dependence and deference. Later, the fool Peter Prosch (chapter 4) was to have similar experiences and would compare the rulers who engaged him in this way to hunter and prey. The king certainly believed that "Wenn man einen Hasen haben will, muss man ihn ja von Universitäten holen" (If one wants a hare [fool], one must fetch him from a university).[2] Yet there were many other penniless university scholars he could have chosen who had written books, were in need of money or a place, and were capable of reading the newspapers aloud and commenting on them. Morgenstern undoubtedly was chosen not only because he looked the part of a fool but because he could play the composite role of fool and scholar that had been Gundling's. Above all, he developed a close personal bond with the king, which, he alleged, made him "immer beliebter" (ever more beloved).[3] It was this that allowed him to work for the recall of Christian Wolff, one of the first acts of Frederick II, Frederick William's successor.

Most of our knowledge of Morgenstern comes from Flögel.[4] There has never been a full-length biography of him, and in contrast to the four devoted to Gundling, the only detailed study of Morgenstern continues to be Richard Otto Leineweber's slim 1890s doctoral dissertation.[5] Most of what we know about Morgenstern's opinions comes from his own published works, which go largely unanalyzed by Flögel, whose account concentrates on the 1737 debate. The issues of the intertwining of foolishness and scholarship that lie at the heart, for example, of Martin Sabrow's biography of Gundling have not attracted their historian in the case of Morgenstern the Halle professor. What appears to be a paucity of sources may have had this effect. Yet, in fact, Morgenstern's published works tell us a great deal about him and his ideas. They also tell us about the tasks Frederick William engaged Morgenstern to fulfill. Flögel tells us that the king took him "into his service to read aloud from the papers and entertain him with old and new stories."[6] So from the beginning, newspaper appreciation and historical knowledge were linked.

Two years before meeting Frederick William, Morgenstern had published his 1735 *Neueste Staats-Geographie, wo jedes Landes natürlicher, politischer, Kirchen- und Schulen-Staat genau abgeschildert.* His bulky text-book, used in his lecture courses in Halle, has an old-fashioned appearance, even for its date. Glosses, for example, appear in small print in the body of the text, rather than in footnotes at the bottom of the page. But the text itself is all about novelty and the search for knowledge and is a far cry from the compilations and lists beloved of Baroque scholars. In the introduction, Morgenstern dedicates the book to those who want to follow the new career of what he calls a "statist," or expert advisor to power, and then rapidly points out how quickly the knowledge contained in books such as his will go out of date.[7] He estimates new editions will need to be published every five years. This is not just a hint to his publisher. It also reflects the way in which knowledge was turning over ever-faster in this era. The people of Morgenstern's time were not simply facing an "information overload," as many modern scholars have pointed out.[8] They were also facing a world in which information simply wore out and had endlessly to be replaced with something better. It is not surprising therefore that Morgenstern stresses to his readers the importance of direct personal experience in the gaining of the knowledge of territories, states, and places. Experience comes from going to the place oneself and gaining firsthand knowledge. Reading is help-ful, especially of authors who have themselves been over the territory, but is not as important as experience. Finally, there comes history, for knowledge of history allows us to weigh competing claims about matters of fact. In this work, Morgenstern is confronting some of the many faces of the knowledge debates of the Enlightenment. In emphasizing experience as the means to knowledge, he was saying no more than the famous Scots philosopher David Hume was to write, for example, in 1748 in his discussion of biblical accounts of miracles.[9] This is not to compare Morgenstern with one of the great figures of the Enlightenment, but it is to say that he had dipped a toe into one of its currents.

Morgenstern's objective of using his book to train "statists" was also to contribute to the growing numbers of "experts" whose expertise was a key factor in the growth of the early modern state. In turn, the state was an important source of legitimation and status for the experts, such as Morgen-stern, as the historian Eric H. Ash has pointed out.[10] His position, though, rested upon a paradox. Frederick William, as we have seen, was the enemy of academic knowledge yet, paradoxically, was reliant on university-trained experts, "statists," such as Morgenstern and Gundling, to carry out his orders and to write the histories on which his claims to legitimate rulership and territorial expansion depended. In doing so, he followed the trend in the larger monarchies. Expertise in French foreign policy, for example, was shaped throughout the seventeenth and early eighteenth centuries by dynasties of "statists," as the historians John C. Rule and Benjamin S. Trotter have recently pointed out.[11] In appointing Morgenstern as *Zeitungs-Referent,* Frederick William was using him as an expert whose expertise should feed directly into his informal equivalent of a cabinet, the so-called Tabakskollegium. Morgenstern's position was only partly legitimated by his expertise, although it played off the way in which the members of the Tabakskollegium were legitimated by the king's trust. In the end, Morgenstern, for all his knowledge, was likewise legitimated by his personal dependence on Frederick William. In this, his position closely resembled that of Gundling.

Morgenstern was certainly a prolific writer. In his situation as an impoverished scholar before 1737, he could hardly afford to be anything else. In 1736, he taught at Halle and published a four-page work entitled *Vorschlag wie die Zeitungen mit Nutzen zu erläutern. Wobey seine Winter-Arbeit zugleich bekannt machen wollen M. Salomon Jacob Morgenstern.*[12] This pamphlet combination of lecture list and reflections on history and the newspaper press, now extremely rare, shows Morgenstern grappling with the intersection of novelty and knowledge. It was not that Morgenstern was in any way original in this. The newspaper press had flourished in the German states since the Reformation.[13] There already existed a substantial body of literature debating the correct reading of newspapers, their claims to impartiality and novelty, and the reading strategies to be employed when newspaper accounts contradicted each other.[14] It was already recommended that attentive readers should make their own notebooks of extracts from newspaper accounts, which was exactly the practice of both Gundling and Morgenstern. Frederick William's decision to create the post of *Zeitungs-Referent* for Gundling, to carry it over (unsuccessfully) to David Fassmann, and then much more successfully to award it to Morgenstern, was thus a logical extension of a state of affairs where newspapers, for all their problems, were recognized as important purveyors of fact and opinion, especially in matters of foreign policy. That Frederick William's newspaper readers also acted as fools shows not only the lability of court positions but also the porousness of the membrane then separating different sorts of knowledge. Taken with the

1737 debate on reason and folly, it also shows the king's attempts to combine in his fools' persons expert knowledge and fool's knowledge.

Newspapers, Morgenstern argued in his pamphlet, were also vital to the understanding of history, close as they were to eyewitnessing. He sees history and news in a symbiotic relationship: "The light of the news serves to tear apart the clouds of ignorance, the light of insight equally drives away the fog of prejudices and utterly harmful dispositions."[15] News knowledge needs to be linked with historical insight to make real knowledge.

Later, he discusses the problems of impartiality: "Because they are not allowed to illuminate partial things properly, their knowledge, instead of a complete picture, becomes only decoration despite collected news; not only insight, however, but the distinction between true and false, esteem and trustworthiness, are lost." Novelty was the enemy of truth, and the origin, as he said in another place, of the contemporary "unstoppable desire always to have extraordinary news."[16] Newspapers were clearly not capable of forming a "canon," and their obsession with the new made their truth-value debatable. A *Zeitungs-Referent,* by amalgamating readings from several newspapers, could to some degree circumvent these problems.

Yet Morgenstern's concern with truth in 1736 is a sad and ironic commentary on his biography of Frederick William published posthumously in 1785. Morgenstern of course grapples with the eternal problem of how to fit Frederick William's reforming reign, frightening, complex character, and sometimes brutal acts into the flow of the history of the dynasty and the fatherland. Morgenstern solves it by simply omitting events that we know to have occurred and that reflected, especially to the sentimental mind of the late Enlightenment, Frederick's cruelty. *Ommissio veri* and *suggestio falsi* are both employed. The execution of Crown Prince Frederick's friend Hans Hermann von Katte, for example, which caused a European scandal, is simply omitted, as is Frederick's attempt to flee with von Katte to England from his father's mistreatment.[17] The biography contains—a great loss for the historian—neither an account of Morgenstern's experiences in the Tabakskollegium nor of the 1737 debate with the professors in Frankfurt-an-der-Oder, which was the high spot of Morgenstern's career as a court fool.

At some points in the biography, he discusses the king's cruelty.[18] He defines cruelty as taking pleasure in the infliction of terror on other creatures. Did the king show such a pleasure? Morgenstern answers his own question by asserting that no one believed such a thing, and: "Further:

Frederick William I, self-portrait, 1737. From the same year as Morgenstern's debate with the professors, this unflattering self-portrait reveals a great deal about the king's inner turmoil. (Staatliche Schlösser und Gärten, Potsdam/Bridgeman Images)

whether a cruel lord could be sympathetic so often and so much that it gives us more proof of sympathy than proof of his alleged cruelty? Nobody can deny that the departed king was indeed most sympathetic to the martyrs to his irascibility. It is not to be denied that he was held to be crueler during his lifetime, because of the blows he delivered, the excesses of his conscription policy, and the strict executions during his lifetime, than he was after he died."[19] Morgenstern, having changed his line of argument about Frederick

William's cruelty halfway through, goes on to recall that one of Frederick William's favorite sayings was, "Il faut donner une victime au bourreau" (You've got to give someone to the executioner).

Submerged allusions tremble under the surface of Morgenstern's account and give the impression that the biography of Frederick William stands at a tangent to the truth. Crown Prince Frederick, the future Frederick II, is never called by his name, and the reader is supposed to know, without being told, the reason for his imprisonment in the fortress of Custrin, and why he is the object of paternal solicitude of a particular kind. Instead of cruelty: "When the Crown Prince was imprisoned in Custrin the Lord Father to keep him occupied gave him criminal cases to review. How could a cruel lord have missed such a beautiful opportunity to torment him, to make his life intolerable and even go so far as to shed blood?"[20]

This account of the king's clemency and mercy has a twofold purpose: it diverts attention from the execution of Hans Hermann von Katte, Frederick's companion in his flight, whose name is also never mentioned, and also from the cruelty with which Frederick William treated his son both before and after his attempted flight to England in 1730. To call Frederick William "der Herr Vater" (the Lord Father) also hooks up nicely with the commonplace idea in the eighteenth century that the king stood as father to his people.[21]

Ueber Friedrich Wilhelm I is thus a deeply problematic work. In spite of all that Morgenstern can do, the king's disturbing character shines through the text. The omissions and contradictions in Morgenstern's account are evidence of the pressure the king was capable of placing, even after death, on history-writing for accuracy and context.

Ueber Friedrich Wilhelm I, Morgenstern's most considerable work, was published in 1793. Yet the high point of his life had been reached decades earlier. In 1737, Frederick William organized a debate over the nature of foolishness and reason between Morgenstern, who was recognized by all as Frederick William's fool, and the assembled professors of the Faculty of Law at the University of Frankfurt-an-der-Oder. The debate carried through the discussion of the relationship between fool and scholar, which we began to explore in chapter 1. There we saw how much to Frederick William's advantage it was to have Gundling, a composite figure containing both foolishness and scholarly knowledge, at his court. Morgenstern can also be seen as such a composite figure. What was specific to Morgenstern was the way that his fool-dom found expression in formal performance. Gundling had only performed formally in front of the Tabakskollegium in Berlin, Potsdam, and Wusterhausen (although it could be argued that his whole life with Frederick William had been a performance of foolishness). Morgenstern commented on the newspapers to the Tabakskollegium too, yet also traveled with Frederick William far outside his usual circuit, to Frankfurt-an-der-Oder in the east of Prussia, and engaged in a public performance in front of professors, schoolboys, and king.

As we look at the Frankfurt-an-der-Oder debate, we look at how foolishness intertwines its truths with contradiction and irony. These truths are made manifest by performance. This chapter argues that performance, in this case the 1737 staging of the conflict between reason and folly, shows struggle between values as much as does debate between printed texts. This is important given recent tendencies to portray an Enlightenment of conversation, reading, and writing instead of one of action; of sensibility rather than of cruelty.

The 1737 debate pitted the professors at the law faculty at the University of Frankfurt-an-der-Oder against Morgenstern, who in this debate was the proponent of foolishness.[22] Frederick William shamed the professors by forcing them into a public contestation with his fool. The king personally orchestrated the debate, and his partiality for black, inventive, and hurtful humor undoubtedly came well into play.

The king had another reason for desiring reform in Frankfurt-an-der-Oder. The eighteenth century saw many new universities founded in the German-speaking lands. In the year of the Frankfurt debate, the new university at Göttingen was to open its doors under the patronage of the Elector of Hannover, who as George II concurrently ruled Britain. The Prussian monarchy had already founded the University of Halle in 1694. Württemberg had founded the Carlsakademie, the alma mater of Friedrich Schiller and Georges Cuvier. These universities and others were in heavy competition with each other for students and star professors. They were expected to produce loyal and expert bureaucrats and clergy for their ruler.[23] Above all, economic advantages were expected to accrue to their towns, as an influx of students led to the growth of getting and spending.

In this context, it is little wonder that Frederick William's attention was sharply focused on what was going on in Frankfurt-an-der-Oder, an ancient university refounded by his father Frederick I, King in Prussia, in 1701. In the light of the strong academic competition among the German states, Frederick William could not afford the failure of an important faculty. What made Frankfurt specific was the difficult situation in its law faculty. The faculty had lost star members, and the university as a whole was neglected in favor of the new university at Halle. Those faculty who were left were undistinguished, earned small salaries, and had few students. To remedy this situation, the king had appointed Johann Jakob Moser (1701–1785), an expert on the public law of the empire, whose quarrels with his colleagues only exacerbated problems in the faculty, and in the university. (Moser had also been appointed its rector.) The difficulties in Frankfurt were thus more important than official irritation at underachieving professors, and to remedy it, Frederick William did something more interesting than sending out an edict from Potsdam.

The debate of 1737 was a deliberately staged performance. Every staging, even (perhaps especially) staging involving a fool, is demonstrative. It brings to the surface and demonstrates, through character, plot, and action, the values behind it. Public debates were not in themselves an unusual form of encounter for an age that delighted in public competitions between musical virtuosi and chess champions, which knew that it was the heir of the great theological debates of the Reformation, and where academic degrees were debated in public. What made the Frankfurt debate unusual was its deliberate staging by a monarch, the response of members of the Frankfurt faculty, and the use of the court fool in a setting well beyond the boundaries of court life. The Frankfurt-an-der-Oder debate took place at the junction of the court and the public. The debate was also important in another sense, mentioned in chapter 1, of being another confrontation between Frederick William, orchestrated through his fool, and the professional scholars of the university. In the same way, Frederick William had publicly bested the scholars of the Akademie der Wissenschaften in Berlin by manipulating Gundling and the silkworm farm. The king was not only brutal; he was clever.

The fool's contribution to the debate was to hold present to each other the contradictory values of *gravitas* (the faculty) and *levitas* (the fool). In this, the fool was doing something that has long historical roots, longer than can be described here, but some of which can be identified in the work of the devoted early sixteenth-century scholar Erasmus. At one point in his *Adages,* a collection of proverbs current in the ancient world, Erasmus discusses the small Roman figurines called *sileni* because they represented the god Silenus, drinking companion of Bacchus, and buffoon to the gods.[24] These figurines can be opened up to reveal objects in their interior that are very different from their external appearance. Erasmus uses them, here as well as in his *Praise of Folly* (1515), as demonstrations of the contradiction between exterior appearance and interior reality. He then makes the more general argument that any given object might therefore need many ways, rather than just one way, to understand it. As an example he points out how easy it was to mistake Socrates for a buffoon, because of his ugly, peasant-like exterior, his unbroken flow of humor, and his frequently uttered contradictory statements, of which the most famous is that there is only one thing to know, and that is that one knows nothing.

Erasmus goes on to point out that, contrary to appearances, there might be more wisdom in an ordinary man than in many pompous theologians, or in professors three or four times over who are stuffed with their favorite Aristotle, and swollen with definitions, conclusions, and propositions. Two hundred years later, we find a Prussian monarch echoing many of these observations, famously remarking—at this very debate—that "ein Quentgen Mutterwitz ist besser als ein Zentner Universitätswitz" (an ounce of mother-wit is worth more than all the university learning in the world).[25]

Here, Frederick William joined the tradition, strong in the seventeenth and eighteenth centuries, of royal mockery of scholars. England, for example, had already seen at least a century of this ridicule. In the late seventeenth century, Charles II and his fool, Thomas Killigrew, mocked the Fellows of the Royal Society of London and the professors of Gresham's College. The king called them "My fools." The monarch and the fool mocked in particular Robert Boyle's experiments with atmospheric pressure ("weighing air") and William Petty's experiments with underwater navigation.[26] The 1737 debate in many ways fits in with this tradition of royal mockery. In mocking the professors, Morgenstern acts as Frederick William's surrogate.

Even without an account by Morgenstern himself, we have several different sources for the 1737 debate. The first is based on the autobiography of a most reluctant participant, Johann Jakob Moser (1701–1785), famous as one of the founders of German public law and holder of a chair in the law faculty of Frankfurt-an-der-Oder.[27] Moser's account is hardly neutral. He was in trouble on all sides by the time of the debate with Morgenstern (also author of a book on public law). Moser was involved in a dispute with the royal education bureaucracy, while at the same time battling the rest of the faculty. This had come to the ears of a monarch bent on the revival of the institution. Moser was summoned to the debate with the fool. Repelled by the thought of the probable loss of his honor arising from debating a fool, he begged to be excused from it or, at the very least, to be allowed to make a serious and not a comic speech.[28] The king replied: "What is this all about? Everyone has his own fool. One has a fool for spiritual pride; one has another for a fool. It is only good clean fun and jokes! If I do not want to drink any wine I should not protest against it but just not drink!"[29]

In the end, Moser was forced to attend the debate. An army sergeant came to his home with the invitation while the family was at dinner, just so there would be no mistaking the king's wishes. Moser's autobiography credits this for causing the severe illness that came upon him immediately after the debate with Morgenstern.

As the debate began, Frederick William mockingly took off his hat to Moser, applauded his entrance, and then took the opportunity of the hiatus caused by Morgenstern's late arrival to interrogate Moser on the difficult situation in the faculty, a pointed interview since Moser had been specifically appointed to deal with its problems. The intimidating debate the king was staging was another attempt to do so, though Moser missed its significance and perceived in it only a threat to his own *gravitas* and honor, as well as that of the university. The king picked the theme of foolish opposites and teased Moser about the foolishness of university scholars. Moser replied to the king's concerns. Thinking that he had dazzled the king with his legal knowledge and suggestions for reform, Moser then made the mistake of asking once more to be allowed to deliver a serious speech on foolishness, using classical biblical texts (e.g., Psalms 14:1; 53:1) At this, the king exploded.

Moser was in any case a difficult man. He had compromised his career with his previous employer, Carl-Alexander, the Grand-Duke of Württemberg, by refusing his invitation to attend a masked ball to open the Carnival season. He had no liking for invitations to public events or for playing games with identity. The double person that was Morgenstern, a professorial fool and a foolish professor, held no attractions for him. Moser was manifesting a severe dislike of staged games and aggressive levity, of the artificial and the contradictory. He would not have appreciated a Silenus figure. What was at stake for him was the enforced confrontation between the levity of the fool with the gravity of the *Lehrstand*. He dreaded being in the same space as that composite being that was Morgenstern. Morgenstern's duality implied that there was really no sharp or necessary distinction between the two roles of fool and professor and that therefore academic forms of reasoning were not separate and superior ways of truth discovery but existed on the same level as the ridicule, paradoxes, riddles, witticisms, irony, folk proverbs, insults, and contradictions characteristic of the interventions of fools.

When Frederick William's fool, Morgenstern, abruptly appeared, he was dressed in an extraordinary costume: a long blue velvet coat with red lapels, and a red vest, both embroidered in silver with hares, one of the animal emblems of foolishness. In a parody of contemporary fashion, reminding us of the costume Gundling had been forced to wear, an enormous wig hung down to his waist. In place of the aristocratic sword, he hung a fox's tail. On his hat, he had pinned a hare's mask. The costume had many functions. It mobilized ancient symbols such as fox (cunning) and hare (foolishness) against the professoriat. It meant that Morgenstern appropriated to himself symbols that were animal rather than rational and that were drawn from everyday sayings and folk life rather than learned discourse.

For the actual conduct of the debate, we turn to our second source. This is a manuscript letter bound in with the Göttingen University Library copy of Morgenstern's published theses.[30] The letter, dated November 1737, appears to be an eyewitness account. There is no indication of the writer or its recipient, but the language and spelling indicate a writer of Swabian origin. The writer is concerned with the printing of Morgenstern's theses ("wir fahren mit dem Druck fleissig fort" [we are industriously carrying on the printing]). The writer is explicit about the king's personal intervention in the debate. He had "den ganzen actum allerhoechst selber dirigiret" (conducted the whole performance by himself). The professors, previously individually invited by soldiers bearing the royal command, debated Morgenstern's theses before a noisy audience of university and gymnasium students. Every time a thesis was debated, the king gave a signal by clapping his hands and blowing on a pipe for the students to show their pleasure or displeasure. The king was demonstrating his power outside the court. He was showing that he could control his subjects in the public world. And that his fool was powerful enough to join him in this.

Naturally the outcome of the debate was not in doubt. The Swabian writer noted that the king had bowed to Morgenstern and had allowed "es lebe Morgenstern!" to be shouted. These were two high honors from Frederick William. The writer concludes, perhaps ironically, that the same honor and "*hohe Gnade*" would figure in the annals of the University of Frankfurt-an-der-Oder as in those of no other German university. Morgenstern received a doctorate from—of course—the University of Frankfurt-an-der-Oder, as a reward for his part in the debate. The 1737 debate seems also to have solidified his hold over Frederick William, at whose side he became a fixture. Even Frederick William's successor, Frederick II (1740–1786), gave him the lucrative official post of *Vizekanzler* (vice chancellor) of Silesia, the province that Frederick seized from Austria in 1740.

The extraordinary events of the debate were followed by the publication of Morgenstern's theses, our third source of knowledge about the debate.[31] The theses are thirty-eight in number. Of these, eleven are directed specifically at the pretentions of the *Gelehrtenstand* to superior wisdom. (We have no record of the counterarguments advanced by Morgenstern's unfortunate opponents.) He sustains the thesis that while all the major *Stände* (social groups), that is, the farmers, the soldiers, the courtiers, are prone to their own forms of folly, the *Gelehrtenstand* has no rival in its foolishness. This was a position of course not lost on the audience in Frankfurt-an-der-Oder. Theses one through six define as a fool someone who has ideas that are out of touch with reality, or who uses inappropriate means to gain his ends. Morgenstern does not relate foolishness to mental illness or pure stupidity, as became increasingly common after the midcentury.

In thesis seven, Morgenstern sustains the very commonplace that Frederick William had used in his outburst against Moser, one found since antiquity (and that is the motto of this book), that foolishness is universal: "Fools are everywhere. The whole world is full of fools / from shepherds to priests!"[32] Morgenstern's thesis mixes an adage originating in Cicero's letters with a modern satirical popular verse. This mixing is very characteristic of foolish discourse. Fools' reasoning does not include the scrupulous weighing of different sources and their division into different genres characteristic of professorial knowledge, the definition and division to which so much energy was devoted in this century. Second, Morgenstern's thesis, though hardly original, inverted the characteristic contrary argument of the Enlightenment that it is the universality of the capacity for reason that defines the human race.

The eleventh thesis continues Morgenstern's thoughts on the nature of foolishness. Fools, he argues, can be frequently encountered, indeed even the so-called "clever" can become fools, unless they work hard: "Demnach ist ein Klüger, nichts anders, als der seinen Trieb zur Narrheit überwindet" (Hence a clever person is no more than somebody who has overcome his impulse to foolishness). "Cleverness" is the result of perpetual struggle with its opposite, foolishness. Its origin is dialogic, not singular. And rather than being an inherent property of the clever, it is one that even they can maintain only by struggle. Intellect, like life, is inextricably linked to its opposite. Cleverness can tip over into foolishness, happiness into misery, as Morgenstern sustained in this thesis: "One can assume without misjudgment that being clever is not an art: but mixed up with foolishness as happiness is with unhappiness."[33] Knowledge arises from contradiction. Like and unlike are bound together in the same person, just as they are in the *sileni* figures, or in the composite persons who are Morgenstern and Gundling. Morgenstern's theses are like the *sileni,* whose external appearance belies their content. He used the appearance of an academic disputation not to make a display of erudition but to call into doubt the distinctive knowledge claims of his opponents. One final contradiction here: Morgenstern had been given the mission of disciplining by ridicule and humiliation. But he himself was manipulated by Frederick William, just as were all the other actors in the debate. Not only did the fool utter paradoxes, but he also embodied them.

Could the Frankfurt-an-der-Oder debate have happened anywhere other than in the German lands of the early eighteenth century? Perhaps not. Most of the more than three hundred German states, of which Prussia was among the largest, were tiny. This meant that German princes were closer to every decision than were those of the great monarchies such as France or Austria. Subjects (like Moser or Morgenstern) could have, whether they appreciated them or not, very close encounters with the princely holders of power. Issues that would have been lengthily decided in Versailles by infighting between court factions were decided in Berlin by direct princely order or, in Frankfurt an-der-Oder in 1737, by aggressive levity organized by the ruler himself. That Frederick William should take an interest in the affairs of the University of Frankfurt-an-der-Oder and decide to reorder things there by the application of his own particular sense of humor was therefore not surprising.

The Frankfurt-an-der-Oder debate also gains significance in its relation to another tradition, that of the ridicule of scholars by scholars, in this case of the law professors by Professor Morgenstern. This is a different tradition from that of the learned fool that we explored in chapter 1. Ridicule was one of the main ways in which scholars dishonored their opponents and made them impossible to take seriously, whatever the intrinsic value of their arguments. That Morgenstern was a professor as well as a fool, a composite creature, meant that he could speak from both inside and outside the profession. While he might be foolish as a professor, as a fool he was professorial. His double role deepened the ironies that could be extracted from his statements and made his ridicule hard to shrug off. The position of the ridiculer was also in any case a strong one: through ridicule he yet aimed to take away seriousness from opponents and reserve it for himself.

So widespread was the ridicule of one scholar by another that self-appointed guardians of the Republic of Letters issued many vain exhortations to their brethren to abstain from ad hominem arguments and aggressive ridicule. In 1720, Moser himself had had the experience of being laughed out of a public disputation in Tübingen by audience and professors alike. He described the opponent who triggered round after round of laughter against him as a "hare's cousin," foreshadowing the silver hares embroidered on Morgenstern's blue coat. It may have been this experience in Tübingen that caused his opposition to the Frankfurt-an-der-Oder debate seventeen years later. Ridicule was a device for establishing dominance, and an effective one at that. If intense ridicule was worth using, something serious must be at stake, something like the professorial character of the Frankfurt-an-der-Oder faculty. Reputations could be made and broken in the public debates. To lose was dishonoring, and it was responded to as such by typically unkind audiences.

Successful ridicule broke down one scholar's honor and built up that of another—as discussed in chapter 1—and left the scholar who was bested without the social recognition that would enable him to continue his intellectual work.[34] Ridicule was the dialogic companion of the emergence of scholarship as a self-standing occupation with its own norms of behavior. It declines as a routine aspect of scholarly life when academic disciplines begin to separate out from each other. But that is another story.

Fools also made claims to be heard, claims that were strongly linked to the idea that a fool could, like a scholar, speak the truth without acknowledging the superior claims of the social hierarchy. There is a parallel between *Philosophenfreiheit* and *Narrenfreiheit*. They are each subversive in their truth claims. Frederick I, King in Prussia, and the father of Frederick William, recognized this clearly. After the death of his official fool, Pussman (Flögel gives no Christian name), the Lutheran clergy of Berlin refused to give him burial in sacred ground, as a person practicing a shameful profession. Frederick, however, ordered that Pussman be buried in the Petruskirche zu Cölln, and buried, at that, among the graves of the priests who had served the church, not far from the altar. Frederick pointed out that "Pussman was a preacher of the truth, and didn't spare even me, the king, the lash of his tongue. He deserves therefore to be buried in the middle of a church, where surely nothing but the truth will be preached."[35] In an eighteenth-century world abounding in conflicts over superiority, inferiority, and precedence, such as those between philosophers and theologians, fools' humor was leveling and melted hierarchy. For Frederick I, fools' truth was as good as theological truth, and his fool, who had not spared the king, and by definition reached the truth he preached by nonrational ways, deserved to lie among the educated men who dedicated themselves to the truths of theology.

Eighteenth-century fools in the German lands worked against the background of conflicts over reason and foolishness, from within a culture of ridicule. They also worked at a time of conflict between theologians on the one hand, and philosophers on the other, where the theologians demanded that the philosophers acknowledge the superiority of theology, and the philosophers refused to do so. Fools' truth was a third form of truth. In the last of Morgenstern's 1737 theses, he pointed out that foolishness was necessary and universal, and universally necessary, and concluded that in these respects all men are equal: "Foolishness is necessary, nay essential to the world. Almost all joy and happiness originates from, through, over and with fools! . . . Nature has attributed to everyone their due allotment of foolishness. This is an opportunity for men to remember their humanity; and the 'little people' find thereby the consolation that others too can barely pull themselves up above normal human weaknesses."[36] Morgenstern, the king's fool, the manipulated manipulator, was essential to sustaining the disciplinary staging of foolishness. Not only is it difficult to imagine the 1737 debate occurring outside the German lands, but it also could not have happened without the foolishness that the king wanted and the professors, of whom Moser was simply the most outspoken, certainly did not. Mockery killed *gravitas*, brought down status, and killed *Doktorwürde*, the honor bestowed by a doctorate.

It was also important that this debate took place in public. Frederick William's presence, his very deliberate staging, and the presence of university and gymnasium students, took the matter of the 1737 debate well outside the court. It shows how little Frederick William regarded the boundaries between the court and the world. Court and public in fact were shifting ground in early eighteenth-century Prussia. The same shift was taking place in Saxony, as the career of Hofnarr Joseph Fröhlich demonstrates (see chapter 3). One of the most important indications of that shift was the public demonstration of foolishness. This was a unique communication between Frederick William and some of his people, well seconding Andreas Gestrich's thesis that not all such communication in the early eighteenth century occurred through written media.[37]

But what do we mean by the public in this period? Historians have devoted much attention to this question ever since the publication of Jürgen Habermas's *The Structural Transformation of the Public Sphere: An Enquiry into a Category of Bourgeois Society*.[38] Yet the extraordinary career of this account has perhaps blocked real assessment of its relevance to the early modern period. Was what Frederick William and Morgenstern were doing part of a development of a "public sphere" of bourgeois critical debate, or was something else going on at this nexus of the king, his professorial fool, law professors, students, and schoolboys? Habermas's "bourgeois public sphere" was constructed as an ideal type, a counterpoint to what he saw as the corruption in late capitalist society of the critical public sphere, due to the fading division between state and society. The bourgeois public sphere in Habermas's reading was a public space, where "propertied people reasoned in public on private interests which were of general relevance, such as the rules of markets and economic production, and referred these interests back to the state."[39]

Habermas's view of the early modern era has, however, been strongly criticized. It is important to note for the purposes of this chapter that he places the development of the "bourgeois public sphere" critical of the state far later in the century than the 1737 debate, whereas it clearly existed from at least 1700. Historians have also asked whether that "public sphere" was, in fact, bourgeois. They have newly found that it actually was dominated by the aristocracy. There also seems to be no reason why a public sphere should necessarily be critical. Feminist historians have also pointed out the near exclusion of women. Often the administration, or the ruler, initiated debate and criticism of the current state of affairs rather than facing opposition from the bourgeoisie. Tim Blanning has gone so far as to argue that the "public sphere was both the creation and the extension of the state."[40]

Four Fools in the Age of Reason

Andreas Gestrich argues, in what has become the new orthodoxy, that "there are two processes which form the foundation of any type of modern media-based public sphere: the printing press as a means of multiplying relevant information for a wider public, and efficient and regular postal routes for its distribution." It has already been mentioned how early the newspaper press developed in the German states. Far from being the trivial publications alleged by Habermas, they contained both news and criticism from an early stage. That was why the thrifty Frederick William employed newspaper readers and commentators. That newspapers stayed in being shows that they must have been tolerated by rulers who on other occasions insisted that politics were no matter for the common people.[41] They were useful as channels of information that could be controlled by rulers through censorship. News could be disseminated through the public by the all-important postal service. Morgenstern's well-selling pamphlet on the 1737 debate, certainly published with Frederick William's approbation, can be considered as a news announcement from the ruler, whose two editions and Dutch translation show the public's interest had been tweaked. The 1737 debate fits this model perfectly and shows how the state and the prince can be put back into play in our thinking about the early modern public realm. It also, and therefore, seems to draw the historiography back toward the classical German historical models of state building.

The 1737 debate thus reveals considerable congruence with the new orthodoxy about the early modern public realm proposed, in replacement of Habermas's theories, by Andreas Gestrich. It also, however, has several features that fit neither Gestrich's nor Habermas's models. Public oral debate in the presence of the monarch does not fit Gestrich's model of absolutism as constituted by paper communication, or Habermas's idea of a separation of state and public sphere. The presence of the fool is even harder to fit into Gestrich's model. We may say that Morgenstern acted as Frederick William's surrogate throughout the debate. But that observation doesn't explain much about why the king set up a public debate in the first place, let alone why he involved a fool in it. He could have just sent out an angry edict from Potsdam. Part of the answer must relate to the king's character: he enjoyed inventive, black humor. To set up a debate offered considerable potentialities, particularly a forced debate, and particularly with a fool, interaction with whom was considered dishonoring. The professors would be shamed, and thus disciplined.

The character of this debate also does little for recent attempts by the historian Benjamin Marschke to "normalize" Frederick William.[42] The pipes and handclaps and riotous schoolboys of 1737 show nothing "normal," nor does disciplining by means of a fool. Morgenstern was Frederick William's surrogate. His arguments about foolishness pointed out that there was another level of knowledge than the professorial one. They thus went over the same ground that Frederick William had already covered with Gundling and the Berlin Akademie der Wissenschaften. Perhaps we end by saying, with a bow to Gestrich, that knowledge wars also constituted part of the constitution of monarchies and states in this period. Fools' knowledge was in the end paradoxical, mirroring professor against fool, folk sayings against academic knowledge, discipline formation against the sileni. Morgenstern's presence, clothed in silver hares, was necessary to carry that work forward.

♦ THREE ♦

Joseph Fröhlich

Of Owls and Other Animals

Two formal owls together sat,
Conferring thus in solemn chat
"How is the modern taste decayed
Where's the respect to wisdom paid?
Our worth the Grecian sages knew
They gave our sires the honor due;
They weighed the dignity of fowls,
And pried into the depth of owls
Athens the seat of learned fame
With general voice revered our name;
On merit title was conferred
And all adored th'Athenian bird . . ."
—John Gay, *Fables and Other Poems* (1727)

Court and city, modern and archaic, human and animal, Joseph Fröhlich
lived between worlds. He was resident at the court of Saxony, in the German
east, as "*Hof-Taschenspieler*," or Court-conjurer (the "*Tasche*" referring to
the small bag at his side used to carry the conjurer's requisites). He was
also well-known in the surrounding city of Dresden for sharp wit, pungent
utterances, and his Tyrolean costume of baggy trousers, suspenders, slouch
boots, long hair, and pointed hat with flowers in the band. At ease in the
contemporary world, he nevertheless lived surrounded by the oldest animal
attributes of the fool such as the hare, the monkey, the ass, and the owl.
Fröhlich was rarely seen in life without an owl (falcon-like) on his wrist. Two
statues of Fröhlich, both frightening, one with a bird's head and another

a Dresde Gravé par CF Boetiu. Avec Privil. du Roi. 1729.

A widely reproduced broadsheet showing Fröhlich in his typical costume sur-rounded by fools' animals (owls, monkey, and swine), as well as bags containing the tools of his trade as a *Taschenspieler*. (inv. no. ES 165, photo no. D152761; © Bayeri-sches Nationalmuseum München)

showing him with grim expression and wearing an iron crown out of which sprout antlers and asses' ears, may be seen in Dresden in the famous Grünes Gewölbe museum.

To be surrounded by animals or animal attributes—like the silver hares embroidered on Salomon Jacob Morgenstern's gown in 1737, and the mon-keys that harried Jacob Paul Gundling, in image and reality, and the ass that Peter Prosch (chapter 4) was given—was certainly one of the main signs by which one might know a fool. It will be one of the tasks of this study of Fröhlich to question this association between animal and fool, and ask what it can tell us about the nature of fooling, even that of such a modern fool as Joseph Fröhlich.

Four Fools in the Age of Reason

The story of Fröhlich's life has attracted few historians. Apart from Rainer Rückert's labor of love, which in any case gives over many of its pages to the relationship between Fröhlich and Meissen china (of which more later), there is no extended biography of him.[1] Flögel devotes only a few pages to him and even then gives much space to material that really relates to Gundling. Nineteenth-century histories of the fool based on Flögel reproduce the master's lack of interest. More work began to be done only in the nineteenth and more particularly the twentieth century, when regional historians took over biographical writing on Fröhlich. From the 1930s onward, aspects of his life were treated in a shower of brief articles and small pamphlets, some written by historians of Meissen porcelain, some by historians of magic, and some, for some reason, by amateur commentators retained in the pages of the journals of postwar political parties. As one might expect, a strong strand of Saxon patriotism is mingled in here. Articles written in the 1930s and 1940s have a *völkisch* tinge, emphasize Fröhlich's humble beginnings, and take seriously his rustic jokes as an indication of someone who had kept his roots in the soil even while living at court. There is no search for consensus on the nature and meaning of Fröhlich's life or its context. Rückert's biography, the only full-length book about Fröhlich, to which I am indebted, must contain every fact about Fröhlich that it is possible to excavate from libraries and archives, and every representation of him extant from the Saxon palaces and the archives of the Meissen porcelain factory. But it fails, again, to put Fröhlich's life into a wider context, notably contexts of court and public arenas. It certainly does not ask the questions of the relationship between fool and animal that were obviously so important to Fröhlich himself.

Almost the whole of Fröhlich's career was passed at the court of two monarchs, Augustus II ("the Strong") (1670–1733) and Augustus III (1696–1763), successive rulers of the composite kingdom of Saxony-Poland. Like many fools, Fröhlich began life in a rural setting, in Bad Aussee in Tyrol. There he trained as miller and baker, receiving guild approval in both arts. It was a side of his life that he never forgot (among his books can be found volumes on the building of mills and the conduct of bakeries). We have no evidence that would allow us to account for the way in which he metamorphosed from miller to *Hoftaschenspieler*, after stints in the country fairs and town weekly markets, at the very small court of the Dukes of Weissensee, and at the bigger, but lonely, court of Christiane Eberhardine (1671–1727), Augustus II's estranged wife.[2]

It was the court of Augustus II that really commanded his life. It could not have been more different from the court of Frederick William I. In Saxony, the life of the court revolved around brilliant festivities, masquerades in Carnival time and winter sledging parties on the frozen Elbe. Hunting, shooting, horseback games, music, amorous intrigue, gambling, and self-conscious court versions of rural festivities filled in any spare moments. In all this, Fröhlich was a participant, along with the several court dwarves, the court "Moor," the court poet Johann Ulrich König, and, of dubious antecedents, "Baron" Schmiedel, another "merry companion" of the king, and Fröhlich's bitter rival. However, it was only Fröhlich's features, well-known to both townspeople and courtiers, which were drawn with fireworks in the elaborate display that took place on 21 February 1730.[3] Fröhlich himself designed the display (his library contains several books on fireworks), which outlined him decked out in his iconic Tyrolean costume of pointed hat, slouching boots, short jacket, and trousers whose suspenders bore the letter *H*. Colored sparklers in the end burned away the figure of Fröhlich and released nothing less than a real owl, which fluttered away into the dark.

What was the motivation for this splendor at court that set the stage for Fröhlich's life? It was there partly to gratify the personal tastes of the king. Michael von Loen, a great connoisseur of courts and thoroughly smitten with Dresden, described Augustus II as "being born to create human pleasure and joy."[4] For von Loen, Dresden was "the most splendid and most gallant court in the world," an enchanted country where the dreams of the ancient poets were exceeded. It was certainly at this court that Augustus II could act out his imitation of his model, Louis XIV of France, whose claims to absolute rule appealed to many German princes. Splendor at court also bolstered diplomatic initiatives and made claims to the throne of Poland by Augustus the Strong more plausible. There was constant interchange between politics and festivities. In 1719, four weeks of celebrations marked the high point of Augustus's diplomacy, the marriage of his only legitimate son, Friedrich August, to Maria Josepha, daughter of the ruler of Austria. In 1728, Augustus II journeyed to Potsdam to be impressed by reviews of the Prussian army. The converse journey was marked with immense splendor—as well as discreet espionage. Extravagant court life also helped to win back a Saxon aristocracy deeply disapproving of the king's conversion to Catholicism (a pitch to the Polish nobility), the expensive military adventures that followed his election to the Polish Crown, and the steps he had taken to reduce their representative institutions.⁵ Historians have called these struggles the "domestication" of the aristocracy, by which they mean reducing their propensity to conspire against the monarch, reducing their opposition to the monarch's demands on their representative institutions, and to the judicial powers that they exercised over their serfs. Victory in such struggles was essential to the foundation of a monarchy with real and unchallenged control over the territory, the sort of monarchy claimed by Louis XIV of France (1638–1715), emulated by Augustus II, and struggled for by Frederick William. In this situation, the investment of the Saxon-Polish kings in dazzling court displays becomes comprehensible.⁶

Court life, however, was not just a space for aristocratic play. It was also a space where social lines might be crossed. Court festivities, for example, included not only aristocratic versions of country dances but also the participation of numerous real peasants and townspeople in rustic dances and feasts. It was here that Fröhlich played a role. He took part in the court festivities. Yet as a *Taschenspieler* of humble origins, he was closer to the conjurers, jugglers, and traveling healers of the town fairs and country markets than to court life. Every 1 April, the date surely not coincidental, he engaged in a public egg fight with the townspeople. His appearance and permanence at the Saxon court was a sign of attempts by Augustus II to bring all classes of society together under an "absolute" ruler, such as that very Louis XIV on whom he modeled himself. At court, the social classes were displayed to each other in a magical world of splendor, abundance, and order, which denied the existence of inevitable social and political tensions and conflicts.

It has seemed worthwhile to insist on the nature of the Saxon court to establish the context in which Fröhlich worked and in which his peculiar brand of humor had to find purchase. Its contradictions mirrored his own. His repartee was often more countrified than courtly or urban, and as a self-defined country boy, he stood in contradiction to the court. This made him stand out and, paradoxically, was one of the causes of his success in the courtly world. His presence was a guarantee against the hectic, frightening intrigue characteristic of court life.

It was at *Tafel*, or the royal table, that Fröhlich exercised his craft. Access to the *Tafel* meant the possibility of unlimited conversation with the ruler and of the exercise of *Narrenfreiheit*, or "fools' freedom." Fröhlich earned this privilege by his astounding manual dexterity and sharp repartee. He brought something from the country, something new and refreshing to the courtiers gathered at the *Tafel,* something that was not a mere repetition of stale old jokes and fools' conundrums. Fröhlich, for example, would put a thaler onto a man's open palm and then tell him to close his fist. On opening it, all the man would find there would be three grains of corn—a rustic joke, and a suitable reminder of Fröhlich's early avocation.[7]

Narrenfreiheit could also be expressed verbally. Once, at the royal table, Fröhlich rhetorically asked what the difference was between King Frederick II of Prussia (this dates the joke to a period after Frederick's accession in 1740) and Heinrich Graf Brühl (1700–1763), Augustus III's long-dominant first minister. The answer to the riddle was that King Frederick was his own first minister, whereas Brühl was his own king. This was only one of the numerous jokes that Fröhlich made at Brühl's expense. It trod on the verge of slander and *lèse-majesté* but expressed important truths traditionally told by the court fool and that no one but his replacement, the court *Taschen-spieler,* could have gotten away with.

Fröhlich also used *Narrenfreiheit* away from the *Tafel,* taking the sort of risky liberties that the fool traditionally ventured upon with the high and mighty. Writing, for example, in November 1727 to no less a personage than Augustus the Strong, he demanded the delivery of a horse he had been promised by the ruler. Perhaps realizing he was skirting dangerously close to the unspoken line between bravura and disrespect, even *lèse-majesté,* he described himself as clinging like a mere limpet to the king's grace and favor. He also promised to repay loans made him by the king himself, which otherwise "will turn me into a Fool." Signing himself "Der Burger Meis-ter [*sic*] von Narrendorf" (mayor of Fooltown), he compares himself to a hare, one of the traditional symbols of the fool, and also to a "*Hering*" (*sic*), surely short for the *Pickelhering* that Flögel lists as one of the alternate titles for a fool.[8]

This letter illustrates in a single document not only the interplay of debt and demand between king and fool but also the fine line trodden by the fool between respect and disrespect, demand and abjection, between a house near the palace, a fine horse, seventeen government ministers and court ladies at the baptism of his eldest son, and the king's gift of extraordinary numbers of *Hanswurst* costumes on the one hand, and on the other, an exis-tence, even for the mayor of Narrendorf, at the whim of the monarch who could humiliate him at every turn if so minded.[9] That was the structure of

Fröhlich's life at court. For even the mayor of Narrendorf had to entertain the *Tafel* by taking part in the sort of mock fights nowadays practiced only by circus clowns. Charles Hanbury-Williams, George II's ambassador to the Saxon court, noted in 1747 that Augustus III "always dines in company, and his buffoons make a great noise and fight one another during the whole repast." Two years later, Hanbury-Williams noted: 'His Polish Majesty has always five or six buffoons in waiting, who are obliged to be in his dressing room every morning by four o'clock, and who never quit him the whole day, unless when Count Brühl comes into the room."[10]

This contest for the king's attention between the fools and Brühl gave rise to extreme hostility between Brühl and Fröhlich, as Fröhlich's post-humously published *Politische Kehraus* (roughly translatable as "political clearing out") of 1757 makes very clear. Attendance on the monarch could be demanding. Bears were led around the seated diners. Dining at the *Tafel* could demand not only refined manners but also considerable courage. Just like the experiences of Jacob Paul Gundling in Prussia and, as we will see, of Peter Prosch in Würzburg (chapter 4), the *Tafel* could be a place even for the famous to experience test, trial, and staged humiliation.

The Saxon court also had a reputation for alchemy, the test and trial of materials, said to be practiced even by the king himself. Out of that "alchemy," in other words, after years of dedicated experimentation with materials at royal expense, came the first successful efforts in Europe to produce the fine translucent ware called porcelain, hitherto made only in China. The first production workshop was set up in the small village of Meissen, close to Dresden, in 1710, and porcelain produced there has ever afterward been known by that name. Meissen became a trade good among monarchs. It was also a medium for the commemoration of genre scenes from court life, in groups defined by brilliant color and extraordinarily detailed modeling by artists such as Johann Friedrich Böttger (1682–1719), the discoverer of porcelain, and Johann Joachim Kaendler (1706–1775).

Meissen was important to Fröhlich. He is immortalized in many porcelain groups featuring scenes from his court life and his role as a fool. His depiction in so many porcelain genre pieces cemented his position as leading "*lustiger Rath*" at court. Several portray interactions with his rival "Baron" Schmiedel, always with Fröhlich gaining the upper hand. In one, Fröhlich and Schmiedel are in a sled together, going down the frozen Elbe. Schmiedel is dressed in women's clothes. In another, Fröhlich exploits Schmiedel's known fears and terrorizes him by thrusting a mouse in his face.[11]

Nor was Fröhlich simply depicted for a court audience. As we have already seen, firework displays represented his well-known features to spectators from court, town, and country alike. But how did they come to be so well-known? Porcelain portrait figures reproduced in large numbers his trademark Tyrolean costume of pointed hat with flowers in the band, baggy trousers held together by braces, and black slouch boots. Often an owl, one of the symbols of foolishness, was modeled as sitting on his shoulder or perched on his arm. Much attention was given to the modeling of his face, framed by the long hair out of fashion in the eighteenth century. His snub nose, jutting chin with a small black growth on it, and small black eyes were characteristic features. Such figurines were so popular that they continued to be made long after Fröhlich's death in 1757. Often reproduced in cheaper materials such as earthenware, their existence meant that his "image" was recognizable by people of many different social classes.

Fröhlich transcended the world of the Saxon courts in Dresden and Warsaw. His audience lay both with and without the court, and he formed a bridge between the court and the world. His career is quite different from that of Gundling, who was kept close at court by Frederick William I. In this sense, they refer to the classical age of fooling, where the fool inhabited only the court, and was dependent politically, emotionally, and financially upon the monarch. In the second half of the century, Fröhlich was still dependent on the court, but at the same time faced outward to the world, as we are to find Peter Prosch doing at a later date. The world of the fool was transforming itself.

This meant that Fröhlich's role was labile. He delighted in playing his fooldom off against other roles. Living in an era where undergraduates wore uniforms, he impersonated a University of Wittenberg student, inscribing his name in the matriculation record during August II's 1728 journey from Dresden to Berlin. This jape caused widespread laughter, not just from the nobility accompanying the king but also from students and local people, who relished the incongruence of the conjunction of the fool and the university. This is a recurring theme in these pages. Japes verging on *lèse-majesté* reached their height in 1729 with the publication of the Saxon *Staats-Calendar,* or list of court officeholders, where in place of the usual portrait of the ruler as a frontispiece, Fröhlich himself was portrayed, standing with his usual attribute, an owl. The king had become the fool.

In Carnival time, his changes of role became even more dazzling. He was noted for his appearances in costume as the character Scaramouche in the Commedia dell'Arte, which was very close to the German Hanswurst character of a conniving, greedy, and scheming servant (see chapter 5). Even more significantly, he would appear in Dresden in a bearskin identical to the all-over animal masks worn at Carnival in his native Tyrol, where Carnival re-created the "world turned upside down" and confirmed the identification of the fool with animals.[12] The "bear" led through the streets, often by a chain through its nose, during Carnival time (Epiphany until Lent), was a common figure in both north and south Germany. In some villages in Tyrol, the "bears" were accompanied by "wild men," each signifying the untrammeled in human nature.[13] Part of the overall message of Carnival was exactly this display of man's willfulness and sin through the animal forms that proliferated in it. Scholars have commented on the centrality of the fool to these Carnival sights. They tell us that in towns and villages, ordinary people did their own fooling. It was open to all to spectate, act, or impersonate. Carnival reminds us that, important as the court fools were, they were only one form of fooling. Ordinary people in town and country made foolery that was both other, ancient, complex, and grounded in animal forms.[14] In his own person, Fröhlich thus united the court fool and the country fool, the human and the animal, and made nonsense of any remaining disposition we may have to believe in a gulf between "high" and "low" culture in the early modern world.

It was the animal rather than the human that was stressed when Fröhlich, like Gundling, went through a mock version of being elevated to the aristocracy. He was addressed by the title of "Count Saumagen" (Count Sow's Stomach) during a stay in Poland in Augustus III's entourage in 1742.[15] In 1730, under Augustus the Strong, Fröhlich had been granted his own coat of arms. A shield shaped like a heart and divided into four sections was surmounted by the three golden cups of the *Taschenspieler*'s favorite trick. At the center of the shield, a mill wheel alludes to Fröhlich's original profession. In the first field, a silver pig springs in the air on a golden ground, recalling the many pigs that accompany Fröhlich in porcelain and ivory pieces. In the second and third fields, threshing flails, perhaps in allusion to the making of flour, stand on a red ground. In the final field, a silver dog on a golden ground is defecating. The shield refers to Fröhlich's biography

Fröhlich's coat of arms as "Count Saumagen." Yet again, Fröhlich is associated in an intimate way with an animal.

and links it with animals fond of dirt and gross appetites, images recalling their traditional association with the fool. Over the golden beakers a fool's cap in a bright harlequin pattern is draped. On top of this, two goats' heads appear. The whole is crowned with the figure of a rider, drawn from the back as though riding away from the spectator, and sporting the pointed hat with the bunch of flowers in its band that was part of Fröhlich's own costume. In place of the usual Latin motto, his name runs on the bottom of the shield. Of course, none of this conforms to any of the rules of heraldry.

What did it mean for Fröhlich to have a title and a coat of arms? We are reminded of those given to Jacob Paul Gundling at the Prussian court, which carried the dual function of humiliating Gundling and teasing the aristocracy. And just as in Gundling's case, their existence put Fröhlich in an ambiguous position at court. In Dresden, just as in Potsdam, many were the

Four Fools in the Age of Reason

dubious hangers-on, all of whom also claimed titles. Böttger, the discoverer of the porcelain process, did not disdain a fictive Barony. These hangers-on, with their fictional titles, were the reverse of the genuine aristocrats, who all had armorial bearings (conforming to the laws of heraldry).

But things were happening outside the court. Conflicts between prince and aristocracy ran alongside another, largely middle-class drama, the *Lesewut,* or reading fever, of an increasingly literate "public" who enthusiastically absorbed the rising printed output of the German lands. Most importantly, they read the "moral weeklies," which, on the model of the English *Spectator* or *Rambler,* shaped opinion by discussing morals, manners, literature, and public issues.[16] Rising literacy meant that more books were either bought or lent. Library records, wills, the inventories of booksellers and the sales records of the great book fairs in Leipzig or Frankfurt tell us that nonfiction works concerning science or travel had begun to overtake theology as preferred reading.[17] Nor was this reading only for the educated middle class. Novels, scientific works, and travel accounts were printed alongside popular poetry, political satire, how-to books, reference manuals, books of piety, and almanacs for farmers and sailors. And, of course, the newspapers whose analysis was the political work of Gundling and Morgenstern.

Fröhlich himself was caught up in the *Lesewut.* We are lucky enough to possess the inventory of his possessions taken after his death in Poland in 1757, which includes a sizeable number of books, whose titles and contents give us an unusually intimate glance into the mind of the *Hoftaschenspieler.*[18] More than six hundred books, in German, French, and Latin, filled his shelves. One might dismiss the Latin books as there for show, or as gifts not reflecting his personal taste, for Fröhlich's life would have given him few opportunities for learning that language, were it not for the presence of a Latin dictionary in the inventory.[19] This leaves us with an image of Fröhlich picking out words as he read among his many Latin works of piety. Fröhlich not only traveled the world of words, but his mind went far afield. He possessed numerous travel narratives, atlases, charts and maps, copper engravings of landscapes, and of pictures of exotic natives in national or tribal dress. The sheer size of this collection makes it difficult to regard it merely as Fröhlich's response to the contemporary fashionability of the travel narrative. It points to a real interest of the village-born in the wider world.

The smaller confines of the court also of course had a great impact. Books about fireworks and masquerades (#591, #537), and copies of the court Calendar, printed by his friend the court bookseller, Georg Moritz Weidemann, which often mentioned Fröhlich's presence at court festivities, accompany many reference works on history and current affairs. Although Fröhling never held the role of *Zeitungs-Referent,* or court newspaper reader, part of his reading covered the same areas as had Morgenstern's and Gundling's. He possessed the invaluable *Huberners Staats- und Zeitungs-Lexikon* of 1735, *Struvens Universal-Historie* of 1733, and a life of Augustus the Strong by the ever-productive David Fassmann, Gundling's biographer.[20] Histories of Hungary, Spain, Venice, and Denmark accompanied them on the shelves. Fröhlich's library was partly that of an "expert," an expert aiming to shine as Morgenstern and Gundling had. His expertise was thus twofold: as an expert and as fool. Fools are paradoxical indeed. To shine as a master of repartee and allusion at court depended, as we have seen in the case of jokes against Graf Brühl, on knowledge of current affairs. Other professional material including conjuring manuals and joke books are present in large numbers. One book promised more than two hundred jokes suitable to be told "in honorable company," or even from the pulpit.

There are also indications that Fröhlich reflected on the meaning of being a fool, in a way that went beyond joke telling, repartee, and sleight of hand. He owned Fassmann's biography of Gundling, a sustained disquisition on one sort of fooling, though not of Fröhlich's experience. We also find in his possession two books by Jacob Schmidt (1689–1740), Jesuit preacher, novelist, teacher, and author of the first collection of saints' lives from the Baroque era. These narratives are filled, to an extent highly unusual in Western Christendom, with the image of the "fool for Christ," of those who live outside society and outside rationality, the better to imitate Christ. The first collection of legends, called the *Die spielende Hand Gottes* (The playful hand of God) tells stories of those who in the middle of impious games had been filled with the Holy Spirit and returned to Christian belief. Fröhlich might have thought here of his own playful hands. The second collection is full of legends of holy men who have been "fools for Christ" in the sense of taking no thought for the morrow, of living apart from the future-oriented worries of the mundane world, in order the better to focus on the example of Christ. No idea could have been further from the reality in which Fröhlich lived, whether in the court or the town. This was not the sort of fooling of which he was master, and these ideas would in any case have been difficult to put into practice in the notoriously worldly courts of Saxony-Poland. Yet

these books appear in his private library. We can only speculate that to Fröhlich this very ancient idea of fooling as a religious act was of value.

Nor are the religious works in Fröhlich's library works only of Catholic
devotion. His religious life did not merely read off the doctrinal divisions
of his age. Born and raised in the strictly Catholic Salzkammergut, Fröhlich
took as his second wife the Protestant Eva Christina Zöblerin, and owned a
1571 edition of Martin Luther's "Table Talk." He also had contacts among the
Jews of Dresden and possessed several books on their faith.[21] Fröhlich in fact
embraced the conspectus of the religious worlds of Enlightenment Saxony.

Fröhlich's relationship with the history of his profession also is revealed
in the first piece published under his name, the 1729 *Gespräch mit Claus
Narr im Reiche der Toten.* Originating in the work of the Roman author
Lucian, the genre of fictional conversations between well-known inhabitants
of Elysium had become highly popular by the time Fröhlich wrote. Its most
famous contemporary exponent was Gundling's nemesis, David Fassmann,
though there is no evidence that Fassmann had a hand in the writing of
Fröhlich's work.[22] It was published in Hamburg, in a small octavo volume
of sixty-four pages. The frontispiece shows Claus Narr and Fröhlich in conversation in a large, palace-like room. Fröhlich is dressed in his characteristic costume, and Claus Narr in a costume whose harlequin-patterned top
recalls the traditional clothing of medieval fools. Claus Narr, a real historical
character, had had a long and distinguished career, having served after 1486
four successive rulers of Saxony, as well as the archbishop of Magdeburg.
The little book, which is really a double biography, had quite clear purposes. Fröhlich aimed to gain legitimacy from history, from his talk with
Claus Narr, the archetypal fool of the German-speaking lands. By putting
their life stories side by side, he hoped to raise his own status: "Wer dieser
Joseph sey, und wer Claus Narr gewesen / Kann man ausführlich in dem
Gespräche lesen" (Who Joseph is and who Claus Narr was can be read in
detail in these conversations).

The subtitle of the little book is "conversation between two fools from
the court of Saxony" and calls Fröhlich *"bekannt und beliebt"* (known and
loved). Jokes and witty talk are promised the reader, who is assured that no
obscenities will spoil its pages. Quickly, Claus Narr and Fröhlich are trans-
ported to the banks of the river Lethe. Without an owl readily to hand, Fröhlich feels lost and alone until he meets a blessed soul, whom he persuades to
sing and dance by breaking into Bavarian dances ("Lustig seyn und jubiliren

/ Mit den Pfeiffen musiciren und darzu noch tantzen, ist der Narren Art und Weise" [Be happy and make merry, play the pipes for the dancers, for that's what fools do]). The soul turns out to be that of Claus Narr, whose closeness to Fröhlich is underscored: "Ach wie wunderlich fuget doch das Glück Leute gleiches Humeurs zusammen" (Oh how wonderful that chance brings people of the same character together). Fröhlich explains that he comes from the Saxon court, where he has made himself beloved by his "sharp speaking" (*argute Reden*). But will he, he asks, have as much respect, let alone as much to eat and drink, in the land of the dead as he did among the living? Claus Narr tells him that no one eats in the underworld, and there are only the stinking waters of the Styx to drink.

Fröhlich then mentions court personages, concluding that whatever his status in the underworld, he is more honorable than they, since he has been given "die hohe Ehre, bey königlichen Tafeln zu erscheinen und frey zu reden" (the high honor of appearing at the king's table and being able to speak freely).[23] The fool's search for honor, seen so often in the lives of previous fools, is fully revealed here. Fröhlich cannot be accurately described as a social climber. He did not want to stop being a fool, and his purchase of a mill in Poland connected him to his first trade. But he was a searcher after honor, and as Burgermeister of Narrendorf, had an acute sense of his own place on its slippery pole. He shows Claus Narr his coat of arms and his full list of titles, so that Claus Narr can write to him when he leaves the underworld. Literacy on both sides is presumed. (Here the conventions of the genre "conversations in the kingdom of the dead" are departed from. Usually both participants are already dead and stay in the underworld at the close of the conversation.) Fröhlich's titles include "undignified Mayor of Fooltown-on-the-Elbe, famous conjurer, master of all dancing bears, king pig in scoffing and slurping. Taker-in of customs-duties for fools and the loquacious. Judge of all fools, knight of the golden spur, judge over all dog-food."[24] He explains to Claus Narr, "I also got the order of the knight of the golden spur, which I wore on my leg, to impress all other fools in the world."[25] The titles maintain the link for Fröhlich between fooling and the animal world. They also show us the propensity for fools to manipulate a system of honor that runs parallel to, and reflects upon, the "proper" honors of kings and aristocrats.

Claus Narr asks him some more about his career. This an important question, because it allows us to find out what Fröhlich thought were the main duties of his calling. He tells Claus Narr of occasions when he had

been an important intermediary between king and aristocracy, and had peti-
tioned Augustus II to bring back into favor many who fallen from his good
graces. This is part of the traditional work of the fool, to act as mediator and
turn aside the wrath of the monarch. In the end, Claus Narr gives Fröhlich
some wine that sends him to sleep. Annoyed at being awakened by Claus
Narr sometime later, he rudely tells him that his high reputation as a fool is
undeserved. Mercury and a crowd of followers arrive in the underworld, and
it is time for the two fools to part.

What were the purposes of Fröhlich's visit to the underworld? The little
book is not strenuous reading, and it is definitely not written only for a
court audience. It was easy to commit to memory or read aloud. The book's
simple language and illustrations meant that it could be read by many different sorts of people. It is amusing, without containing anything deep or
inaccessible. Definitely, one purpose of Fröhlich's visit to the underworld
was to spread his "image" among as broad a segment of the reading pop-
ulation as possible. His conversation with Claus Narr thus broadly raises
his status from a rural *Taschenspieler* to the equal of Saxony's most famous
historic fool. By engaging with Claus Narr, he could draw off accusations
that he was merely a country bumpkin, a Tyrolean *Taschenspieler,* someone
with deft fingers and rapid patter who had caught the eye of Augustus the
Strong when the king was looking for diversion, and when "merry companions" from the Tyrol with their rural accents, droll costumes, and down-to-
earth humor were in fashion.

Fröhlich had greater ambitions. Just as he had not feared to demand his
horse from Augustus the Strong, he did not fear to commit *lèse-majesté* by
linking himself to the king of the fools, Claus Narr. Fröhlich wanted higher
status and went after it by associating himself with Claus Narr. It is likely,
given the interest in the history of fooling revealed by his library holdings,
that this was an entirely conscious maneuver on his part. The catalogue of
Fröhlich's library paints a remarkable picture of the unexpected complexity
of the mind of a fool, one who disguised intellectual, professional, and spiritual curiosity with a capacity for sharp, even coarse, repartee, behind the
mask of a country boy from the Tyrol.

What are we to make of the persistent appearance of animals and animal
symbols in Fröhlich's life, which seems at odds with his literacy and literary production? Are Habermas's ideas useful for us in answering this

question? It is clear that the court life of Augustus the Strong is that of a classical "representative" monarch. Personal display was all. But it is also clear that elements of the public sphere were present in Saxony, or Fröhlich would not have been able, or have wanted, to bring his written works to publication. Yet Fröhlich's own world can also be seen as that of "representative" power. His firework display, which showed a large audience his face and his owl, makes this point. The extraordinary numbers of china figures carrying his face do the same. Nor do Habermas's ideas work well when we consider the mixture of worlds in which Fröhlich lived. A fool who lived at court who could also be a writer of political satire who also wore a bear's coat at Carnival time is difficult to fit into Habermasian accounts of the public sphere. To whatever extent one subscribes to them, it still provides little or no handle on the interlocking visual symbols still so forceful in the Enlightenment.

Fools lived surrounded by animals. It was not for nothing that Gundling was portrayed surrounded by monkeys and hares and was forced to acknowledge a real monkey as his son; that Morgenstern wore his blue robe embroidered with silver hares and carried a foxtail during the 1737 debate; or that Fröhlich wore a bearskin, was never to be seen without an owl, was several times modeled in Meissen groups of pigs, and had pigs and a dog on his coat of arms. These animal symbols, often equated with human vices, are pervasive and powerful. Eighteenth-century people were not simply swayed by verbal debates among the philosophes. They were also swayed by symbols that were far older than their own times. An important example is provided by Louis XIV of France, who proclaimed the risen sun as his symbol, thereby placing himself in a whole line of cosmic imagery both Christian and classical of the *oriens augusti*, the emperor, or Christ, rising like the sun.[26]

It is important to ask about the relationship between Louis and his symbol. Seventeenth-century and early eighteenth-century people may have seen Louis as close to it in ways that we do not. They could see Louis as partaking in the fruitfulness and omnipresence of the sun. His *Mémoires* make it clear that he consciously chose his sun symbol, knew what he wished it to convey, and chose the cultural forms by which it did so. Having once done so, he also accepted, and indeed desired, that the fruitfulness and omnipresence of the sun would adhere to his own person, even down to having his sleeping chamber in the palace of Versailles orientated on the rising sun.[27] As Louis wrote in his *Mémoires,* composed for the use of his heir:

> I think that, without becoming bogged down in details, my duties as a prince should yet always be present to me. Thus I could hope to fulfill them. I choose the most noble symbol of all: the sun. It is unique. It spreads light to other stars, which are like courtiers to the sun monarch. With equal justice, the sun dispenses light all over the different climates of the word. It does good everywhere, producing always and everywhere joy and vivacity, by his unceasing movement. Yet he appears, nevertheless, always calm, set on a constant and invariable course, from which he never deviates. This is, surely, the most living and beautiful part of a great monarch.[28]

Even if this magnificent explication of the relation between symbol and monarchy was not intended for wider consumption, the extraordinary and numerous artistic and architectural works that were produced as a result of it no doubt encouraged Augustus the Strong to copy Louis XIV to the extent of choosing the attribute of the sun. At the wedding celebrations of 1719, Augustus II appeared arrayed as the sun-god Apollo.

In the same way, early modern culture made available the ambiguous and multilayered symbol of the owl (among other animal attributes) to the fool. The owl gathered together reason and unreason. It was not only linked to fools and foolishness but also, in Roman mythology, to Minerva, goddess of wisdom. Images of an owl in flight through the darkness were especially used in the early modern period as a symbol of the illumination given by reason.

The owl allowed Fröhlich the freedom of contradiction. Fröhlich lived surrounded by owl images. A Meissen figure, for example, modeled before his arrival at the court of Augustus the Strong, shows a fool riding the heavens on the outstretched wings of an owl.[29] Fröhlich himself possessed a picture of an owl, as we find in the inventory of his goods taken after his death in 1757.[30] One could continue elaborating the early modern symbolism of the owl. But the really important point to make here is that the owl is contradictory and therefore inclusive, combines wisdom and foolishness, Till Eulenspiegel and Minerva. It is worth remembering the similarly contradictory structure of Fröhlich's firework display, where the owl was released into the night air through a burning outline of Fröhlich's own face. Fool and owl became visually one. The owl took that flight through the dark, which was connected with the illumination of reason. Natural objects carried power, and especially the power to reconcile opposites. This is probably the reason why one of the Meissen statues of Fröhlich shows him with an owl's head. It is a powerful representation of the fusion of fool and symbol.

How different the ceremonial of Augustus the Strong. It is clear that he attempted to model his monarchy on that of Louis XIV, and more particularly on the younger incarnations of the Sun King. Dance, music, art, decoration, and drama were used to attach the attributes of the sun to Louis's person. In the same way, Augustus used natural and cosmic symbols to attach their powers to him. In February 1695, for example, in the middle of Carnival, Augustus took part in the so-called *Götteraufzug*, or procession of the gods. His current mistress, Aurora von Koenigsmarck, was, appositely, given the role of the goddess of the dawn. In 1719, to give another example, the festivities marking the Austrian marriage included a *Planetenfest,* where Augustus moved as the sun among courtiers arrayed as the planets.[31]

Both monarch and fool used ancient emblems. The fools' symbols linked them particularly to animals that display gross appetites (pigs and dogs), frailty and cowardice (hares), cunning (foxes), stupidity (asses), terror (owls), while those of the monarchs linked them to cosmic forces in ways that were already ancient in the Roman world. The monarchs "naturalized" their power, that is, made it seem as ineluctable and eternal as nature herself, by aligning themselves with the planets.

But the fool and his symbol are doing different things from the monarch and his planets. If we turn to the two ivory statues of Fröhlich that are held in the Grünes Gewölbe in Dresden, we are in a different world. Unlike the porcelain genre portraits of Fröhlich, these could never have been put into mass production. The circumstances of their production, sometime between 1727 and 1730, are unclear. Yet their power to impress and even to frighten still remains. One of these statues portrays Fröhlich in characteristic costume, with an owl perched on his wrist. However, this statue does not have human head but an owl's. Fool and symbol could be seen as corporally merged. Animal and human may not be far apart. This is how the statue gains its power, and its power to challenge us in the modern world, where animals have been overwhelmed by taxonomy.[32]

Dating from the mid-1730s, these two representations of Joseph Fröhlich in ivory, bronze, wood, and pearls show him in characteristic costume. The first shows Fröhlich as owl-headed, as though the owls with which he surrounded himself in real life had fused with him. The other, however, shows him with grim expression, wearing an iron crown, asses' ears, and antlers. While the asses' ears are traditional parts of a fool's dress, the antlers are not, leading to speculation about ancient connections between the fool and the animal dances present from the classical world onward. (bpk-Bildagentur/Grüenes Gewölbe, Staatliche Kunstsammlungen/Jürgen Karpinski/Art Resource, NY)

The second figure shows Fröhlich with donkey's ears and a headband resembling a crown supporting formidable deer antlers. His thick leather jerkin is encrusted with representations of animals—donkeys, owls, hares, pigs and apes—strongly associated with fools. The former should come as no surprise. It is the antlers that are surprising, since deer nowhere feature among the emblems associated with fools. Antlered animals, which return us to the forest, also appear on Fröhlich's coat of arms.

How do these symbols fit in with our understanding of the Enlightenment? If the Enlightenment is understood as a matter of the middle class, of the written word, of reading, writing, and the Republic of Letters, then these emblems hardly fit at all. If the Enlightenment is understood as a modernizing movement, then we also encounter difficulties. Louis XIV's emblem of the sun brought its viewer back to the Roman world. The animal symbols of the fools are difficult to date. They may take their origins from the animal dances of the medieval era, of which we find the first traces in the tenth century. Each has origins and meanings well before and well outside the Enlightenment. The eighteenth century does not only possess one chronology.

Much has been written on the meaning of animal symbols, little of which applies to Morgenstern's silver hares or Gundling's monkeys or Fröhlich's owl. We may have to abandon the idea that animal symbols are a "natural" resource for saying things about humans. Famous statements such as Claude Levi-Strauss's comment that animals are not only "good to eat" but also "good to think with" may have to be ignored for our purposes. It may be that we follow John Berger's insight that "what we are trying to define, because the experience is almost lost, is the universal use of animal signs for charting the experience of the world." Yet even this does not capture the full force of the animals, real and symbolic, which accompany the fools and especially Fröhlich. It can be argued that the eighteenth-century urge to classify plants, animals, (and minerals) effectively drained the living being of its "experience and secrets." Fools' animals lived outside this classificatory enterprise. That is why they retain their power to shock and surprise. They still have their own force fields of power.[33]

We thus may have to understand the Enlightenment public sphere as a series of labile practices that allowed the fool to slip between its many layers. It had many parallel chronologies. It was not intrinsically critical, as Habermas would argue. Fröhlich encountered Enlightenment modern technology in the shape of Meissen manufacture and fireworks, and its modern art in the shape of Canaletto. He was a denizen of court entertainments who was also the subject of frightening statues and who frightened others as a bear at Carnival time. He was a manipulator of his own image who never forgot his owl attribute, and whose portrait was diffused in thousands of porcelain objects. He was the mayor of Narrendorf and a demanding supplicant to his monarch. He was a baker and a miller who died possessed of more than six hundred books. He managed to combine all these layers in his own person. He was a "personality" because, although clinging like a limpet to his monarchs, he still stood between the court and its "representative" culture, the world of the town, and the world of the past. His life demonstrates the poverty of the Habermasian model of the Enlightenment public sphere. Fröhlich became one of the places where the contradictions of Enlightenment were most demonstrated. His foolishness held at bay definition and division: the classifying energies of the Enlightenment, its taxonomical reason.

FOUR

Peter Prosch

The Last Court Fool

Peter Prosch made his living by provoking laughter. That laughter was alien to our own sense of the comic. It provoked laughter when Peter Prosch was, among many other things, set on fire, tied to an unruly horse, tormented with electric shocks, and given an enema in public.[1] He himself provoked laughter when he urinated out of a window and carried out the duties of a *Nachtstuhlverwalter* (chamber pot administrator) to the bishop of Würzburg (67–68, 72, 91–92, 69, 146, 84, 76). Roars of laughter greeted these merry japes, laughter violent enough to have lords and ladies rolling on the floor, heaving and shaking, tears running down their cheeks, unable to utter a word. For Peter Prosch was a fool, and this was how, traveling from one court to another, he made his living.

It is the purpose of this chapter to question that laughter and that life, and to apply the meanings we discover to the interwoven history of courts, control, and cruelty, in what Peter Prosch, perhaps not without irony, called "our enlightened age" (9).

Prosch described his life in his 1789 "autobiography," his *Leben und Ereignisse* (Life and events). This work, in spite of its many editions, has often been treated by scholars as a mere literary curiosity.[2] Prosch's occupation as a fool seemed to remove him from serious consideration by scholars. He tells his story by punctuated anecdotes, "events," rather than by the flow of history. His resolute unwillingness to wrestle explicitly with the problem of his own identity means that he seemed not to belong in the Romantic era, and his preoccupation with the *Herrschaften*, the "Lords and Ladies," seemed out of place in the bourgeois era of the nineteenth and twentieth centuries. Prosch's often scatological humor meant that when the text was reissued in the nineteenth and early twentieth centuries it could only be in

Portrait of Peter Prosch, the itinerant fool, wearing livery given to him by an aristocratic patron. Artist unknown, 1788. (Tiroler Landesmuseums, Innsbruck; reproduced in Peter Prosch, *Leben und Ereignisse*)

bowdlerized versions. The first complete edition of the text in modern times (though published without the list of subscribers) is that of 1964, which is the one used in this chapter, and the parenthetical page citations refer to the 1964 edition.

The Swiss playwright Felix Mitterer has recently recast Prosch as a folk hero of the Tyrol.[3] Otherwise, Prosch's autobiography has maintained a shadow-life in literary history, always mentioned but never systematically analyzed. Ralph-Rainer Wuthenow, for example, calls the text "a curiosity," "without deep reflection," and written with "a fortunate degree of naivety" (which, however, even Wuthenow points out, may be more asserted than real).[4] Prosch himself writes: "I'm really not an author / I have neither rhyme nor poetry / I scribbled my life / and wrote it down / the style was after my Tyrolian custom" (9).[5] For Wuthenow, the question of Prosch's motivation is resolved by seeing him as selling himself to the *Herrschaften*. Little is made of the psychology of Prosch's position of fool or of what it tells us about the courts in which Prosch labored and suffered. Prosch in this account is a mere reflection of courtly society.

Günter Niggl argued in his pathbreaking work that autobiography in the years from 1740 to 1790 is characterized in general by an increasing secularization, and the introspective polarization of "I and the world."[6] For him, Prosch's account is naïve and unmarked by these introspective tendencies. Calling the autobiography a "fable," Niggl argues that it is stylized as a fairy tale of the success of poor Peter, rather like Jack the giant-killer going from rags to riches. This account, according to Niggl, has a threefold purpose: to publicly thank his protectors and patrons; to entertain the reader; and to create a self-presentation, continuing the fairy story, of a man from the lowest social class who became beloved and successful in court society. It will be argued here, however, that Prosch's account is far more complex—and interesting—than either Wuthenow or Niggl recognizes.

Contributing more than anything else to the neglect of Prosch's account, however, was its problematical content. Prosch recounts tale after tale of public humiliation that portray him as the passive, pliable tool of a court society always in want of entertainment and often finding it in japes with Prosch that to us frequently seem cruel, almost monstrous. The aristocratic laughter that accompanies each episode seems too intense to be quite adult and does more than anything else to make it hard to feel sympathy or understanding for the characters of the text. Descriptions of this laughter also support the theories of historians who have seen in the laughter of this period a reaction characteristic of the aristocracy (the bourgeoisie increasingly favoring the self-controlled smile rather than the expansive laugh). It is also argued that aristocratic laughter was seen at the time as cruel and exclusionary. Much, though not all, of Prosch's account justifies this perception. The peals of laughter that ring through his text have a bitter politics of their own.[7]

Prosch's writing in fact presents us with a problem that historians often shy away from: how to come to grips with material that is "opaque" because at the farthest remove from the moral sensibilities of our own time. There is a danger of a failure of that sympathy that is the basis of our relationship with the text. What happens to Prosch often appalls. It makes our reading of his autobiography an exercise in dealing with the sheer strangeness of the past, of being confronted with moments of opacity, as Robert Darnton called them, where it seems impossible to find a means of translating from the past to the present.[8] Part of the work of this chapter will be to attempt to find that translation, to understand Prosch and the laughter that surrounded him in a way that restores our sympathy. This happens when we find a way to talk about Prosch as part of the normality of that culture without reducing his particularity.

It is thus not surprising that Prosch's text should often be treated as part of what Walter Benjamin called *"der Abfall der Geschichte"* (the rubbish heap of history), meaning everything that fell by the wayside as history progressed: texts without long-term influence, doomed belief systems, social practices that bourgeois manners would stamp out.[9] By the time of his death in 1804, Prosch's own profession had become part of that *Abfall*.

What sort of historical source has Prosch given us? Prosch's world, first of all, is remote from "big history." His autobiography was published in 1789, and he visited Paris in 1786, but the work gives no hint of the coming storm. No one would guess from this text of the existence of the Seven Years' War (1756–63) or the American Revolution, which began in 1776. Unremarked is the War of the Bavarian Succession (1778–79), which pitted against each other two of his major patrons, Electors Max III Joseph, Elector of Bavaria, and Karl Theodor, Elector of the Palatinate. The only "historical" events mentioned are the deaths of the Emperor Francis at Innsbruck in 1765 and of Empress Maria Theresa in 1780, and the visit of Pope Pius VI to Vienna in 1782. Prosch's own chronology is often unclear. Long passages in the text are devoid of dates or even references to Prosch's own age by which we might fix the multiple events of his account. They alternate with paragraphs where dates are defined down to the day.

The text is anchored in quite another way than the chronological. It teems with names. Names of persons drawn from all social strata, from the Empress Maria Theresa down to the guests at his village wedding (62–65). All his patrons are there. It is these witnesses that are our security for the authenticity of this text. The *Herrschaften,* the individual lords and ladies who figure so largely in the autobiography, must indeed have recognized themselves, for good or ill, in its pages. Prosch wrote: "Es leben noch Herrschaften genug die davon Augenzeugen gewesen sind" (There are enough lords and ladies still alive who were eyewitnesses). The text is also anchored, and saved from being a merely a collection of loosely connected anecdotes, by its retelling of Prosch's own life, which he himself sees as exemplary. As he wrote in the rhyme that introduces the book: "In unser aufgeklärten Zeit / Kann meiner Lebens Seltenheit / Vielleicht noch manchen dienen" (In our enlightened age / my life's peculiarity / can perhaps be of use to some).[10]

In spite of the strangeness of his life, he believed that there were things in it that could serve others. Prosch was not concerned with the exploration of the recesses of his own personality, although he gives us plenty of clues to it that we can access without very much psychological penetration. But he was concerned that his life, seemingly so in thrall to the *Herrschaften,* should be understood in a more balanced way, and to that end, the autobiography is as much concerned with village happenings, even with "our enlightened times," as it is with the practical jokes to which Prosch was subjected at court. In his village, Prosch reveals himself as quite another person than Peter Prosch the court fool, as a canny peasant who like many others took to the roads of Tyrol, Bavaria, and other parts of southern Germany in the off-seasons, selling gloves and medicinal oils.[11] Prosch was successful at both trades, filling simultaneously the quite different demands of fooling and of selling in the courts of Paris, Vienna, Munich, Würzburg, Ansbach, Ellwangen, and Regensburg, so much so that having begun life as an orphaned child beggar in his native Tyrolean village of Ried im Zillerthal, he ended as its leading inhabitant.

In his life, the gaining of the patronage of the lords and ladies, the *Herrschaften,* was crucial. Prosch's account is a sampler of patronage. In the Enlightenment almost everyone was enveloped in a web of patronage. Without patronage—however much the *Aufklärer* raged against it as corrupting and degrading—Prosch would not have survived. Prosch's life often resembles a literary commonplace. Orphaned at a very early age, Prosch was cast out upon the world, like many an eighteenth-century hero, and became a marginal figure in the village, enduring deep poverty, begging in the winter, and herding sheep in the summer. He was rescued by his first patron, Graf Ignaz von Tannenburg. "He saw me, I pleased him" (15): the quickness of the adoption process recalls that of Morgenstern by Frederick William I. He went trembling to his second patron, Fürst Alexander von Taxis, who had just come in from hunting and saw before him "another strange wild creature, a small broad-trousered Tyrolese" (24–25). Like a wild beast, Prosch was captured by a courtly hunter. Prosch here also portrays himself as an anthropological specimen, a Tyrolese, a person distant from the world of the courts in which he was destined to live out a role as, among many other things, a fashionable rustic.

After hearing that Prosch was an orphan, Taxis caused him to be brought to his castle (25). And there Prosch, an impoverished child, was consumed with excitement because: "I had often heard that whoever had to do with rich people would themselves become rich, and that from the lords and other great ones favours [*Gnaden*] flowed on every side" (26). But equally powerful were other kinds of bonds. After more adventures, the orphaned Prosch came into contact with the high official Geheimrat Kirchmayr, who adopted him, together with his wife: "[He] took me under his protection, and had me serve at his table. He regarded me as his child, especially so as both he and his wife came from Tyrolean families." Prosch, however, unable to adapt himself to courtly manners, succumbed to homesickness, deserted Graf Taxis and Geheimrat Kirchmayr, and made his way back to Ried im Zillerthal, only to reencounter there "my evil neighbor, hunger" (35). Having lost his birth parents, and deprived of the support of his fictive parents, Prosch turned to the universal mother, Empress Maria Theresa, whom Prosch called "the immortal Empress Maria Theresa, loved by all her subjects as a real mother. And I heard as well, that she had a special fondness for Tyroleans" (35). He became obsessed with thoughts of the empress. A few nights later, he had a dream that would influence much of the rest of his life. He dreamt that he had been to see the empress, with his hat under his arm, that she had filled his hat with gold and allowed him to build on a certain spot in the village a house and a brandy still (37). In spite of the jeers and laughter that greeted him in the village when he spoke of this dream, he had no peace with himself until he set out to Vienna to see the empress (38).

Having walked to Innsbruck, he was recommended there to the ladies of the royal foundation in Hall. Pleased by his determination, the aristocratic ladies there recommended him to Graf Leopold Künigl, the father of Gräfin Taxis, and court chamberlain to Maria Theresa's son, the later emperor, Archduke Leopold. In September 1757, he traveled to Vienna with Künigl (41). There, the showers of patronage came thick and fast: "I was recommended from one lord to another, and came thereby to Cardinal Migazzi" (44). At the cardinal-archbishop's table, he met Graf Johann Kotegg, who became another of his protectors. He and his wife allowed Prosch to call them Mother and Father (44).

The making of fictive families was important in the working of patronage, and more than anything else Prosch's account confirms this. Fictive families emphasized, strengthened, and extended the "family" lines of patrons and bound clients to them because of the very strength of their affective bonds.[12] They thus could also be corrupting, offering many opportunities for moral and emotional blackmail—and not only in one direction. They could also be supportive and affirming. The rage of the *Aufklärer* against patronage was a rage against the loss of autonomy. But in Prosch's world, particularly for the poor, to be without a patron was no laughing matter, and the autonomy so favored by Rousseau would be nothing but a death sentence.

However, Prosch's entry into his second fictive family did not divert him from his project of meeting the empress. When that same month Kotegg followed the court to the palace of Schönbrunn, just outside Vienna, Peter went with him and, having learned how to read and write at Graf Taxis', wrote a letter to the empress about his dream (46). Laughing, Graf Künigl gave it to the empress, who, laughing, read it. On 23 September 1757, Prosch, astoundingly, met the empress in the chapel at the palace of Schönbrunn. He was filled "with joy, fear, terror and shaking," slipping and sliding on the polished floor (incidentally, a trope referring to the uncertainty of court life). Prosch was astounded by the huge mirrors that reflected him in every direction and made him question "ob ich bei mir selbsten wäre" (whether I was beside myself). Everyone who was there laughed "because they saw that I didn't know what I was doing" (50–51). He fell at the empress's feet. "Are you the young Tyrolean who was recommended to me?" she asked and gave Prosch her hand to kiss (51). Meanwhile the double doors through which the empress had entered were jammed with people (*voller Köpfe*) laughing so loudly that the empress twice had to signal for silence before she could hear Prosch's supplications. Astoundingly, she gave him his wish and arranged to have it confirmed in writing (52).

A few years after this, in 1765, came another of the great events of Prosch's life, the sudden death of the Emperor Francis, the husband of Maria Theresa. Prosch's account neatly balances the world stage inhabited by the empress and emperor with his own small projects. The court was at Innsbruck, and Prosch made gloves ready to give to the emperor. When, through aristocratic intermediaries, Prosch encountered the emperor, it was a Tuesday. Prosch gave him the gloves. He told Prosch to come back on Wednesday, for then he would give Prosch, and his wife and child, "something to live on." There was laughter when an overjoyed Prosch attempted to catch the emperor's hand in order to kiss it. He fooled for the emperor at his table for a long time, until the dessert was removed (101–3). At the end of the meal, the emperor quite suddenly collapsed and died. Prosch gives a minutely detailed account of the next hours, as courtiers unavailingly tried to keep the news from the frantic empress. He himself becomes an eyewitness.

Prosch's own reaction to the death of the emperor was extreme. If the empress was the universal mother, that made the emperor the universal father, and his death seems to have caused the orphaned Prosch deep disturbance. He became severely depressed. He attempted suicide and was cut down just in time. Even then, his troubles were not at an end, for the public knowledge of his suicide attempt led to a prosecution, and he was sentenced to two years in jail in Innsbruck. He was no longer a *Spassmacher,* a fun-maker, but a "melancholy fool" (132).

Prosch, however (sustained by meals sent in by his aristocratic patrons), revived sufficiently to break jail. He succeeded in reaching the city of Munich in the neighboring state of Bavaria, and thence he traveled to the small city of Ellwangen (141). There, the Fürst, who had heard already about the prison break, had no qualms about welcoming an escaped felon and promised Prosch his protection, food, and lodging. Now, Prosch relates, "Fear and care had left me" (145). Cautiously, however, the Fürst forbade Prosch to go beyond the walls of the castle garden. He stayed in Ellwangen for six months. In this protected environment, excited only by the performances of the count's new "electrical machine," Prosch improved, "and the Fürst was happy to see that I was healthy again" (145). But this time of protection and recovery was not to be prolonged.

Prosch began to travel again, this time taking with him his much-neglected wife. He explains why he had not done so before: "My wife was young and pretty, and we know how it is with the *Herrschaften* when they see a strange wild creature." This passage, with its reminiscence of Prosch's own encounter with a courtly hunter years before, opens the darkest episode in the autobiography. The positive depiction of Prosch's sympathetic patron in Ellwangen is replaced by a view of the aristocracy at Würzburg, a small ecclesiastical principality, as hunters of the naïve country girl. Prosch appeared at court in Würzburg with his wife tied to him by a rope. The Count-Bishop Adam Friedrich von Seinsheim (1708–1779) gallantly drank a toast to his wife.[13] Prosch was pleased that the courtiers were happy to have him there. But as the drinking continued, the rope was cut by cathedral provost Frankenstein, and Prosch lost control of the proceedings while his wife, Maria Fiechtlein, was spirited away. He burst into tears, knowing that all was not well with his wife. As he writes: "The night, a sad one, at length passed" (149). The compression says everything. It is never entirely clear in Prosch's account what happened to his wife that night, but it was nothing positive, of that we can be sure. Her shyness when they met again the next morning confirmed his worst fears (150–51). "I am her possessor!" he burst out (150). He lived, after all, in a world where patronage meant that everyone possessed someone, everyone, that is, but the lowest of the low, the very poor, or, lastly, fools who had no social support apart from the prince. And even among fools, husbands possessed wives.

Astoundingly, Prosch later returned to Würzburg. A rude shock awaited him. Tired from the journey, he went immediately to his lodgings in the town and delayed making an appearance at Adam Friedrich's table, the table where, as Prosch says, the prince-bishop recruited himself from his cares of state. This was an important lapse. Prosch was arrested by six grenadiers carrying fixed bayonets and taken by force to the court and, while Adam Friedrich watched through the blinds, was marched to the guard room in his palace and kept there for several hours without food. "The *Herrschaften*," he drily comments, "were sitting at table for a long time" (177). At length, he was taken under guard to the prince-bishop's table, where Adam Friedrich punished him for his delayed appearance by playing what can only be called mind games. When Prosch went to him and kissed his hand, he referred to him as "this gentleman" and refused to "see" or recognize Prosch, insisting that "My Peter is quite another person, who has the understanding of an angel." Then Prosch's tormenter Frankenstein took up the game and asked, "Where does this gentleman come from?" When Prosch replied that he came from the Tyrol, he is asked whether he knows "our court Tyrolese (*Hoftyroler*), Peter, a charming man and the king of the Hoftyroler." When Prosch replied that he was that man, Frankenstein called him a liar. The young men at the table conversed with him only in compliments "as one would to a stranger" (177–78). Adam Friedrich sent a messenger to Prosch's lodgings to ask where he was, whether he was ill, and where he was eating that day. When Prosch continued to repeat, "Here I am!" it changed nothing. Prosch tried to reassure himself of his own existence by going to a large mirror and seeing himself, thus continuing a pattern of references to mirrors in the text, nearly all in the context of questioning of the self. Nobody "recognized" him when Adam Friedrich moved into the audience chamber for coffee. Going back to his lodgings, his landlady also did not "recognize" him and bade him be gone. In a panic, Prosch went to the Capuchin church, thinking to find truth there, and asked the prince-bishop's confessor, "Who am I?" "I don't know you," was the reply. The next day, he went back to the *Residenz* but was not allowed to enter the building without undergoing a lengthy written interrogation about his identity. No one else would speak to him or appear to notice that he was there. Going to the count's table, only after a considerable interval did Adam Friedrich "see" him once more. Then, suddenly, all the courtiers could see him too (179). But by this point Prosch felt himself truly invisible. This small story shows the extent to which his sense of identity entirely depended on being "seen" by the *Herrschaften*. And it provides some explanation for the dependency that took him back even to Würzburg, where his wife had probably been prostituted. Prosch does not comment on this last cruelty, and this refusal to comment is a comment in itself. It leaves an empty space in which the reader can find her own horror, or humor.

This incident also shows how Adam Friedrich's table, like all the "tables" we have so far encountered, was not simply a place of rest and relaxation.[14] The table could also be a place of disciplining, a place where lowly subjects who did not immediately make themselves "available" to the ruler could be punished before the whole court. The table could also be a *theatrum mundi*, with Adam Friedrich as a more or sometimes less benevolent spectator god, where those players who are "unseen" simply do not exist.[15] Without the gaze of the spectator, the play and its actors vanished. This is exactly what Adam Friedrich's game with Prosch's identity sought to demonstrate.

Once the constituting spectator is removed, the potential of the *theatrum mundi* to cause loss of identity, to be something that creates, represents, and responds to uncertainties about how to constitute and maintain a stable and authentic self, is revealed. No wonder Prosch fears that he has lost himself, and that even a mirror will not be able to restore him to himself. It is in this way that Prosch explores the questions of identity that agitated the "high culture" of his age. In looking at the courts of eighteenth-century southern Germany, we see a conjuncture of rigid etiquette, wild outbursts of laughter, and aggressive practical joking. They seem to have nothing to do either with the "sensibility" of the *Goethezeit*.[16] Yet laughter and etiquette, in appearance so different, were both instruments of control: etiquette, of courtiers by the ruler: laughter, of subjects by the court.

Meanwhile, Prosch's wife, Maria, died, and Prosch, unromantically seeking a mother for his children, quickly remarried. Back on the road, Prosch found a new princely patron, the Margrave of Ansbach-Bayreuth (186).[17] Christian Friedrich (1736–1806) has often been portrayed as a typical enlightened German prince, who founded a porcelain factory, gave much time and thought to the agricultural improvement of his small principality, and founded a state bank (the distant ancestor of the modern Hypo-Vereinsbank). Yet Christian Friedrich, so much in other ways a participant in "our enlightened times," was also partial to Prosch, who received a handsome reward from him for the poem he recited on the margrave's birthday. It recalls the ancient truth-telling function of the fool: "Children and fools say what is true / what is true always nice and fine / And now to come to the truth / Peter will uprightly confess / to being a double fool" (203).[18] These references to truth are given added resonance by Adam Friedrich's mind games, which depended on distortions and the untruths he was able to create around him.

Prosch also references the contemporary poets Johann Wilhelm Gleim (1719–1803) and Albrecht von Haller (1708–1777). As well as being the butt of courtly society, Prosch had also picked up some of its culture: "Hier sollen Gleim und Haller reden / Und nicht ein Stockfisch von Poeten / Wie Peter ist" (Here Gleim and Haller should talk / and not an amateur poet / like Peter) (202-3).[19] There were several more verses, one even making a reference to his suicide attempt, which must by now have become common knowledge. "Everyone shouted and laughed" after Prosch's recitation, a recitation that recalls Morgenstern's theses in its mixture of folk sayings and "high culture" poetry. Like Morgenstern and Fröhlich, Prosch moved between many cultures. The margrave joined the ranks of Prosch's patrons with an invitation to breakfast the following day, an annual pension of twenty-five guilders, and board and lodging when at court. Prosch left the court after a six-week stay, carrying letters from the margrave to the prince-bishop in Würzburg.

Being now the father of five children, two from his first marriage and three from his second, Prosch began to feel his means inadequate to provide for their support. Accordingly, he took the two small boys, Jacob and Philip, tricked out in Tyrolean costume, on his next journey. Arriving at the court in Munich, the boys were so naïve that they tried to walk through mirrors to meet the people they saw reflected in them (218). Prosch set them to wrestling in front of the *Herrschaften*. The Kurfürst and Kurfürstin laughed and offered to take care of one of the children. Having sealed the bargain by kissing the hands of the Kurfürst and his wife, Prosch arranged to leave Jacob behind with them. Without manifesting much sadness at the separation, he remarked, "Now at least I had one fewer mouth to feed" (219).

Going on to Würzburg, he built on a previous remark from Adam Friedrich, that he would like Prosch to bring him a "*Gemsbock,*" or chamois, from the Tyrol. He carried Philip into court in a sack, telling him to make goat-like noises, and then released him suddenly, telling him to bleat his way straight to the "short fat man with a golden cross round his neck, and to kiss the hem of his cassock": "Everyone laughed at the mountain goat." Adam Friedrich agreed to take care of the boy as long as he lived (220–21). This condition was common for the pensions awarded to Prosch, their donors being careful to stipulate that he held them for their lifetimes only. Nothing could make clearer than these "favors" the personal nature of their rule.[20]

This was to be the last time Prosch entertained the prince-bishop, who died shortly thereafter. As Prosch lamented, with a typical mixture of cupidity and genuine feeling: "Adam Friedrich, May God console him! (226). . . . I was inconsolable, that I would not see him again, for half my living had now gone" (231). Adam Friedrich's death in 1779 opened a new era for Prosch, one where his relationships with patrons became more insecure. He did not win the struggle for primacy with another "*Hoftyroler*" already in residence at the court of the new Elector of Bavaria, Karl Theodor, and departed after only a few days (227). At Bamberg he was initially refused his usual board and lodging, though this was later restored. The new bishop there agreed to let the arrangement go on for another year but warned Prosch, "mit Narren kann ich nicht umgehen" (I can't stand fools) (233) and told him that that he would probably be turned away at the end of the grace period. Prosch returned to his village, where he bought property valued at the substantial sum of 4,540 florins and organized the casting of a bell for the church through one of his patrons, Graf von Tannenburg (237). Now, he exulted, he was a farmer, an innkeeper, and a brandy distiller, possessing eight cows and two horses, one of the richest men in the village (239).

Yet at the suggestion of the Margrave of Ansbach-Bayreuth that he should join him on an Italian journey, with a rendezvous in Venice, he willingly set off again. At Venice, having walked from Trento, he saw the open sea for the first time. He also heard the news of the death of Empress Maria Theresa (on 29 November 1780). This was enough to have the margrave turn back and abandon his Italian project, leaving Prosch in the lurch in Venice. The margrave reimbursed him for his expenses, but Prosch was inconsolable at the death of the empress, "our immortal mother," and also, as ever, at the loss of his trade in gloves at the court in Vienna. Her successor, her son the Emperor Joseph II, disliked fools, and it was clear that Prosch had lost his opening there (240–41).[21]

This loss was followed in 1781 by a devastating flood in the Zillerthal, which Prosch would not have survived financially without a loan—later forgiven him—from the Margrave of Ansbach-Bayreuth (251). Increasingly, he stayed at home in the village, in spite of thereby losing several little pensions, and in spite of the fact that this reduced his trade in gloves. He made one last trip, to Anton-Ignaz, the Prince-Bishop of Regensburg, who for thirty years had been "meinen besten Vater" (my best father) (276). The prince-bishop was not well, "und so brauchte er mich desto besser zur Aufmünterung" (and so needed me to raise his spirits). This was the last time he saw the prince-bishop (259–65). On a final visit to a now ancient Graf Kotegg, he saw the papal entrance into Vienna in 1782 (264–65).

His retirement ended, however, and a new—alas short-lived—era opened, when in October 1785, he received a letter from the Margrave of Ansbach-Bayreuth, who was at that time the lover of the famous French actress Mlle Clairon.[22] He invited Prosch to accompany him to Paris. Prosch wanted to see the young Queen Marie Antoinette, a daughter of Maria Theresa, and obtained an assurance from Prince Max of Zweibrücken that he would be given an entrée at the French court (279). So fortified, Prosch, even though not speaking a word of French, made his way to Paris. At length, on 17

November 1786, at nine in the evening, he entered Paris, marveling at the bustle and noise and the lamps lighting the streets (281). Finding an inn, he was shocked at being asked, as was normal, to share a bed with a stranger, and he fell out of bed in his efforts not to sleep too near his enforced neighbor (282). Next day, he could not find out where the margrave was lodging or the location of the bank to which the margrave had directed him for his financial needs. The next few days were taken up with these inquiries. On arriving at last at the margrave's Hôtel in Issy, Prosch was so exhausted that he lay two days in bed before seeing the margrave, who laughed heartily at his misadventures. He delivered to him a letter from the Markgräfin (286). Prosch was assured of his board and lodging, and seeing his disorientation in Paris, the margrave assigned him a permanent escort. Now began a very happy time of eating and drinking and sightseeing in Paris. When the margrave returned to his hotel at night, Prosch's duty was to stay up until all hours and amuse him, Scheherazade-like, by telling him all he had seen during the day, whether the Palais royal, the Comédie française or the Bastille, Nôtre Dame, or St. Geneviève. Prosch remarked that these were the best days of his life, days whose equal he would never see again (288).

On 12 December the margrave went to Versailles, carrying with him a letter that Prosch had brought from Prince Max to the great French noble, the Duc de Polignac. Prosch asked the margrave to recommend him to the duke and ask him if he could come to court. He was overjoyed when this permission was granted, and he went to Versailles the next day, accompanied by an interpreter and a letter from the margrave. Polignac told him to attend in the evening where the queen would pass through on the way to a concert. So, taking many dozens of gloves with him, Prosch waited until he could talk to Marie Antoinette. She asked him for news of her family, and Prosch praised Maria Theresa as a true mother of her lands. Marie Antoinette bought Prosch's gloves, and the Duc de Polignac gave Prosch a "present" in return (289). This incident shows how Prosch's connections could even transcend the court of Vienna and launch him into the world of the international aristocracy.

On 17 January, Prosch left for Germany, his journey paid for by the margrave, and arrived back in Ansbach on 13 February. Passing on to Fürstenried, he performed a gala-day song for Maria Anna, the widow of the previous Elector of Bavaria, containing the verse: "We small puppets / can only do what the Father wills / Enjoy yourselves and learn to pray" (299).

Prosch then returned to Ried, where even those who had never heard of Paris wanted to hear about his wanderings. But Prosch could never stay at home very long. He set off again for Innsbruck and the nobility there (301). This is the last trip that we hear of. Prosch's working life was coming to an end. Even the Margrave of Ansbach would have disappointed as a patron, for in 1791 he was to sell his small territories to the king of Prussia and retire to England with Lady Craven, his new favorite, to breed race horses. In conclusion, Prosch asks, in another verse in his poem to Maria Anna: "The fate of man is wonderful / Virtue is the heart's wages, / This have I experienced. / Without you, what is a Throne?" (304). An ironic way of closing an account so full of earthly thrones and princes, and their peals of laughter.

Even this abbreviated account of the incidents in Prosch's autobiography should show how rich is this source. But it is important for the reader to avoid being seduced by it. Prosch manages to do what all great storytellers do, which is to construct a self-sufficient universe. It is tempting to stay inside it. But such microhistorical sources also pose problems. How typical were the events described? What other points of view can be imagined? What can the fate of a single individual tell us about the rest of the history of larger entities such as courts and governments? What links can we make between the structures of individual personality and the world that they describe? How can we tell the story so that it retains its individuality and yet can help us approach larger patterns?

Prosch's account is complex. In spite, for example, of its orientation toward the *Herrschaften* who were the major subscribers—more than three hundred in all—to its publication, it contains incidents, such as the public enema, which could be doubtful even to a robust sense of humor, and even very dark ones such as Prosch's suicide attempt and the fate of Prosch's wife at the hands of those very *Herrschaften*. Many of Prosch's gala-day poems contain ironic implications aimed at the lords and ladies among whom he spent so much time. In spite, too, of Prosch's concern as a fool with the lords and ladies, there is much to read here, which alas has had to be abbreviated, about his life as a peasant in his village of Ried im Zillerthal. A third thread is provided by his stories of life on the road. These stories provide buffer zones between the accounts of what happens to Prosch at each court.

All these threads are bound together in complex ways. Village and court intertwine, most dramatically in the meetings between Prosch and Empress

Maria Theresa, most sadly and darkly in his suicide attempt and in the story of what happened when he took his young wife with him from her village to Würzburg. Prosch's struggles in the village show Prosch as quite a different person from the long-suffering fool who had the *Herrschaften* rolling on the floor with laughter. Prosch's account, which appears on the surface naïve and picaresque, little more than a succession of anecdotes whose deeper significance he explicitly refuses to discuss (303), in fact is a complex weaving together of three strands: his life at the courts that patronized him, his life in the village, and his life on the road, and a meditation on the variability of personality in its interaction with circumstance. The references throughout to mirrors, to hunting, and to electrical machines help to enhance the unity of Prosch's autobiography in a way that shows him as an artful writer. Was this man risen from the depths of poverty in fact the author of the *Leben und Ereignisse* (Life and events)? My judgement is positive. Too many small private details stud the text, such as the exact amounts given to him by each of his wedding guests (61–66) or the more than three hundred names of nobles and court officials great and small mentioned in the text who could stand witness to his account. By the time that Prosch wrote, he was clearly fully literate, reading books his patrons had given him (enough to fill a room in his house in Ried), and making references to major poets of the era, such as Gleim and Haller.

Yet Prosch was isolated by laughter, left as an outsider, in spite of the fact that his "adoption" by some of his patrons might seem to make him simultaneously an insider. For the courtiers, during their japes, Prosch is the "other," an otherness that is increased by his intermittent role as a *Hoftyroler* expected to be on hand not just for merry japes but also for amusing Tyrolean dialect, "native" dances, and snippets of folklore and fairy tales. If the new "anthropology" at this very time was constructing the exotic person, the Pacific Islander or the American Indian, as the "other," this process of "othering" was also going on in the small German courts using people who lived only a few miles away. It helped a great deal too that Prosch is well known to be a peasant and an itinerant salesman, in other words, a subject from one of the lowest social classes. Cruel laughter demonstrates the courtiers' ability to control their social inferiors. In this way, Prosch's position is like that of medieval and Renaissance court fools who combined in their persons an insider who had unequalled access to the ear of the monarch, and an outsider who slept on the floor amid the rushes. Prosch is one of these kept outsiders, such as the court poets and the court Jews (159), outsiders on whom the court relied to maintain its own identity. What makes him different from them is this "autobiography," and the songs he produced and sang at his patrons' gala days, which are full of ironies under their surface of praise for the ruler concerned, and of references to the functions of the fool as truth teller (9–11, 202, 213–16, 22).

It is notable that Prosch himself seldom says anything during the japes to which he is subjected. He denies himself ways to negotiate himself out of them, and his muteness leads us straight to the question of the ambivalence of Prosch's desire. Does he positively wish to be the butt of jokes and japes, even the most cruel, dangerous, and demeaning, even those involving his wife? Does he undergo them as part of a profitable role? Or is he somehow, even suffering, unable to extricate himself from sometimes life-threatening situations?

Prosch is paid to establish this role. His own personality allows him to sustain it. The courts he visited needed him as much as he needed them. They needed kept outsiders, to give them definition. He in his turn needed the reputation they gave him as a *Spassmacher,* or fun-maker, not only in financial terms but also for the emotional relationships he formed with members of the *Herrschaften,* whose "child" he became. Even rulers with whom he had not formed this fictive family relationship clearly maintained highly emotional relationships with him. In Munich, for example, under Max III Joseph, Prosch recounts how he was sitting in the early morning in Electress Maria Anna Sophia's private room.[23] In came her brother, who was glad to see that Prosch was there and showed it after Prosch's greeting by taking him by the shoulders, shaking him, kissing him, and making the sign of the Cross over him. Maria Anna commented: "He is the only fool that I can put up with—he is honest, doesn't gossip, and can be discreet. We should trust him" (155). This response to Prosch, with its very physical expression, stems from the deep ambivalence of Prosch's position at court. Prosch can be bullied into delivering up his wife and subjected to enemas and electrical experiments, yet he and his children are also sheltered, supported, and treated as temporary court insiders with access to the private rooms of the *Herrschaften,* not just to the public table; in a trusted position, he might see and hear enough to have occasion to be discreet; and could yet be treated as a favorite child, to be safeguarded by the sign of the Cross.

Much has been written about the etiquette-bound nature of the German courts and their obsession with establishing orders of precedence.[24] But Prosch's interventions occurred in a way that for a few minutes broke down hierarchy. All the lords and ladies laugh together without apparent discrimination of rank, delighted to play this game of a moment, even if they knew that at the end of the day the joke would die away—and would actually confirm their relative positions in the hierarchy. Prosch's japes occur often at the "table," the meal at which, often after going to Mass, the lordly family would re-create themselves. By the time that Prosch retired, this "table," which had once had the power to become a *theatrum mundi,* had lost the old etiquette that had dictated the order of precedence in eating and sitting.[25] Perhaps it could be argued that Prosch the kept outsider was needed more than ever at this time of increasing fluidity and flux in court life, to focus the court and increase its cohesion by the designation of one single focus of controlling laughter. One is unavoidably reminded of Gundling's functions at the Prussian court decades before. At the greater, self-consciously enlightened courts of Prussia under Frederick II and Austria under Joseph II, court ceremonial and etiquette were being set aside at a rapid pace exactly at this time. But the utilitarian kingship practiced in Berlin and Vienna, which justified itself by doing, not being, had not yet come to the small courts in which Prosch lived and moved. They were in a transitional position, and that was the niche in which Prosch the fool performed.

This is why his account of the aristocracy is contradictory. The word "contradiction" is crucial for Prosch, as it is for all fools: he was not only loved, helped, and supported but also and at the same time treated cruelly by his patrons and at their courts. He himself saw his patrons both as sources of love and of profit. His personality enabled him to intervene in the power structures of the courts he frequented. He proves Elias's point about the way in which courtly structures both created and depended upon the emergence of appropriate personality types. Personality and power interlock.

In his account of those courts, Prosch can even be seen as playing into the contemporary debate on the position of the aristocracy, the so-called *Adelsfrage.* For it was not simply that the courts were in flux. The position of the *Herrschaften* themselves was under attack. From the 1770s, a growing number of middle-class writers, such as Adolf Knigge, Johann Heinrich Merck, or, most violently, from the standpoint of poverty, Johann Gottfried Seume,[26] attacked the privileged position of the aristocracy, arguing that their frivolous and irresponsible lives should disqualify them from their social and economic privileges and that the middle class formed the true elite, that of virtue and practical learning.[27] Prosch's work, though it contains few overt criticisms of the aristocracy, can be read against this background. His autobiography is in part an account of aristocratic irresponsibility, as its anonymous reviewer in Friedrich Nicolai's *Allgemeine Deutsche Bibliothek* pointed out.[28] No ruler in Prosch's account appears in their ruling capacity, no agricultural practices are reformed, workhouses, hospitals, or porcelain factories founded, to cite only some of the most usual activities of enlightened German rulers. Prosch's tale is punctuated by peals of laughter rather than by the deliberations of statesmen. By implication, then, it supports the bourgeois side of the debate on the aristocracy. Whether this is by accident or by design is difficult to decide. Prosch was certainly capable of irony in relation to the *Herrschaften*. Whether the whole text could be read as an intervention into the debate is unclear. A decided reader could certainly take it as such. The lords and ladies who contributed to it as subscribers clearly did not, seemingly overlooking its dark passages, ironies, and complaints and their own representation as cruel practical jokers. They thus, ironically, showed how much they needed for their self-definition this representation of subordination through laughter and cruelty.

In this context, let us take a further look at Seume's writings as they can be run against Prosch's.[29] Johann Gottfried Seume, from Hesse-Kassel, was born in 1763. He had good reason to hate the *Herrschaften*. His family fell victim to harsh landlords and the famine years of 1770–71. In 1781, he was kidnapped and pressed into the army of Hessen, whose soldiers, as is well known, were sold as mercenaries to the English for deployment in the American Revolutionary War. He was returned to Germany in 1783. Fearing to be sold again, this time to the Prussian army, he fled, only to be captured as a deserter and imprisoned for four years in Emden whence he escaped in 1787. Making a living in the German equivalent of Grub Street, he studied law with the help of his first patron and in 1791 was given the degree of magister. Six months later found him in Russia working as a translator, tutor, and legation secretary. Returning to Leipzig in 1795, he became a schoolmaster near Grimma. This obscure literary hack originating in the same social stratum as Prosch, only became well known through his autobiographical writings,[30] and died in poverty in 1810. Many of his works were heavily censored due to their outspoken comments on the *Herrschaften*. Seume, for example, wrote, in direct counterpoint to Prosch's own earlier emphasis on *Gnaden* (favors): "Where the prince gives favors he is never just and therefore is always a bad ruler. Favors are only for criminals."[31]

Prosch's account of his life and events is thus far from the rubbish heap of history or from being a mere literary curiosity. It tells us much about the nature of fooling and hence the nature of power. It also presents the historian with acute problems of response. "Enlightened times" should not produce discourses like that of Prosch's ambivalent and often painful life history. To get to the bottom of their structure means overcoming initial moments of horror, sadness, and shock. Yet these are the very moments in which we somehow build sympathy with Prosch's life with its structure of contradiction and ambivalence.

That life encourages us also to examine more closely the meaning of Prosch's phrase "our enlightened times." It is clear that the majority of the incidents Prosch relates would not fit any definition of "enlightened." Taking joy in another's pain goes against the Enlightenment rationale of benevolence, and the intense, childlike mirth of courtiers and rulers alike belies values such as rationality or progress, let alone bourgeois self-control.

We have recently been faced with very different accounts of the Enlightenment in Germany, France, and England. An Enlightenment has been discovered that is devoted to polite rational amusement, to print-based self-improvement, to the cult of sensibility that measures enlightenment by sensitivity to another's pain. It is the world of Goethe's 1809 great novel *Wahlverwandtschaften* (*Elective Affinities*) rather than of Peter Prosch. But Prosch's text is not canceled by *Wahlverwandtschaften*—published only five years after Prosch's death—which many have also read as an ironic account of aristocratic irresponsibility, or even as a direct intervention in the debates around the *Adelsfrage*. Rather, Prosch's autobiography might even fit Goethe's own definition of a work of art, which, he argues, should lack all didactic purpose: "It neither approves nor censures, but instead develops sentiments and actions in sequence and thereby illuminates and instructs."[32]

The Enlightenment faced problems that aristocratic humor encapsulated and exacerbated. Aristocratic laughter at inferiors endorsed cruelty and put a brake on the idea of the independent individual entitled to respect. It shored up the privileged classes. It acted against the idea of the (male) human as a self-standing locus of rights, which the French and American Revolutions were in their different ways in Prosch's lifetime to invent. The itinerant fool is far from the rubbish heap of history.

FIVE

Two Deaths

The Hanswurst and the Fool

"Inconsistencies," answered Imlac, "cannot both be right; but imputed
to man, they may both be true."
—Samuel Johnson, *The History of Rasselas, Prince of Abissinia* (1759)

Court scholar-fools, court newspaper reader–fools, court magician-fools,
municipal fools, and Carnival fools ran the gamut of fooling in the Enlightenment. It is not surprising that contemporaries found it difficult to make
firm distinctions between different categories of fools, and one of the most
slippery distinctions was that between fool and "Hanswurst." As we have
seen, Peter Prosch was often called a Hanswurst, and Joseph Fröhlich possessed ninety-nine Hanswurst suits, each embroidered with a large capital
H on its suspenders. So what or who was a Hanswurst?

The Hanswurst played onstage. As Peter Prosch or Joseph Fröhlich
played to an audience on the stage of the court, so the Hanswurst was a
familiar figure not only in the private theaters of the aristocracy but also
on the stages of the commercial theaters.[1] There was a continuum between
the famous actors who specialized in Hanswurst roles, and the fools who
performed Hanswurst-like actions to entertain their courts. The role itself
was outrageous. The Hanswurst, a peasant-like servant figure in a brightly
colored costume, usually carrying a large sausage and a wooden sword,
was a "walking appetite," consuming food, drink, and sex in large quan-
tities. His nearest modern equivalent is probably the persona developed
by Harpo Marx. As one historian has recently noted: "He eats and drinks
himself through enormous portions and grotesquely long lists of food and
booze. . . . Whether love intrigues are spun round him, whether battles are

being fought and corpses having to be collected, or whether he only has to stand guard or deliver a letter . . . images of devouring or carousing are perpetually arising in him. His character is willing to do anything for money except work. He is happy to lie, thieve, act as a hired killer, or marry an old and ugly woman for her money."[2] The Hanswurst is also on a permanent quest for sex. The sausage and the wooden sword he carries have barely disguised phallic connotations. Many dramatic plots thus revolve around the Hanswurst chasing women, or being chased by them.

It is easy to see why the Hanswurst appealed to a wide audience. By eating enormously and desiring greatly, he was showing its members their fantasies and desires, just as the court fools were often depicted as close to creatures of mud and gluttony such as the pig. Flögel vividly describes the Hanswurst: "a chameleon that takes on all colors and that in the hands of an intelligent man could be the leading role on the stage. . . . He is . . . cowardly, loyal, active but takes on all sorts of fraud and tricks out of fear and self-interest."[3] In the "chameleon," all could find something of their own colors. We have a good idea of what a Hanswurst play was like from an eyewitness account by the English writer and traveler Lady Mary Wortley Montagu (1689–1762). In 1716, she wrote to her friend the poet Alexander Pope (1688–1744) describing a Hanswurst play she had attended in Vienna:

> I thought the house very low and dark; but I confess the comedy admirably recompensed that defect. I never laughed so much in my life. It began with Jupiter's falling in love out of a peep-hole in the clouds, and ended with the birth of Hercules. . . . But I could not easily pardon the liberty the poet has taken of larding his play with not only indecent expressions, but such gross words as I don't think our mob would suffer from a mountebank; and the two Sosias very fairly let down their breeches in the direct view of the boxes, which were full of people of the first rank, that seemed very well pleased with their entertainment, and they assured me that this was a celebrated piece.

This letter, immediately printed, had a long-lasting influence, because it is one of few eyewitness accounts of a Hanswurst piece by a literate person.[4]

The laughter raised, including Lady Mary's own, was clearly uproarious. But it was not rational, wholesome, or serene laughter. Lady Mary herself was torn between her own overwhelming urge to laugh and her disapproval of what she laughed at. The role of the Hanswurst stood in direct opposition to those in the Enlightenment who would "clean up" laughter. It is a truism that calls for purity are integral to the shaping of class or national unity: the Hanswurst plays, so full of impure laughter, were an obvious target for reformers who were trying to do both.

It was not long before a moral crusader arose who was willing to take on the struggle. Johann Christian Gottsched (1700–1766) came to Leipzig in 1724 after university studies at Königsburg, on the run from the Prussian army draft, and there saw a play for the first time. It was a Hanswurst play, and it aroused visceral revulsion in him, expressed as scorn and fear. He spent much of the rest of his life in public opposition to the "walking appetite." His 1732 play *Der sterbende Cato* (The dying Cato), based on Roman history, carried a preface that violently attacked the Hanswurst plays. His 1751 *Versuch einer kritischen Dichtkunst für die Deutschen* (An essay on critical poetry for the Germans) tried again to clean up laughter and decried the earthy humor of the Hanswurst comedies, full of "*Narrenpossen*" (fools' practical jokes). The same message had been conveyed in his 1748 *Grundlegung einer deutschen Sprachkunst* (Basics of German rhetoric). Together with the actress Frederike Neuber (1697–1760), he formally and publicly "banished" the Hanswurst from his dramas. All this took place in 1737, the year in which Morgenstern, dressed in a blue velvet robe embroidered in silver with the fool's symbolic hares, debated the professors of Frankfurt-an-der-Oder. Things happening at the same time need not point in the same direction.

The Hanswurst role not only broke down distance between audience and actor with loud uncontrolled laughter at *Possen* (practical jokes), but it casually mixed tragic and comic. Plebeian Hanswurst "interludes" broke into the action even of heroic dramas concerned with the doings of kings and aristocracy. Gottsched wanted to corral the comic and to contain its unpredictable energies. He saw censoring and controlling the action on the stage as synonymous with educating and restraining the people in the audience. Plays should show middle-class characters to a polite, silent, self-contained middle-class audience. This would be very different from most eighteenth-century theaters, full of noise from the groundlings in the pit and from the chatter, often amatory in nature, that could be heard throughout the play from the upper classes in the theater boxes. Only after all this noise and misconduct was removed could the educational potential of theater through the display of correct manners and morals be fulfilled. Above all,

Gottsched wanted to produce a theater that was "rational" and that insisted on the clear separation of categories like comedy and tragedy, audience and performers, aristocracy and groundlings. It was a drama where there was no role for fools or Hanswursts.

The struggle against the Hanswurst was a long one in the German states. It was paralleled in other countries. The Venetian dramatist Gozzi and the Milanese dramatist Goldoni struggled over the issue of the popular theater in Italy, for exactly the same reasons. Gozzi writes in his autobiography that Goldoni professed himself the champion of theatrical reform, including the project of "cutting the throat of the innocent commedia dell'arte, which had been so well supported in Venice by four principal and deservedly popular masks: Sacchi, Fiorilli, Zannoni and Darbes. . . . Accordingly I opened fire with a dithyrambic poem, praising the extemporary comedians in question, and comparing their gay farces favorably with the dull and heavy pieces of the reformers."[5] In Austria, Hanswurst plays were banned in the licensed theaters in Vienna after 1770.[6]

The plays that replaced the Hanswurst were indeed unattractive, as the Berlin publisher and *Aufklärer* Friedrich Nicolai found in 1781: "What has replaced the outlawed Hanswurst plays? Mainly stiff-sounding translations, tasteless imitations, weak original dramas. . . . [T]hese plays are far weaker than the Hanswurst pieces ever were."[7] Other famous names weighed in, and their interventions undoubtedly did much to lengthen the so-called *Hanswurststreit* (Hanswurst conflict). The Osnabrück jurist Justus Möser (1720–1794), a friend of Nicolai's, for example, contended in his much-reprinted and -translated 1761 *Harlekin, oder Verteidigung des Groteske-Komischen* (Harlequin, or a defense of the comic-grotesque) that laughter and joy, which he saw as deeply grounded in human nature itself, justify the existence of the comic figure of the Hanswurst. Möser placed this defense of the Hanswurst in the context of a defense of the grotesque in general. He attacked critics who saw laughter merely as satire or an attempt to correct human folly, while in reality laughter is basic to our understanding of what it means to be human.[8] The grotesque, that which mixes categories, is a living area of the incongruous and the irrational, which Gottsched saw as incompatible with both the audience and the drama of the reformed, Hanswurst-free theater.

Karl-Friedrich Flögel, that great historian of the funny, the foolish, and the grotesque- comic, came down heavily—if a little late—on the side of the Hanswurst and the grotesque. Many of the arguments of Möser's *Verteidigung* find an echo in his work. In his *Geschichte des Grotesk-Komischen* (History of the comic-grotesque) (1788), Flögel argues about the relationship of the Hanswurst and Enlightenment: Why do men wish to ban the comic, he asks, "that is more deeply embedded in human nature than any other, why would you introduce despotism, when human nature can oppose it, even must oppose it? The pleasure of the grotesque comic is to be found even in unenlightened times very frequently, but its existence is not any evidence of lack of enlightenment; for one meets it just as often in enlightened nations as in individuals who do not lack enlightenment."[9] By 1788, "despotism" was a fighting word. Though it was often applied to Gottsched by his opponents, using it allied the struggle over the Hanswurst to much bigger conflicts looming in the political world, conflicts for which German reformers, like others all over Europe, were preparing during the next decade.[10] For Flögel, Gottsched had got it wrong, through misunderstanding the deep roots of humor in human nature and misunderstanding the relationship between Enlightenment and the funny.

The great playwright and critic Gotthold Ephraim Lessing (1729–1781) also staunchly defended the Hanswurst. Like Gottsched, Lessing was concerned with the remaking of the German stage. His play *Miss Sara Sampson* (1755) has often been viewed as a prototype of the later development of the bourgeois drama. Between 1767 and 1770, Lessing was the theater critic of the Hamburg National Theatre, Germany's first permanent theater. His reviews, collected as the *Hamburgische Dramaturgie,* allowed him the opportunity of supporting the Hanswurst (though it is to be noted that Lessing never wrote a Hanswurst role for any of his own plays). Did not, he argued, the ancient Greeks and Romans also have a Hanswurst role, also dressed in a special costume? Why should we think we are so superior in taste to them? Lessing sharply rebuked Gottsched, asserting that Gottsched "did not so much want to be the reformer of the German stage, but rather wanted to be the creator of a wholly new one. . . . It is to be wished that Herr Gottsched had never mixed himself up with the stage."[11] Both Gottsched and his junior, Lessing, saw themselves as reformers of the German stage, and in their competition, the Hanswurst was the breaking point. Even by the beginning of the early nineteenth-century Romantic movement in Germany, when Gottsched no longer was viewed as the reformer of the stage but as a tiresome, dictatorial pedant, the critic August Wilhelm Schlegel (1767–1845) wrote in 1811, "Without doubt, Hanswurst had more understanding in his little finger, than Gottsched in his whole body."[12] Schlegel wrote that the Hanswurst would always "pop up again as an allegorical figure."

Yet, in spite of Schlegel's recognition of the eternity of the Hanswurst role as a social and psychological archetype, the *Hanswurststreit* did have an impact. The Hanswurst role in the drama did change. The age of the great Hanswurst actors, such as Stranitsky in Vienna, was plainly over. The Hanswurst was increasingly called "Little Hans" in theater programs, and the character laid aside the brightly colored costume he had flaunted, to dress all in white, the color of innocence. Increasingly, too, the work of separation and definition continued, and the Hanswurst lost his role in the main action of the play. Comic miniplays, *Hanswurstiaden* or Harlequin pantomimes, were relegated to pre- or postplay entertainments and merely existed to frame the more serious drama of the evening. Gottsched's ideas in fact had triumphed: it just took a long time for them to do so. They had triumphed in making public the work of separation and distinction. They had also triumphed in creating the preconditions for modern laughter by making the relationship between audience and performers more distant, so that audiences tended to laugh at, rather than with, the performers. They had removed the explosion of social energy inherent in improvisation, and the plays they shaped became predictable and scripted. They had formed our own understanding of restrained conduct in the theater and of the meaning of laughter in the drama. They had led up, in fact, to the twentieth-century invention of canned laughter.[13]

The reasons for the length of the struggle over the Hanswurst are thus not far to seek. A much-loved stage role is difficult to kill, especially when it has the support of both groundlings and aristocracy. In Vienna, when the Hanswurst was banned in 1770 from the licensed theaters on the grounds of the potential of improvisation to disturb public order, his supporters followed him to the unlicensed theaters in the suburbs. The struggle over the Hanswurst and all he represented was also Europe-wide. In Italy, the playwrights Gozzi and Goldoni struggled over the same questions as had the pro- and anti-Hanswurst factions in the German states. In Austria, the royal censor Sonnenfels worked hard to ban the role, to ban improvisation, and to ban traveling theatrical troupes, all as threats to public order. It was only in 1770 that he succeeded in doing so. Eminent critics and literary men intervened, and this only lengthened the conflict.

Yet, given the length of the struggle, it still remains difficult to explain why the Hanswurst came to an end as a viable stage role. Pressure from governments and from serious-minded theatrical reformers does not wholly explain why this happened. We are dealing here with a much more wide-spread change, geographically and socially, in attitudes toward rationality, laughter, classification, and the body. Without those changes, the work of the reformers and governments would have been pointless.

The very existence of the struggles over the Hanswurst shows the depth of the conflict and anxiety that laughter could provoke in the Enlightenment. Thus it also says something important about the Enlightenment itself. The Hanswurst struggle, and those like it, took place virtually simultaneously in many different European countries, countries that varied widely in religion, social structure, wealth, economic development, and government. Does this mean that ideas and attitudes in the Enlightenment float free from such factors? Or, rather differently, is it that the long-term shaping of the national middle classes by placing them in a particular relationship with a purified drama, is similar across many European states and obeys similar agendas? Posing such questions may allow us to understand a little more about the formation of a nation-state culturally dominated by the middle class partly depending for definition upon the presence—or absence—of rude laughter.

And yet: I have told a story about the decline of the Hanswurst that is dependent on another story, that of the rise and self-definition of the middle class. Of course, the middle classes are well-known to be always rising. It is the particular way in which they do it that is interesting. Why did "the" German middle class find it so imperative to banish the Hanswurst in particular? What was it that they were constructing by doing so? I am not suggesting here that the very idea of the "rise of the middle class" is incorrect. What I am doing is trying to ally that story with other things than the *Lesewut* (reading fever), polite conversation, moral weeklies, sensibility, and schemes of social and economic improvement. I believe, quite differently, that the violent attacks on the Hanswurst came from the absolute resistance of the role to the taxonomic urge toward definition and division that lay at the heart of middle-class self-making. It had to differentiate itself from those both below them and above them, and to do so at a time when many middle-class people in the German states earned their livings in state employment. They were thus also caught up in the search of many states for simplification and legibility. This made the struggle over the composite role (remember Morgenstern!) of the Hanswurst one of truly threatening proportions. Thus the struggle against the Hanswurst has strong political overtones. Not just in the weak sense that his improvisation was seen as an inducement to disorder, for example, but in the strong sense that it was bound up with state making. The social energies released by Hanswurst performances were fundamentally opposed to the social disciplining on which state making depended.[14]

As noted, the role of the fool and the role of the Hanswurst often overlapped. It is not surprising, therefore, that just as the Hanswurst role became a pallid shade of its former self by the end of the Enlightenment, so the role of the fool was also lost by the same period. All over Europe the social energies released by comedy were repressed. Fröhlich, for example, was a Dresden personality and major figure at the Saxon court in the 1730s. By the end of the century even the well-known Peter Prosch was struggling to find patrons. Just as Hanswurst-like roles declined, after much struggle, all over Europe in the course of the eighteenth century, so the decline of the fool was a pan-European process. By the end of the seventeenth century, England and France had already lost their court fools. By the beginning of the nineteenth, only the Russians, for whom the fools had been so important in Peter the Great's projects of reform, kept theirs.[15] Yet there were also significant differences. The Hanswurst's decline came after a long period of open and explicit struggle. For the court fool, the process went on more quietly. Prosch, for example, was usually rebuffed from courts where he sought work with simple formulas such as the ruler "didn't like fools," unaccompanied by any further explanation. Frederick II's strongly worded decree abolishing the office of court fool is unique. By the 1790s the passing of the fool seemed complete. Ludwig Tieck, for example (1773–1855), set his 1797 retelling of the story of "Puss in Boots" (*Der gestiefelte Kater*) in the kind of small court where Peter Prosch had performed, ruled by the same sort of irascible ruler he had often encountered in real life. In act 2, a wandering fool appears and tells his sad story: "I am a poor exiled refugee, someone who a long time ago was funny, who now has become stupid and forced to earn his living in a foreign land where he is anew found funny for a short time. . . . My countrymen have become so clever that all fun is legally punished. Wherever they see me, they give me shameful names, like tasteless, improper, bizarre—whoever laughs at me was persecuted like me, and so I had to go into exile."[16]

Many were the attempts to account for the disappearance of the fool. Flögel, in his masterpiece, *Geschichte der Hofnarren* (1789), put it down, logically enough, to changes in the rulers themselves, to those rulers who "could not abide" fools, or who felt ashamed to employ fools because they wished to be seen to enjoy the more refined amusements of the current age.[17] A plethora of learned antiquarian works on various aspects of the history of the fool, culminating in Flögel's own global survey, tried to answer the question of the fool's current demise from another direction, by portraying his previous flourishing as a mark of the irrationality of past times.[18] These "enlightened" writers often tried to recruit their readers to their own distaste for their chosen subject matter. Excess and irrationality, to which the Enlightenment was most hostile, were presented as characteristic of fooling. The very antiquarianism of accounts such as Jean-Baptiste Lucotte Du Tilliot's showed their readers their distance from the foolish past, and in doing so, helped to construct the self-understanding of the Enlightenment itself. Consciously living the Enlightenment meant seeing fooling as an "other," just as being part of an "enlightened" audience meant finding the Hanswurst exactly what must not be laughed along with.

Modern historians have also struggled, largely unsuccessfully, to find the origins of the decline of the court fool. Some, like Rainer Müller, have argued that the rising power of the royal mistress in the eighteenth century left little space for the attractions of the fool.[19] But this idea has little to say to courts like that of Frederick II of Prussia, who had neither mistress nor fool. In 1744 he not only dismissed his fool, the Freiherr von Pöllnitz (1691–1775), but also abolished the very office itself, decreeing: "We want the position that was entrusted to him to be completely abolished in order to completely erase its memory among mankind."[20] The reaction against his father's court, which had been so full of fools, could hardly have been sharper.

Clemens Amelunxen points to the new practices of pleasure centered on court life in this period. The fool, Amelunxen argues, lost his place at court because hunting, music, dining, art collecting, and patronage, sometimes even the practice of piety, took up the days.[21] Easily adduced to the contrary of this argument are the courts of August II and III of Saxony, whose pursuit of pleasure was legendary and where mistresses played a large role; and yet in Dresden there was nonetheless room not only for Joseph Fröhlich but for a plethora of "buffoons."

Gerhardt Petrat considers the question with more sophistication and thoughtfulness.[22] He argues that the fools extended the power of the monarch and acted as a buffer between monarch and court, as Morgenstern did for Frederick William I. But, we may ask, what happens when the monarch sees himself as the "first servant of the state," as Frederick II of Prussia famously described himself? Joseph II of Austria did not say this but ruled as though he had. The fool as buffer between court and king is no longer desired because the ruler orients himself more toward the state than toward the court. Typical royal amusements are in fact much diminished in this period. It is no accident that many monarchs in this period dismantled the court ceremonial and splendor that had been so important to the "representative" monarchies of the previous generation. Queen Anne radically reduced the splendor of the English court.[23] George III of England lived without splendor.[24] Joseph II and Frederick II spent much time on journeys of inspection. Both in fact became famous for traveling through their territories incognito and usually without a large suite. At these times the court was in abeyance. In Munich, court ceremonies declined, and the rigid hierarchies that had governed access to the *Tafel* were replaced with a free-for-all.[25] Many other examples could be given. Peter Prosch's patron, the Duke of Ansbach, after successfully playing the role of enlightened ruler, cared so little for his hereditary dignities that he sold his territory to Prussia and, with his current mistress, Lady Craven, left Germany to live in England and raise race horses. All this abandonment of splendor and ceremony meant that almost everywhere the court (as distinct from the government) was diminishing in importance. "No one comes to visit us," lamented Queen Marie Antoinette of France, while her husband, Louis XVI, repaired watches and turned table legs for amusement.

The fate of the fool was thus dependent on the changing nature of the court.[26] This means that the fool did not disappear everywhere at the same time and that, just as in the case of the Hanswurst, the decline was a long time coming. Peter Prosch was able to find a last, generous patron in Ansbach even in the 1780s and was able to assume a large readership for his autobiography of 1789, published in the same year as Flögel's masterpiece. This coincidence of dates is not without meaning. Both Flögel and Prosch wrote in the last years of the fool. Prosch's last patron, Carl Alexander, was a godsend precisely because he was finding it so hard to recruit any other. One further suggestion for this state of affairs might be the radical changes brought about in many courts by the Seven Years' War (1756–63), the European and colonial conflict that stressed to breaking point the finances of every state involved in it. The court of Poland-Saxony took refuge in Warsaw for the duration of the conflict. It was the end for Fröhlich, who died there in 1757. There is no record of a fool replacing him. Maybe Prosch could travel among so many courts in the period after 1763 precisely because many courts had changed in such a way as to be no longer interested in employing full-time fools. What looks like a triumphal career may in fact have been a sign of the deterioration of the position of the fool in the German-speaking lands.

Let us look in detail at Flögel's account of the end of the fool. He was recounting the end of a social and artistic form that had been with him ever since childhood, when his interest in fools had been aroused by the performances of the municipal fool in his hometown of Jauer in Silesia.[27] Flögel begins by pointing out that the decline of the fool was not confined to the *Hofnarren*. He discusses municipal fools, such as the one employed by the German Baltic port of Lubeck, whose existence had been guaranteed by imperial privilege, and who "vor wenig Jahren" (a few years ago) had still carried on his fooling, like the municipal fools of some French provincial towns. Yet: "Seit einigen Jahren verlohr dieser Narren seinen Einfluss auf den Pöbel, und seine witzigsten Spässe machten niemand mehr lachen" (A few years ago this fool lost his influence with the people, and his funniest jokes didn't make anyone laugh anymore). [28]

Flögel then tells the reader that he has received a letter from a recently dismissed fool. Whether this letter is real or fictional is beside the point. What is surprising is its nostalgia. The world of Flögel suddenly approaches that of Enid Welsford. In the letter, the ex-fool boasts that such was his free, frank, and friendly advice to his master that the master never needed a first minister. His master had explained his firing by saying that fools were no longer apposite to the times. But, the fool exclaims, have not fools been the companions of emperors and kings, counts and gentlemen, throughout history? What makes "our times" so different? The writer ends in puzzlement, "Now if it had been a mistress treated this way . . ." (perhaps meaning that in that case, there would have been nothing to explain, since mistresses were disposable). The fool in his diatribe points to numerous examples from history of true and loyal fools who had been of more use to their masters than a whole college of legal scholars.[29] We find again the theme of conflict between fool's knowledge and university-trained knowledge, which has arisen many times in the course of this study. At a time of the growth of "cameralism," the science of government taught in the new German universities like Göttingen, the fool's point was apposite.[30] Who made better interventions with the ruler, the fool or the cameralist? And who but fools, he continues, was able to tell the truth to the great ones of the earth? Priests and pastors are too timid, and cameralists too bound up with the projects of the ruler. The fool then blames the attractions of plays and operas for distracting attention from the fools.[31] At this point, his explanation is less than convincing. The Saxon court, for example, had put on numerous plays and operas yet still maintained not only a Fröhlich but a whole penumbra of buffoons.

At the last, the fool (surely representing Flögel's own opinion) describes the decline of his vocation as an "unbeschreiblicher Verlust" (indescribable loss) for the world. However, the fool philosophically concludes, ingratitude is only the way the world wags. The voice of the fool here functions like a native informant for an anthropologist, there, possessively, among "her" people, to catch them at the moment of the passing of their authenticity, which is the moment when they become an "other." The fool continuously confronted the Enlightenment with one of its "others," one that presented another mind in opposition to the rationality seen by some at the time, and by many subsequent historians, as the leading characteristic of the Enlightenment.[32]

In accounting for the end of the fool, we also notice references to the fools, like the town fool in Jauer, whose jokes and capers were no longer perceived as funny, and whose hold over their audiences vanished as a result. Something is happening not just to the courts but also to the sense of humor of the times. More and more this came to be taken for granted. Striking is the way, for example, that rulers who are dismissing fools rarely give any, or sufficient, reason for their actions, or simply, at the end, just refuse to find the fools' jokes funny. Are we dealing here with a growing change in taste, a movement against physical humor and against the humor of violence? Peter Prosch here seems to provide an example. Working later in the century than the other fools we discuss in this study, he begins his career as the butt of practical jokes that we would find, to say the least, coarse. Yet he is not just the butt of jokes but makes some of his own—the reason for the expurgation of many editions of his autobiography—like dropping his trousers at *Tafel* and peeing out of the window, both causes of uproarious laughter. Readers are also supposed to find amusing his bondage to the chamber pot of the bishop of Würzburg, who gives him the office of *Nachtstuhlverwalter*.[33] This thereby confirms the identification of the fool with the grossest human appetites and functions. Yet he ends as a narrator of the tales of Paris.

The end of the fool also coincides with the death of the Hanswurst, whose performances were also full of the same physical humor. For all these reasons, it is not surprising that Prosch's career ends for all intents and purposes in Paris with the Margrave of Ansbach-Bayreuth, telling his employer every evening, rather in the manner of Scheherazade in the *Arabian Nights,* about the sounds and sights of Paris. What begins as a physical vocation ends as a narrator's. It is a tribute to Prosch's intelligence that he could make the adjustment.

Nonetheless, to point to a decline in the acceptability of physical humor does not by itself give an explanation of why something that had been previously seen as funny no longer was so. The reasons for this change are, in fact, complex. Perhaps one could suggest that the eighteenth-century social and learned elites supported not just a turning away from physical humor, not just an allegiance to unfoolish virtue and utility, but ultimately the growth of skepticism. This meant the rejection of the strange, the curious, and the irrational, such as the quest for the philosopher's stone, or the alchemy that had so preoccupied the Saxon court in the 1730s. Henceforward, they were to be ascribed to the lower classes of society. The credible changed its nature and in doing so suppressed many narratives present in society. Foolishness itself is a suppressed narrative, so effectively repressed even in our own times that, as noted in the introduction, even many historians have not picked it up. Is this the real meaning of not being found funny any longer? That finding fools and Hanswursts funny is too far away from the elite self-identification with skepticism? A joke is a small narrative (like an anecdote), and one has to play into it for it to seem funny. Only the nonskeptical can do this. And doing so places them on the wrong side of a social and intellectual boundary line. It is probably at this point that the fool, like Tieck's, is expelled from society, and he and his humor are placed on the trash heap of discarded practices and incomprehensible thoughts.

The period of Prosch's professional activity is precisely the period that many Enlightenment historians, not least in Germany but also in the United States and England, have identified as the "sentimental Enlightenment," an Enlightenment based on contact with the written and printed word, on conversation, and Habermasian "critique" carried forward in coffeehouses, tea shops, Masonic lodges, art exhibitions, and any number of other polite meeting places.[34] In other words, historians have seen it as a very urban, genteel, middle-class phenomenon. It is strongly connected with the so-called rise of the middle class. It is also an Enlightenment connected with new structures of feeling. Sympathy for the feelings of others was lauded. Cruelty to animals was censured. Antislavery feeling (though, with the exception of England, without actual antislavery organization) became widespread in Europe. New models for men of how to express sentiment emerge, as in Henry Mackenzie's (1745–1831) bestselling *The Man of Feeling* (1771), or Goethe's (1749–1832) *The Sorrows of Young Werther* (1774), Samuel Richardson's (1689–1761) *Sir Charles Grandison* (1753), or Jean-Jacques Rousseau's (1712–1778) *Julie, ou la nouvelle Héloïse* (1761). All these renowned novels show men as responsive, sentimental beings, not afraid to give way to emotions with tears and gestures.[35] The same was true for women, who, in their valued roles of wives and mothers, were felt to be close to "nature." Nature, as has often been pointed out, comes close to being a moral norm in this period of the "sentimental Enlightenment," connected as it was to the fight against corruption: corruption in high places, the corruption of "natural" feelings by a corrupt society, and the struggle to preserve uncorrupted indigenous peoples in their natural state from the incursions of Europeans.[36]

None of this fitted easily into the world of the fool. Being a fool meant playing a role, in the sense that Prosch played the role of fool. None of the eighteenth-century fools known to me was a so-called "natural" fool, a weak-minded or "simple" person eliciting laughter by nothing but their very intellectual weakness. Their conscious role-playing opposed the tendency of the sentimental Enlightenment to see all role-playing as inherently corrupt. In this sense comedy is always at odds with the sentimental Enlightenment. This is especially true for the cruel comedy of the fool and those who would use the fool as the butt of their own comedy of cruelty. Sentimental feeling is alien to Prosch's world, just as it is for that of Frederick William I, Gundling, Morgenstern, and Fröhlich.

On another level, the fool's comedy is also opposed to the Enlightenment of those who, like Anthony Pagden, would see Enlightenment as the basis of modern liberalism. It is worthwhile to examine this influential recent overview, to be able to confront the significance of our fools with that of an Enlightenment seen from a different angle.[37] Pagden asks, How did we get to where we are today, to a cosmopolitan, liberal-democratic world informed by internationalist secular principles? (Leaving aside whether the world really does look like this.) How did we come to have value systems that insist on sympathy for those unlike ourselves and thus allow us to live lives very different from the sensibility-free existences of the heroes of this book?

The Enlightenment tried, according to Pagden, to be secular and to link human beings together by sympathy: "a passion which offered a minimum psychological principle on which to base a claim to human sociability, both within individual communities and, what is still more significant for my purposes, across them."[38] Pagden argues that human history reveals that "the final destiny of the species must be the creation of a universal cosmopolitan civilization."[39] There Pagden skirts around lives such as Peter Prosch's. His world swings in his narrative from the intensely local world of his village to the cosmopolitan worlds of Paris and Vienna. While Prosch may have a "patria," it is the very local one of his village, and if he has a "nation," it is the nation of those who acknowledge Empress Maria Theresa as mother and Emperor Francis as father. While the concepts of nation and patria are reprehended by Kant as impeding the "dissemination of general human good-will," it may be that it is the oscillation between the local and the cosmopolitan, home and the world, that makes human existence in any way interesting.[40] Either alone would produce claustrophobia or solitude.

Pagden examines Kant's new thinking about the state, important for this book's major theme of state building, and the fools' intervention in its many tensions. Stripping away the ideas that God was the ultimate source of political authority and that the state was the result of contract, it was clear to Kant that there could be no legitimate political authority other than one derived from consent, and that in a republic where all the citizens were represented, though Kant is not clear about the form this representation should take.[41] Pagden argues that Kant's would be a "truly modern state."[42] In another place, Pagden argues that Kant's state would look "remarkably like" a modern liberal democracy.[43] Kant's thinking is a world away from the small and large states full of inventively irascible sovereigns occupied with the fate of their projects of state building in which Prosch, Morgenstern, Gundling, and Fröhlich had their being.

Kant was writing about his future rather than about his present. One has to ask, though, if the "truly modern state," with its shift of sovereignty from the ruler to the people, was really immanent in old regime states? Could it ever have emerged without the impetus of the French Revolution and its breaking of all political molds? Pagden argues (as he must, to save his case for liberal cosmopolitanism as the child of the Enlightenment) that: "Any direct causal link between the Enlightenment, the Revolution and the Revolutionary wars which followed, although apparently obvious, is, however, a spurious one."[44] Pagden does not say why. All this amounts to Pagden's opinion that the Enlightenment, in other words, must remain unsullied by the Revolution if it is to act as the ancestor of modern liberal cosmopolitanism.

But Pagden leaves to one side the other Enlightenment, the Enlightenment of performances and practices, unsentimental practices, as he is primarily concerned with texts rather than the lived experience of Enlightenment men and women. There are simply too many contrasting strands and contradictory features here to be able to say that liberalism and the Enlightenment have an easy relationship. Or that "we" are its direct heirs. Who are "we"? Pagden's book, replete as it is with "us" and "we," instills a profound uneasiness. It is a not so gentle attempt to co-opt his readers into an Enlightenment project and an Enlightenment identity defined as being without cruelty, humor, class conflict, or gender divide, without religion or specific culture, certainly without foolishness, and to instill feelings of guilt and exclusion into those who are unable to forget them. If "we" means those who are happy members of a liberal, secular, cosmopolitan society, it is permissible to argue about what the value system of such a society might be.[45] This is why Pagden takes issue with Alasdair MacIntyre's 1981 book *After Virtue*. MacIntyre's position that "the Enlightenment" offered no basis for the grounding of morals is clearly contradictory to Pagden's, since it involves seeing serious consequences for the Enlightenment's (alleged) anti-religious cosmopolitanism.[46]

The book you are reading at this moment of course stands in direct opposition to Pagden's "we." It carries the belief that the only real "we" is the "we" of the foolish who wisely acknowledge their foolishness: *numerus stultorum infinitus est.* With this understanding, it is possible to avoid Pagden's argument that "we" live in a very particular, possessive relationship to the past, and especially to the Enlightenment past.[47]

We, the foolish, and foolish readers, need a way of thinking that enables us to balance the Enlightenment and its enemies, and to admit interpretative uncertainty as a way of, paradoxically, arriving at probability. For after all, many analysts in the Enlightenment managed to be both pro and con. Herder, for example, defined man as rational but also noted that the dominance of the high-minded (Pagden's "we") could lead to disaster: "The ferment of generalities which characterize our philosophy can conceal oppressions and infringements of the freedom of men and countries, of citizens and people."[48] Pagden lacks humility. His attitude toward the Enlightenment is a possessive one, which dragoons a historical period into being a fake "contemporary."[49] This makes it difficult to stand back from the Enlightenment and see it, too, as bearing scars and traces of its own past. The idea of a self-consistent "period" without such scars and traces is a construct existing only in the minds of historians. Gottsched and Morgenstern are alive in the same world.

In fact, the Enlightenment was, as Herder implies, struggle, and it is defined by the subject of its struggles. The sentimental Enlightenment was not a given, the result of a natural evolution from gross to refined, from credulity to skepticism, but struggled, as Simon Dickie has recently pointed out, against a world of human-inflicted pain, some of which has been detailed in these pages.[50] Lonely autodidacts struggled against mockery and penury to read themselves into being an enlightened person. Young mothers braved social exclusion to follow Rousseau's precepts on breastfeeding. Those in favor of religious toleration struggled against the strong words of those who could still make consistent cases for intolerance, those in favor of constitutional government shouted against those in favor of divine right rule, those who wished to regulate the grain trade shouted against those who wished to be "natural" and let the market find the price level, no matter what suffering ensued. Fools and Hanswursts struggled against reformers who were so invested in social disciplining that they could not tolerate the social energy liberated by their humor, their improvisations, and their belly laughter.

The idea of rights as inherent in the (white, male) individual (and the very idea of the individual), so important in the liberalism originating in the Enlightenment, is absolutely nonexistent not only for the fools discussed in this study but also for their patrons. The fools, like Fröhlich, cling "like a limpet," as he himself once said, to the grace and favor, the *Gnade,* of their rulers. The will of the ruler overrode theirs at every turn, and only by obeying it could they maintain their role and hence their employment. It overrides, for example, Prosch's well-founded fear that his wife would be prostituted if he brought her to the court of the bishop of Würzburg. "It was only a bit of fun," says the bishop. When Prosch in anguish cries, "I am the possessor" (of his wife), he is responding in the only way he knows, which is to try to insert himself into this world where people gain status by

Four Fools in the Age of Reason

possessing others. Prosch and the bishop struggle over possession rights, and Prosch's prior struggle to evade the bishop's commands to bring his wife to court is an unsuccessful attempt to protect Prosch's right to possess.

Even beyond Pagden's insistence on the Enlightenment as the origin of the modern world, to find oneself the "heir" of a historical period is a very odd matter. The historical period is largely a fiction constructed by historians. It exists to put meat on their claims to possess the past. In reality, every time is the heir not of one historical period but of all previous times. It therefore bears their traces.[51] "Our enlightened times," to quote Prosch's ironical phrase, were no different.

The modern only exists at the price of shutting down the human sympathy that unites us not only to "our" period but to all previous ones. It does nothing to unite us to the fools and Hanswursts, and just as importantly, their audiences, in their human foolishness and contradictory wisdom. It has been the aim of this book to capture that foolishness and that wisdom, and in doing so, point to the many different ways in which history can be written and experienced.

Conclusion

The End of the Journey

> We are now, reader, arrived at the last stage of our long journey. . . .
> And now, my friend, I take this opportunity (as I shall have no other),
> of heartily wishing thee well. If I have been an entertaining companion
> to thee, I promise thee it is what I have desired. If in anything I have
> offended, it was really without any intention.
> —Henry Fielding, *The History of Tom Jones, A Foundling* (1742)

There is sadness in reaching the end of writing a book. Characters and places among which one has lived for so long abruptly vanish. Readers and their responses will soon enough take over the life of the text and change the small world one has labored to create into a different universe of interpretation. And writing is transformative. I am no longer the same person as the one who began fourteen years ago, at the urging of a friend, to write about Morgenstern's debate with the professors, and who slowly realized from that experience—due to the urging of the same friend—that I had stumbled upon the germ of a book. There is sadness in the sheer stretch of that time, and for that lost person.

Writing this book has been a transformative experience. For in spite of its subject matter this book is dark rather than light. Readers who open these pages encounter the shock of the cruelty inflicted on Gundling and Prosch, and the cruelty practiced by Frederick William, always in the service of the joke and the jape, and the making of sovereignty. Even more so, they encounter the shock of the sheer strangeness of a world full of fools, bears, pigs, apes, silver hares, and owls. Not to mention Meissen china, fireworks, and hunters of small game both animal and human.

I have really been writing an immersion in strangeness. I have tried to use that strangeness as a way into understanding the workings of power in early modern German states.[1] Talking about strangeness is really to talk about identification. What is like the universe of what we feel we know, and what unlike? Why do we want to identify with the unlike and therefore continue to turn these pages? Is it merely a form of emotional sensationalism? Or is it a deeper transformation we seek? A relationship with the past that is also a relationship with the present self? For one of the threads of this book has been the writing of a history that does not pretend to objectivity and distance but that identifies with its strange subjects.

I have found major and once fashionable theorists such as Jürgen Habermas and Michel Foucault to be helpful only to a limited degree for the understanding of the triad of fool, prince, and court. The government by paper treated by Andreas Gestrich, and above all the theories of Norbert Elias about the relationship between personality and the working of the court, have given much. But even these historians are unprepared to deal with the life of the fool and its shaping of the strangeness of the eighteenth-century German court. I have also found that historians divide sharply between those who do and those who do not feel at home with strangeness. Sabrow and Marschke for example, ill at ease, take on the ungrateful task of normalizing the strangeness of Frederick William I and his fool Gundling. Those who do feel at home in strangeness might be likened to anthropologists, sitting around sputtering campfires, on the edge of the strange forest of symbols and characters that is Enlightenment Germany.

Through them we ask, Why did court fools last so much longer in the German states than anywhere else in Europe? So much longer in fact, that they could run straight on into "our enlightened times," to quote Peter Prosch. Contemporaries agreed that the most obvious peculiarity of the German states was their very number (more than three hundred), their multiplicity, and their variety.[2] Large, tiny, and small; Catholic and Protestant; monarchies, electorates, city states, and ecclesiastical states; rich and poor; militarized and peaceful: the list of contrasts could run on. Such a background was obviously a necessary condition for the travels from court to court of an itinerant such as Peter Prosch. But it seems to tell us little about Fröhlich, Gundling, and Morgenstern. What unites all four, however, was their dependency on the courts and especially on a human relationship with their rulers. For the rulers, too, the fools were important. Augustus the

Strong, Frederick William I, and Peter Prosch's numerous employers kept fools at their courts not just for entertainment but also to make their courts more attractive and more coherent, by whatever means necessary. As has been argued throughout this book, the fools were the necessary outsiders who focused the inner groupings of the courts, at a time when power was still fluid, when states were in the making, and when rulers relied on fools for some of the tasks of government. The force field of honor, for example, so close to the making of sovereignty, was fully intervened in by the fools.

The German fools, even those of major states like Saxony, Brandenburg-Prussia, or Bavaria, also had another common characteristic, which was ease of access to their rulers. As we saw at Frankfurt-an-der-Oder in 1737, ordinary subjects could have more access to the ruler even than they really wanted. Ease of access to the ruler, especially at the ruler's meal times where *Narrenfreiheit* ruled, were two of the defining characteristics of traditional fools. This made the German courts very different from those of France, for example, where access to the ruler was mediated through a large and complex court, the seat of many warring factions.

Historians of the court in this period have pointed out an overall process, perhaps beginning with Frederick William and ending with the French court of the 1780s, of the reduction of spending on the court, the decreasing numbers of court personnel, the reduction of ceremonial and etiquette, and the separation of court offices from those of the state. There is no indication that German courts were exempt from this movement, but much suggests that many simply took longer about it. The Bavarian court, for example, became notably less formal and populous, but only toward the end of the century. Prosch's difficulties later in his career in gaining employment may well be connected to this reduction and simplification of court life.

So here we have three necessary, if not sufficient, conditions for the prolonged survival of the fool in the German states of the eighteenth century: the multiplicity of courts; the ease of access to the ruler, which allowed a niche for *Narrenfreiheit;* and the slowness of the movement toward court reform. What of "our enlightened times"? It is clear that what we call enlightened attitudes could well be reconciled with the employment of fools. Prosch's last major employer, Christian Friedrich Carl Alexander, Margrave of Ansbach-Bayreuth (1738–1806), is an example here, as are Electors Max III Joseph (1727–1777) and Karl Theordor of Bavaria (1724–1799), all of whom brought significant "enlightened" reforms to their territories.[3]

Fools and Enlightenment, in "our enlightened times," were in fact critical to each other. If we can understand Enlightenment as pockets of debates and confrontations (as I have argued elsewhere), then reason was sharpened by its confrontation with the fool.[4] And in confronting reason, the fool kept alive, as he did in a Prussian town in 1737, traces from the deep history of thought, traces that included Socrates's paradoxes and Erasmus's *sileni*. The fool may thus be seen as one who intervenes in the relationship between past and present and holds the past up to the present. In this way, there is continuity, for example, between the fools and the history of writers such as Baumgarten, whom we have encountered in these pages. In this way, too, we can see the "house-historians" such as Gundling not as hopelessly split personalities but as people who were able to reconcile within themselves conventional history writing and the fool's world of ridicule and contradiction.

This is precisely the importance of the fool in the Enlightenment: his capacity to provide a place where opposites could interact, and to do so at a time when more and more energy was being expended on category separation. Gottsched sought to separate audience and players at exactly the same time as natural philosophers tried to separate the seen and the seer in the name of objectivity, and the leopard from the worm in the name of taxonomy. The transparent and the uncontradictory were seen by thinkers such as Jean-Jacques Rousseau as the equivalent of the good and the true.[5] Simplicity, remarkably, was seen as achievable.

This connects with another theme of this book, of the wars of knowledge that marked the Enlightenment. Frederick William I, who must surely stand as the antihero of this book, was in no doubt that there existed at least three different forms of knowledge: commonsense knowledge, academic knowledge (inferior and problematic), and fools' knowledge. Nowhere appears a place for the *Aufklärer,* that *Kulturträger,* carrier of the battles and ideas of the Enlightenment, unless we are to count the banished Christian Wolff. Fools and *Aufklärer* may even have been seen as overlapping. Fools after all also had the job of speaking truth to power. Even the powerful mind of Frederick II had difficulty making the distinction. Awaiting the arrival of Voltaire, whom he had invited to Berlin, he wrote acidly to a friend: "No great lord's fool ever had such wages."[6]

What has the Enlightenment fool left for us? As remarked at the beginning of this book, the fool could well be part of the monumental rubbish heap of history. I have argued, on the contrary, for the necessity of the fool in gaining a full understanding of the eighteenth century. Nonetheless let us explore a little further into that heap. It is full of barriers and blockades. Shakespeare's jokes are a good example here, probably wildly funny at the time of their writing, now incomprehensible without footnotes full of editorial musings. To able to tell jokes in a new language is often taken for a sign of mastery. We know we have not mastered colloquial Shakespeare. I hope that in this book the recurrent translations and interpretations of jokes, particularly those of Frederick William I, have opened a path into the strangeness of the times in which he and the fools lived and moved, and to the mastery of his black comedy.

The comic was often defined in the Enlightenment as the holding present to each other of unlike things.[7] Prosch's experiences as a fool with the bear, animal versus human, like and unlike, seen as comic in his enlightened times, are examples of this. Thus, the fool, far from being perpetuated in modern satirical TV shows, as is often argued, could in fact question our own definition of humor. The twentieth century, for example, saw the invention of antihumor humor, in the shape of tapes of canned laughter.[8] Canned laughter puts the maximum distance between audience and performance, for the laughter one hears is not generated by the performance going on in front of one's eyes but by the mixing of many tapes containing snippets of laughter recorded in different times and places. In fact, canned laughter continues the trend opened by Gottsched, in his battle with the stage fool, of increasing distance between audience and players. To all this the fool stands opposed, and this is one of his most valuable legacies. Laughter, be it dark and complex as well as direct and brutal, or fresh and funny, can bring down pretension and false simplicity. It releases social energy and questions definitions and distinctions. It challenges social disciplining. The contradictory world is the fool's gift to our times.

Notes

Introduction

1. See also Gottfried Wilhelm Leibniz, *The Art of Controversies,* ed. Marcelo Dascal et al. (Dordrecht: Springer, 2006), esp. chap. 16, "Towards a Heuristics for Persuading." Leibniz, living in the aftermath of the confessional wars of the seventeenth century, worked hard to bring former enemies to the negotiating table rather than encouraging divisive public religious controversy. As he said, "En un mot, l'art de conférer et disputer auroit besoin d'estre tout refondu" (Negotiating and arguing need to be entirely rethought) (Leibniz, *Nouveaux essais sur l'entendement humain*, 4.7.11).

2. Peter Novick, *That Noble Dream: The "Objectivity Question," and the American Historical Profession* (Cambridge: Cambridge University Press, 1988).

3. The *"Abfall der Geschichte"* (rubbish tip of history) is a phrase from Benjamin's *Passagenwerk* (Walter Benjamin, *Gesammelte Schriften*, 12 vols., ed. Rolf Tiedemann [Frankfurt-am-Main: Suhrkamp, 1980], 5:575). It connects with Benjamin's belief in history writing as *bricolage*, as fashioned from *Trödel*, pieces of rubbish that have lost their former use (see Stephan Seitz, *Geschichte als Bricolage: W. G. Sebald und die Poetik des Bastelns* [Göttingen: V & R Unipress, 2011]).

4. Karl Friedrich Flögel, *Geschichte der Hofnarren* (Leipzig: David Siegert, 1789). For enlarged editions, see, for example, Friedrich Wilhelm Ebeling, *Zur Geschichte der Hofnarren* (Leipzig: J. Lehmann, 1864); Ebeling, *Flögels Geschichte des Grotesk-Komischen, neu bearbeitet und erweitert* (Leipzig: Adolf Werl, 1862); Flögel, *Geschichte des Grotesk-Komischen* (Munich: Müller, 1914).

5. Karl Friedrich Flögel, *Geschichte der komischen Litteratur,* 2 vols. (Liegnitz: David Siegert, 1784); Karl Friedrich Flögel, *Geschichte der Grotesk-Komischen,* 2 vols. (Leipzig: David Siegert, 1788). See, for one of the few modern attempts to place Flögel in a literary tradition, Michel Espagne, *"L'Histoire du grotesque et du comique* de Karl Friedrich Flögel (1729–1788)," in *Pitres et Pantins: Transformations du masque comique: De l'Antiquité au théâtre d'ombres,* ed. Sophie Basch and Pierre Chauvin (Paris: PUPS, 2007), 153–68: "Le grotesque n'est pas destiné seulement à

faire rire, mais il est le marqueur d'un envers de la société policée, il revèle des tendances anthropologiques profondes que l'ordre social dissimule, il a une dimension de déchainement dionysiaque" (153).

6. Karl-Friedrich Flögel, *Geschichte der komischen Litteratur:* "In wiefern verdient die Geschichte der komischen Litteratur den Namen einer Geschichte?" (To what extent does the history of comic literature deserve the name of history?) (vol. 1, Zweite vorläufige Abhandlung [second preliminary discourse], 3:1).

7. Johann Heinrich Zedler, *Grosses vollständiges Universal-Lexikon aller Wissenschaften und Kunste, welche bishero durch menschlichen Verstand und Witz erfunden und verbessert worden . . .,* 64 vols. (Halle: Zedler, 1732–50); Johann Christoph Adelung, *Grammatisch-Kritisches Wörterbuch der hochdeutschen Mundart,* 2 vols. (Vienna: A Pichler, 1796).

8. This section is indebted to David Sorkin, *The Religious Enlightenment: Protestants, Jews and Catholics from London to Vienna* (Princeton: Princeton University Press, 2008), 113–63.

9. Christa Knellwolf, "The Science of Man," in *The Enlightenment World,* ed. Martin Fitzpatrick, Peter Jones, Knellwolf, and Ian McCalman (London: Routledge, 2004), 194–206.

10. Friedrich Christian Weber, *Das veränderte Ruszland* [sic] . . . *mit einem accuraten Land-Charte und Kupferstichen versehen,* 2 vols. (Frankfurt: Nicolas Forster, 1739–44).

11. Flögel, *Hofnarren (1789),* 274.

12. Enid Welsford, *The Fool: His Social and Literary History* (London: Faber and Faber, 1935). Also excerpted in *Twentieth-Century Interpretations of the "Praise of Folly": A Collection of Critical Essays,* edited by Kathleen Williams (Englewood Cliffs, NJ: Prentice Hall, 1969), 101–5.

13. Enid Welsford, *The Court Masque: A Study in the Relationship between Poetry and the Revels* (Cambridge: Cambridge University Press 1927), viii.

14. Elsie Duncan-Jones, "Enid Welsford (1892–1981)," in *Cambridge Women: Twelve Portraits,* ed. Edward Shills and Carmen Blacker (Cambridge: Cambridge University Press, 1996), 203–19.

15. I. A. Richards, *Science and Poetry,* originally appeared in 1926, the year before the publication of Welsford's *The Court Masque,* and then in a reworked edition in 1935, the year of publication of *The Fool* (London: Kegan Paul, 1935); Welsford, *The Fool,* 403n.

16. Welsford, *The Fool,* 242.

17. Welsford, *The Fool,* 193–94.

18. Compare with the argument by the American social critic Christopher Lasch (1932–1994) that nostalgia was frowned upon by the 1930s (Christopher Lasch, *The True and Only Heaven: Progress and Its Critics* [New York: Norton, 1991]).

19. Beatrice Otto, *Fools Are Everywhere* (Chicago: University of Chicago Press, 2001), xvii. Otto also denies the existence of fools past the period of the Renaissance: "Perhaps because the European court jesters were so inextricably linked with the

tradition of folly that straddled the Middle Ages and the Renaissance, their time was relatively short-lived, and they died out more or less as the fashion for folly faded" (233–34).

20. Qtd. in Anthony Pagden, *The Enlightenment and Why It Still Matters* (Oxford: Oxford University Press, 2013), 148.

21. Universalism is often tied to a positive evaluation of the Enlightenment (Pagden, *The Enlightenment and Why It Still Matters*, 314).

22. Otto, *The Enlightentment*, 71, 146.

23. See Sonja Laden, "Recuperating the Archive: Anecdotal Evidence and Questions of Historical Realism," *Poetics Today* 25 (2004): 1–28; and Malina Stefanovska, "Exemplary or Singular? The Anecdote in Historical Narrative," *SubStance* 38 (2009): 16–30.

24. Samuel Johnson, *The History of Rasselas, Prince of Abissinia* (1759; London, 1819), 40.

25. Marcel Henaff, "The Anecdotal: Truth in Detail," *SubStance* 38 (2009): 97–111.

26. In Peter Prosch, *Leben und Ereignisse des Peter Prosch, eines Tyrolers von Ried im Zillerthal, oder das wunderbare Schicksal geschrieben in den Zeiten der Aufklärung* (1789; Munich: Kösel, 1964), 9.

27. James Schmidt, *What Is Enlightenment? Eighteenth-Century Answers and Twentieth-Century Questions* (Berkeley: University of California Press, 1996), 2–6.

28. Schmidt, *What Is Enlightenment?*, 53–57, 58.

29. Schmidt, *What Is Enlightenment?*, 59.

30. Schmidt, *What Is Enlightenment?*, 65.

31. Schmidt, *What Is Enlightenment?*, 58–65.

32. Schmidt, *What Is Enlightenment?*, 65–77.

33. See the classic account by Rosalie L. Colie, *Paradoxia Epidemica: The Renaissance Tradition of Paradox* (Princeton: Princeton University Press, 1966), which in spite of its title carries forward its account into the Enlightenment.

34. Qtd. in Dorinda Outram, *The Enlightenment,* 3rd ed. (Cambridge: Cambridge University Press, 2013), 66; see also F. Barnard, ed., *Herder on Social and Political Culture* (Cambridge: Cambridge University Press, 1969), 187, 320.

35. There is no intention here to entangle this account with Hegelian dialectic, (very briefly) the interaction of contraries to reach synthesis.

36. Jonathan Sheehan and Dror Wahrman, *Invisible Hands: Self-Organization and the Eighteenth Century* (Chicago: University of Chicago Press, 2015).

37. Norbert Elias, *Gesammelte Schriften,* 19 vols. (Amsterdam: Norbert Elias Foundation, 1992–2010); vol. 2, *Die höfische Gesellschaft,* ed. Claudia Opitz, 2002; vol. 3, *Über den Prozess der Zivilisation,* ed. Heike Hammer, 1997; more accessibly, see Johan Goudsblom and Stephen Mennell, eds., *The Norbert Elias Reader* (Oxford: Blackwell, 1998); and Jeroen Duindam, *Myths of Power: Norbert Elias and the Early Modern European Court* (Amsterdam: Amsterdam University Press, 1994), 1–34, 159–95.

38. Duindam, *Myths of Power,* 179.

39. Duindam, *Myths of Power,* 179.

40. R. J. W. Evans, "The Court: A Protean Institution," in *Princes, Patronage, and the Nobility: The Court at the Beginning of the Modern Age, ca. 1450–1650,* ed. Ronald G. Asch and Adolf M. Birke (Oxford: Oxford University Press, 1991).

41. Michael Kaiser and Andreas Pecar, eds., *Der zweite Mann im Staat: Oberste, Amtsträger, und Favoriten im Umkreis der Reichsfürsten in der Frühen Neuzeit* (Berlin: Duncker and Humblot, 2003); Wolfgang Martens, *Der patriotischer Minister: Fürstendiener in der Literatur der Aufklärungszeit* (Weimar: Bohlau, 1996).

42. Rudolf Vierhaus, "The Prussian Bureaucracy Reconsidered," in *Rethinking Leviathan: The Eighteenth-Century State in Britain and Germany,* ed. John Brewer and Eckhart Hellmuth (Oxford: Oxford University Press, 1999), 149–65, 153, 159.

43. Benjamin Marschke, "Princes' Power, Aristocratic Norms and Personal Eccentricities: *Le caractère bizarre* of Frederick William I of Prussia (1713–1740)," in *The Holy Roman Empire, Reconsidered,* ed. Jason Philip Coy, Marschke, and David Warren Sabean (New York: Berghahn, 2010), 49–70.

44. Marschke, "Princes' Power," 54, is the only time the fools are mentioned in Marschke's recent articles. See chapter 1 for fuller discussion.

45. Vierhaus, "The Prussian Bureaucracy Reconsidered."

46. Simon Dickie, *Cruelty and Laughter: Forgotten Comic Literature and the Unsentimental Eighteenth Century* (Chicago: University of Chicago Press, 2011).

1. Jacob Paul Gundling

1. Theodor Schieder, *Friedrich der Große: Ein Königtum der Widersprüche* (Berlin: Ullstein, 1998); for the bears, see Anton Balthasar König, *Leben und Thaten Jakob Paul Freiherrn von Gundling* (Berlin: Friedrich Francke, 1795), 111.

2. Marschke, "Princes' Power."

3. David Fassmann, *Der gelehrte Narr, oder ganz natürliche Abbildung solcher Gelehrten . . . nebst einer lustigen Dedication und sonderbaren Vorrede* (Freiburg: published by the author, 1729).

4. Martin Sabrow, *Herr und Hanswurst: Das tragische Schicksal des Hofgelehrten Jacob Paul von Gundling* (Stuttgart: Deutsche Verlag, 2001).

5. Michael von Loen, *Des Herrn von Loen gesammelte kleine Schriften,* ed. F. C. Schneider (Frankfurt: Philip Heinrich Huttern, 1750), 198–218.

6. Siegfried Sieber, ed., *Johann Michael von Loen: Goethes Grossoheim (1694–1776), sein Leben, sein Wirken und eine Auswahl aus seinen Schriften* (Leipzig: Historia, 1922).

7. Sieber, ed., *Johann Michael von Loen,* 198.

8. Flögel, *Geschichte der Hofnarren,* 218–26.

9. Sabrow, *Herr und Hanswurst.*

10. Flögel, *Geschichte der Hofnarren,* 15–30.

11. Dror Wahrman, *The Making of the Modern Self: Identity and Culture in Eighteenth-Century England* (New Haven: Yale University Press, 2004), xi–xviii.

12. Frank Henderson Stewart, *Honor* (Chicago: University of Chicago Press, 1994); Kathy Stuart, *Defiled Trades and Social Outcasts: Honor and Ritual Pollution*

in Early Modern Germany (Cambridge: Cambridge University Press, 1999); David Martin Luebke, "Serfdom and Honor in Eighteenth-Century Germany," *Social History* 18 (1993): 143–61; Friedrich Zunkel, "Ehre, Reputation," in *Geschichtliche Grundbegriffe: Historisches Lexikon zur politisch-sozialen Sprache in Deutschland*, 8 vols, ed. Otto Brunner, Werner Conze, and Reinhart Koselleck (Stuttgart: Klett-Cotta, 1975), 2:1–64.

13. Fassmann, *Der gelehrte Narr.*

14. Herbert Breger, "Närrische Weisheit und weise Narrheit in Erfindung des Barocks," *Aesthetik und Kommunikation* 45–46 (1981): 114–22; Marian Füssel, "'Charlataneria Eruditorum': Zur sozialen Semantik des gelehrten Betrugs im 17. und 18. Jahrhundert," *Berichte zur Wissenschaftsgeschichte* 27 (2004): 119–35; Alexander Košenina, *Der gelehrte Narr: Gelehrtensatire seit der Aufklärung* (Göttingen: Wallstein, 2003).

15. Marschke, "Princes' Power."

16. Schieder, *Friedrich der Große*, 18. "Es ist ihm Zeitlebens nicht gelungen, sich selbst zu disziplinieren und seinen gefährlichen Anlagen zu aufbrausendem Jähzorn, Brutalität und Menschenverachtung, die ihn als das Urbild eines unmenschlichen Despoten erscheinen liesen, den Stachel zu nehmen. Unmässig im Zorn war er ebenso unmässig in Reue und Zerknirschung, hin- und hergerissen von heftigsten Emotionen, mit denen seine plänende Rationalität fast unvereinbar zu sein schien."

17. Sabrow, *Herr und Hanswurst*, 87.

18. Peter Baumgart, "Der Adel Brandenburg-Preussens im Urteil der Hohenzollern des 18. Jahrhunderts," in *Adel in der Frühneuzeit: Ein regionaler Vergleich*, ed. Rudolf Endres (Cologne: Bohlau, 1991), 141–61.

19. Andreas Gestrich, *Absolutismus und Öffentlichkeit: Politische Kommunikation in Deutschland zu Beginn des 18. Jahrhunderts* (Göttingen: Vandenhoeck and Ruprecht, 1994).

20. Salomon Jacob Morgenstern, *Ueber Friedrich Wilhelm I: Ein nachgelassenes Werk* (Braunschweig, 1793), 189; Sabrow, *Herr und Hanswurst*, 85.

21. König, *Leben und Thaten Jakob Paul Freiherrn von Gundling*, 120, 129.

22. Marschke, "Princes' Power"; Reinhold August Dorwart, *The Administrative Reforms of Frederick William I of Prussia* (Cambridge: Harvard University Press, 1953).

23. König, *Leben und Thaten Jakob Paul Freiherrn von Gundling*, 39–47. "Merkmahle der Ehren. . . . und Wir dann in Consideration unsers Ober-Ceremonien-Meisters Jacob Paul von Gundling, vielfaltig, und Uns zum offtern Vergnügen nützlichen und unverdrossenen Dienste, Wie auch zu Bezeigung des sonderbaren Allergdsten [*sic*] Wohlgefallens, so Wir an seiner grossen und die Capacität Tausend anderer in Europa höchst berühmt gewesener Leute, weit übersteigenden Gelehrsamkeit und durchbringenden Verstandes, Lecture und ühmblichen [*sic*] Conduite, tragen, aus Eigener Bewegenus [*sic*] resolviret, denselben in den Freyherrlichen Stand zu setzen und zu erheben."

24. König, *Leben und Thaten Jakob Paul Freiherrn von Gundling*, 44–45.

25. "unvergleichlichen Frey-Herrn von Gundeling [*sic*] der gelehrten Welt vorzubilden."

26. König, *Leben und Thaten Jakob Paul Freiherrn von Gundling*, 43–44: "damit vorzustellen das der Frey-Herr von Gundeling [*sic*] von Jugend auf, in den Schriften gelehrter Leute rechts und links um sich gegriffen, und sich dadurch einen guldnen [*sic*] Schatz erworben, selbigen auch nachgehends, aller Welt, zur stupenden admiration, durch den Druck offentlich mitgetheilet und dargeleget habe." Insofar as Gundling was seen as a fool, he was exercising a "dishonorable" trade (see Stuart, *Defiled Trades*). The philosopher Christian Thomasius (1655–1728) argued for the abolition of the idea of the "dishonorable trade," specifically mentioning the "*Pickelhering*," or fool, in his essay "Ob und wie weit Comödianten, Pickelheringe, item Scharfrichterssöhne ad dignitates Academicas zuzulassen," in *Ernsthafte aber doch muntere und vernünftige Thomasische Gedanken und Erinnerungen über allerhand auserlesene Juristische Handel*, by Thomasius, 2 vols. (Halle, 1721), 2:185–94.

27. König, *Leben und Thaten Jakob Paul Freiherrn von Gundling*, 203–4, 129.

28. François Marie Arouet de Voltaire, *Candide, ou de l'optimisme* (Geneva: Cramer, 1759), 1.

29. Qtd. in Marschke, "Princes' Power," 49: "die heroldische Kunst wie das Zeremonialwesen als ein Feld des Witzes und Spottes."

30. Ute Frevert, *Men of Honor: A Social and Cultural History of the Duel* (Cambridge: Cambridge University Press, 1995).

31. Frank Gose, "Das Verhältnis Friedrich Wilhelms I zum Adel," in *Der Soldatenkönig: Friedrich Wilhelm I in seiner Zeit*, ed. Friedrich Beck and Julius H. Schoeps (Potsdam: Verlag fur Berlin-Brandenburg, 2003).

32. König, *Leben und Thaten Jakob Paul Freiherrn von Gundling*, 90–91.

33. Zedler, *Grosses vollständiges Universal-Lexikon aller Wissenschaften und Künste*, vol. E, column 441, columns 415–16.

34. Charles-Louis baron de Montesquieu, *L'esprit des lois* (Geneva: Barrillot et Fils, 1748), 1:24–25.

35. Michael von Loen, "Die närrische Ehre," in *Des Herrn von Loen Gesammlete kleine Schriften*, ed. Schneider, 64–69.

36. "Du Narr! Du Pavians-Physionomie! Visage à faire rire, oder du lächerliches Gesichte! Du Affe! Du Haase! Du Pedant! Du Ignorant! Du Limmel! Du Tolpel! Du Pantoffelholz!"

37. William Clark, *Academic Charisma and the Origins of the Research University* (Chicago: University of Chicago Press, 2006); Lorraine Daston, "The Moral Economy of Science," *Osiris* 10 (1995): 3–24; Dorinda Outram, *Georges Cuvier: Science and Authority in Post-Revolutionary France* (Manchester: Manchester University Press, 1984); Justin Stagl,"Die Ehre des Wissenschaftlers," in *Ehre:Archäische Momente in der Moderne*, ed. Ludgera Vogt and Arnold Zingerl (Frankfurt-am-Main: Suhrkamp, 1994), 35–56.

38. Michael von Loen, "Der unglückliche Gelehrte am Hof, oder einige Nachrichten von dem Freyherrn von Gundling," in *Des Herrn von Loen Gesammlete kleine Schriften*, ed. Schneider, 198–218.

39. My thanks to Martin Gierl for conversations on this point.

40. Qtd. in Marschke, "Princes' Power," 49; for example: "The history is written in a direct, manly style. He relates not only that which happened, but shows at the same time the reason why it happened in this way, or through which intrigues, or through which Imperial laws. He enlarges on all this by using few but well-chosen witnesses. This, the best history of the Empire that could be expected, is founded on a correct and well-organized telling of the story, without at the same time allowing himself to get himself mixed up in it" (anonymous review of Gundling's *Leben Kaysers Conrads des III* [Halle, 1719], in *Unpartheyische Urtheile von juridisch-und historischen Büchern, zweites Stück* [Frankfurt, 1722], 15).

41. König, *Leben und Thaten Jakob Paul Freiherrn von Gundling*, 148–59.

42. König, *Leben und Thaten Jakob Paul Freiherrn von Gundling*, 132–33.

43. König, *Leben und Thaten Jakob Paul Freiherrn von Gundling*, 19.

44. König *Leben und Thaten Jakob Paul Freiherrn von Gundling*, 39.

45. König, *Leben und Thaten Jakob Paul Freiherrn von Gundling*, 36–37; von Loen, "Die närrische Ehre," 201.

46. König, *Leben und Thaten Jakob Paul Freiherrn von Gundling*, 37.

47. König, *Leben und Thaten Jakob Paul Freiherrn von Gundling*, 116; for the bears, see 111.

48. Flögel, *Geschichte der Hofnarren*, 243.

49. Norbert Elias, *Über den Prozess der Zivilisation* (1939; Frankfurt-am-Main: Suhrkamp, 1980); "Scham und Peinlichkeit," 397–409.

50. Elias, *Über den Prozess der Zivilisation*, 397–409.

51. König, *Leben und Thaten Jakob Paul Freiherrn von Gundling*, 64.

52. Morgenstern, *Ueber Friedrich Wilhelm I*, 172.

53. König, *Leben und Thaten Jakob Paul Freiherrn von Gundling*, 17–18.

54. Hannelore Lehmann, "Wurde Jacob Paul Freiherr von Gundling (1673–1731), in einem Sarg begraben, der die Gestalt eines Weinfasses hatte?," *Jahrbuch für Berlin-Brandenburgische Kirchengeschichte* 58 (1991): 199–217.

55. Marschke, "Princes' Power."

56. Beck and Schoeps, eds., *Der Soldatenkönig*, 119: "Ich komme zu meinem Zweck und stabilire die Soveranität und setze die Krone fest wie ein Rocher von Bronze."

57. Elias, *Über den Prozess der Zivilisation*. But see the critical Jeroen Duindam, *Myths of Power;* and *Vienna and Versailles: The Courts of Europe's Dynastic Rivals, 1550–1780* (Cambridge: Cambridge University Press, 2003).

58. Marschke, "Princes' Power."

59. The routine hazing and disorder at Frederick William's court, including hooligan-like behavior even in the Tabakskollegium, should lead us to question the thesis of Michel Foucault and Gerhard Oestreich that this period was one of increasing "social disciplining" as a prerequisite for state building. Gundling was the way in which Frederick William tried to discipline the court (see Gerhard Oestreich, *Neo-Stoicism and the Early Modern State* [Cambridge: Cambridge University Press,

1982]; Michel Foucault, *Discipline and Punish: The Birth of the Prison* [London: Tavistock, 1977]; and Michel Foucault, "Governmentality," *Ideology and Consciousness* 6 [1979]: 5–21).

2. Salomon Jacob Morgenstern

This chapter is partly based on my article "The Work of the Fool: Enlightenment Encounters with Folly, Laughter, and Truth," *Eighteenth-Century Thought* 1 (2003): 281–94. I am grateful to the editors for permission to use material from this work. I would also like to acknowledge my indebtedness to Mack Walker, *Johann Jakob Moser and the Holy Roman Empire of the German Nation* (Chapel Hill: University of North Carolina Press, 1981), 93–95, though my interpretation differs and of course emphasizes the work of the fool rather than Moser's discomfiture. Frederick William: a free translation by Mack Walker using Moser's *Lebensgeschichte*, 4 pts. (Frankfurt: 1777–83), 1:175–77, reads, "It's just a joke and we can have it" (95).

1. Salomon Jacob Morgenstern, *Jus Publicum Imperii Russorum* (Halle, 1737); Richard Otto Leineweber, *Salomon Jacob Morgenstern: Ein Biograph Friedrich Wilhelms I* (Leipzig: Duncker and Humblot, 1899), chap. 1.

2. Flögel, *Geschichte der Hofnarren*, 248.

3. Morgenstern, *Ueber Friedrich Wilhelm I*, iv.

4. Flögel, *Geschichte der Hofnarren*, 245–51.

5. Leineweber, *Salomon Jacob Morgenstern*.

6. Flögel, *Geschichte der Hofnarren*, 46: "in seine Dienste, das er ihm die Zeitungen vorlesen, und ihm aus der alten und neuen Historie unterhalten sollte."

7. Salomon Jacob Morgenstern, *Neueste Staats-Geographie, wo jedes Landes natürlicher, politischer, Kirchen- und Schulen-Staat genau abgeschildert* (Halle, 1735), 2.

8. For example, Ann M. Blair, *Too Much to Know: Managing Scholarly Information before the Modern Age* (New Haven: Yale University Press, 2010).

9. David Hume, *An Enquiry Concerning Human Understanding*, X, "Of Miracles," pt. 1, secs. 86–89 (London: A. Millar, 1748).

10. Eric H. Ash, "Expertise and Practical Knowledge in the Early Modern State," *Osiris* 25 (2010): 1–24.

11. John C. Rule and Benjamin S. Trotter, *A World of Paper: Louis XIV, Colbert de Torcy, and the Rise of the Information State* (Montreal: McGill-Queens University Press, 2014).

12. I thank Martin Gierl for his assistance in obtaining a copy of this rare pamphlet from the library of the Franckesche Stiftung in Halle.

13. Thomas Schroeder, "The Origins of the German Press," in *The Politics of Information in Early Modern Europe*, ed. Brendan Dooley and Sabrina A. Baron (London: Routledge, 2001), 123–50.

14. For example, Holger Boning, "Vom Umgang mit Zeitungen: August Ludwig Schlözer und die neuen Medien des 18. Jahrhunderts," in *August Ludwig von*

Schlözer in Europa, edited by Heinz Duchardt and Martin Espenhorst (Göttingen: Vandenhoek and Ruprecht, 2012), 133–55.

15. Morgenstern, *Vorschlag wie die Zeitungen mit Nützen zu erläutern. Wobey seine Winter-Arbeit zugleich bekannt machen wollen M. Salomon Jacob Morgenstern* (Halle, 1736), unnumbered pages [2 verso]: "Das Licht derer Nachrichten dienet, die Wolken der Unwissenheit zu zertheilen: das Licht der Einsicht hingegen, vertreibet die Nebel derer Vorurtheile, und hochschädlichen Neigungen."

16. Morgenstern, *Vorschlag wie die Zeitungen mit Nützen zu erläutern,* [3]: "Denn indem ihnen nicht erlaubt, partheyische Dinge recht zu beleuchten; so wird ihre Erkentnis statt eines Zusammenhanges, aller gesammleten Nachrichten ohngeachtet, blosses Stuckwerk; die Einsicht aber, und der Geschmack am Wahren und Falschen, nichtweniger Ansehen und Glaubwuerdigkeit gehen verloren . . . unwiedertreibliche Lust, immer ausserordentliche Neuigkeiten zu haben."

17. Tim Blanning, *Frederick the Great, King of Prussia* (New York: Random House, 2016), 27–49, gives a detailed account of Frederick's relationship with his father. For the court-martial commission that adjudicated both Frederick and von Katte in 1730, see Jürgen Kloosterhuis and Lothar Lambacher, *Kriegsgericht in Köpenick! Anno 1730: Kronprinz-Katte-Königswort* (Berlin: Geheimes Staatsarchiv Preussicher Kulturbesitz, 2011).

18. Morgenstern, *Ueber Friedrich Wilhelm I,* 140.

19. Morgenstern, *Ueber Friedrich Wilhelm I,* 140: "Ferner: ob ein grausamer Herr mitleidig seyn könne, und zwar so oft und viel, dass mehr proben des Mitleids, als der angeblichen Grausamkeit herauskommen? Wobey niemand leugnen kann, dass der hochstseelige König gegen die Martyrer seines Jähzorns just am meisten mitleidig gewesen. Freylich ist nicht zu leugnen, dass derselbe bei seinem Leben mehr, als seit seinem Ableben, vor grausam gehalten worden, und zwar wegen des Schlagens, wegen der Werbe-Excesse, und wegen der strengen Executionen."

20. "Als der Cron-Prinz in Custrin sich aufhielt, weiss der Herr Vater um ihn zu beschäftigen, ihm alle Criminal-Processe und Urtheile zur Confirmation, oder Reformation zu. Wie konnte ein grausamer Herr eine so schöne Gelegenheit, mit (illeg) zu quälen, das Leben sauer zu machen und gar Blut zu vergiesen, so leicht under ohne Roth von sich schieben?"

21. See the bestselling novel *Der Vater,* by Jochen Klepper (Berlin: Deutscher Verlagsanstalt, 1937).

22. *Vernünftige Gedanken über Narrheit und Narren* (Frankfurt-an-der-Oder, 1737); 2nd ed., Schwabach, 1739. No variations between these editions. A Dutch translation also exists.

23. Anthony La Vopa, *Grace, Talent and Merit: Poor Students, Clerical Careers and Professional Ideology in Eighteenth-Century Germany* (Cambridge: Cambridge University Press, 1988).

24. William Barker, ed., *The Adages of Erasmus* (1500; Toronto: University of Toronto Press, 2001), 241–68, 296.

25. Flögel, *Geschichte der Hofnarren,* 248.

26. W. E. Knowles Middelton, "What Did Charles II Call the Fellows of the Royal Society?" *Notes and Records of the Royal Society of London* 32 (1977–78): 13–16; Simon Schaffer, "Wallification: Thomas Hobbes on School Divinity and Experimental Pneumatics," *Studies in the History and Philosophy of Science* 19 (1988): 275–98.

27. Johann Jacob Moser, *Lebens-Geschichte Johann Jacob Mosers, . . . von ihm selbst beschrieben,* 3rd ed., 4 pts, (Frankfurt-am-Main, 1777–83).

28. Flögel, *Geschichte der Hofnarren,* 247.

29. "Was ist es denn? Jeder Mensch hat seinen Narren. Einer . . . hat den geistlichen Hochmuts-Narren; ein andrer hat wieder einen andern Narren. Es ist ja nur rein erlaubter Spass und Scherz! Wenn ich keinen Wein trinken will, muss ich nicht lange dagegen protestiren, sondern eben nicht trinken!" (qtd. in Outram, "The Work of the Fool"); Walker's loose translation from his *Johann Jakob Moser and the Holy Roman Empire of the German Nation:* "So what? Everybody's a fool about something. I'm a fool for a soldier, somebody else . . . is a fool for pious vanity, somebody else is a fool about something else" (90).

30. Morgenstern, *Ueber Friedrich Wilhelm I.*

31. Morgenstern, *Ueber Friedrich Wilhelm I.*

32. Cicero, *Ad familiares* 9.22.4. ". . . stultorum plena sunt omnia! Die ganze Welt ist voller Narren / Vom Hirten an bis auf den Pfarren!"

33. "Daraus ist ohne Hererey abzunehmen, wie das Klug seyn kein Handwerk: sondern das solches bey jedem Menschen mit Narrheit, wie das Glück mit Unglück immer vermischet."

34. See Steven Shapin, *The Social History of Truth: Gentility and Science in Seventeenth-Century England* (Chicago: University of Chicago Press, 1994).

35. Flögel, *Geschichte der Hofnarren,* 218.

36. Die Narrheit ist in der Welt nothwendig und unentbehrlich . . . beynahe alle Freude entstehet von, durch, über und bey Narren! Ein Narr macht durch närrischen Vortrag dessen was ein Narr, einen Narr fröhlich . . . hat die Natur die Anstheilung der Narrheit allgemein gemacht; und jedem seinen bescheidenen Theil gegeben. Denen Vornehmen wachst daher die Gelegenheit zu dass sie Menschen zu seyn sich erinnern; und die Geringen ziehen daraus den Trost das andere durch den Stand nicht eben zugleich uber die allgemeinen Menschlichen Schwachheiten erhoben (Morgenstern, *Ueber Friedrich Wilhelm I,* 24).

37. Gestrich, *Absolutismus und Öffentlichkeit.*

38. Jürgen Habermas, *The Structural Transformation of the Public Sphere: An Enquiry into a Category of Bourgeois Society,* trans. Thomas Burger and Frederick Lawrence (1960; Cambridge: MIT Press, 1989).

39. Andreas Gestrich, "The Public Sphere and the Habermas Debate," *German History* 2 (2006): 413–30, 415.

40. Tim Blanning, *The Culture of Power and the Power of Culture: Old Regime Europe, 1660–1789* (Oxford: Oxford University Press, 2002), 13.

41. Gestrich, *Absolutismus und Öffentlichkeit*, 168ff.

42. Marschke, "Princes' Power," 49–70.

3. Joseph Fröhlich

1. Rainer Rückert, *Der Hofnarr Joseph Fröhlich 1694–1757: Taschenspieler und Spassmacher am Hofe Augusts des Starken* (Offenbach-am-Main: Volker Huber, 1998). Fröhlich's modern renown is carried forward in Hans Joachim Schädlich, *Narrenleben: Roman* (Reinbeck bei Hamburg: Rowohlt, 2015).

2. Helen Watanabe-O'Kelly, "Religion and the Consort: Two Electresses of Saxony and Queens of Poland (1697–1757)," in *Queenship in Europe 1660–1815: The Role of the Consort*, ed. Clarissa Campbell-Orr, 252–75 (Cambridge: Cambridge University Press, 2004).

3. Rückert, *Der Hofnarr Joseph Fröhlich 1694–1757*, 230.

4. Johann Michael von Loen, "Der Hof zu Dresden," in *Des Herrn von Loen Gesammelete kleine Schriften*, ed. F. C. Schneider (Frankfurt: Philip Heinrich Huttern, 1750), 152.

5. Karl Czok, "Der Adel in Kursachsen und August der Starke," in *Adel*, ed. Rudolph Endres (Vienna: Bohlau, 1991), 119–40; Wieland Held, *Der Adel und August der Starke: Konflikt und Konfliktaustrag zwischen 1694 und 1707 in Kursachsen* (Cologne: Bohlau, 1999).

6. Helen Watanabe-O'Kelly, *Court Culture in Dresden from Renaissance to Baroque* (Basingstoke: Palgrave, 2002).

7. Rückert, *Der Hofnarr Joseph Fröhlich 1694–1757*, 228.

8. Rückert, *Der Hofnarr Joseph Fröhlich 1694–1757*, 174–78; Flögel, *Geschichte der Hofnarren*, 183.

9. Rückert, *Der Hofnarr Joseph Fröhlich 1694–1757*, 138–44.

10. Qtd. in Rückert, *Der Hofnarr Joseph Fröhlich 1694–1757*, 225. See also Earl of Ilchester and Mrs Langford-Brooke, *The Life of Sir Charles Hanbury-Williams, Poet, Wit and Diplomatist* (London: T. Butterworth, 1928).

11. Fritz Fichtner, "Darstellungen des kursachsischen Hofnarren J. Fröhlich," *Belvedere: Monatsschrift für Sammler und Kunstfreunde* 8 (1929): 1–24; Eva Czernis-Ryl, "The Golden Years of Meissen Porcelain and Saxon Jesters: The Schmiedel Bust in Australia," *Mitteilungsblatt Keramik-Freunde der Schweiz* 104 (1989): 5–11; Rainer Rückert, *Meissener Porzellan 1710–1810: Austellung im Bayerischen Nationalmuseum, München: Katalog* (Munich: Hirmer, 1966).

12. Dietz-Rüdiger Moser, *Fastnacht-Fasching-Karneval: Das Fest der "Verkehrten Welt"* (Graz: Styria, 1986), 137–63.

13. Moser, *Fastnacht-Fasching-Karneval*, 139.

14. Moser, *Fastnacht-Fasching-Karneval*, 137.

15. Rückert, *Der Hofnarr Joseph Fröhlich 1694–1757*, 230.

16. Wolfgang Martens, *Die Botschaft der Tugend: Die Aufklärung im Spiegel der deutschen moralischen Wochenschriften* (Stuttgart: Metzler, 1968).

17. Rolf Engelsing, *Der Burger als Leser: Lesergeschichte in Deutschland 1500–1800* (Stuttgart: Metzler, 1974); Outram, *The Enlightenment*, 14–16.

18. Rückert, *Der Hofnarr Joseph Fröhlich 1694–1757*, 333–61; Johannes Glotzner, *Die Lesergewohnheiten des sachsischen Hofnarrn Joseph Fröhlich (1694–1757): Eine barocke Bücher Schau* (Munich: Edition Enhuber, 2007).

19. Glotzner, *Die Lesergewohnheiten des sachsischen Hofnarrn Joseph Fröhlich (1694–1757)*, #605.

20. David Fassmann, *Das glorwürdigste Leben und Thaten Friedrich August des Grossen, Königs in Pohlen und Churfurstens zu Sachsen* (Hamburg, 1733).

21. Glotzner, *Die Lesergewohnheiten des sachsischen Hofnarrn Joseph Fröhlich (1694–1757)*, #530 (Luther); #578 (Jacob Schmidt); #614 (Fassmann); #624 (Synagogues).

22. Rückert, *Der Hofnarr Joseph Fröhlich 1694–1757*, 154–68; *Gespräch mit Claus Narr im Reiche der Toten: Besonders curieuses Gespräche in dem Reiche derer Todten zwischen dem Königl. Pohln. und Churfurstl-Sachsen Hof-Taschen-Spieler und kurzweilen Rath, Joseph Fröhlich* . . . (Hamburg, 1729). The second work published under Fröhlich's name, the *Politischer Kerhaus* of 1767, is posthumous. A section is devoted to a biting satire on Graf Heinrich von Brühl, Fröhlich's inveterate enemy in life. The piece could not have been published in either Brühl's or Fröhlich's lifetime. Twenty-four pages long, it begins with typical fools' contradictions: he writes, "mit Freud und Leid, süss und sauer . . . als eine Prophezeihung auf gegenwärtige Zeit" (with joy and sorrow, sweet and sour . . . a prophecy about the present).

23. Rückert, *Der Hofnarr Joseph Fröhlich 1694–1757*, 162.

24. "unwürdiger Burgermeister zu Narrendorf an der Elbe, berühmter Taschenspieler . . . Obrister aller Bahrenheuter, Ausschus aller Flegel, Hauptschwein in Fressen und Sauffen . . . Zolleinnehmer der Maulschellen und Narrenstuder, Geordneter Richter aller Narren, und Erb-und-Gerichts-Herr aller Hundsfutterey, Ritter von goldenen Sporn" (Rückert, *Der Hofnarr Joseph Fröhlich 1694–1757*, 163).

25. "Ich bekam auch den Ritter Orden von goldenen Sporn, so ich am Beine trug, womit die Narren in der Welt warden geschorn."

26. Ernst Kantorowicz, "Oriens Augusti: Lever du Roi," *Dumbarton Oaks Papers* 17 (1963): 117–77.

27. See Yona Pinson, *The Fool's Journey: A Myth of Obsession in Northern Renaissance Art* (Turnhout, Belgium: Brepolis, 2008), 137–39.

28. "Je crus que, sans s'arrêter à quelque chose de particulier et de moindre, il devait representer en quelque sorte les devoirs d'un Prince, et m'exciter éternellement moi-même à les remplir. On choisit pour corps le soleil, qui, dans les règles de cet art, est le plus noble de tous, et qui, par la qualité d'unique, par l'éclat qui l'environne, par la lumière qu'il communique aux autres astres qui lui composent comme une espèce de cour, par le partage égal et juste qu'il fait de cette meme lumière à tous les divers climats du monde, par le bien qu'il fait en tous lieux, produisant sans cesse de tous côtés de la vie, la joie et l'action, par son movement sans relâche, où il paraît néanmoins toujours tranquille, par cette course constante et invariable, don't il ne s'écarte et ne

se détourne jamais. C'est assurément la plus vive et la plus belle image d'un grand monarque" (Jean Longnon, *Louis XIV: Mémoires pour les années 1661 et 1666* . . . [Paris: Tallendier, 1978]; François Bluche, *Louis XIV* [Paris: Fayard, 1987], 233).

29. Rückert, *Der Hofnarr Joseph Fröhlich 1694–1757,* 259.

30. Rückert, *Der Hofnarr Joseph Fröhlich 1694–1757,* 357, inventory #907.

31. Karl Czok, *August der Starke und seine Zeit: Kurfurst von Sachsen, König in Polen* (Munich: Piper, 2006), 123–34.

32. I would like to thank the curators of the Grünes Gewölbe.

33. Welsford, *The Court Masque,* chap. 1; Steve Baker, *Picturing the Beast: Animals, Identity, and Representation* (Manchester: Manchester University Press, 1993), 10–11, 47, 91; John Berger, *About Looking* (London: Writers and Readers, 1980), 6; Claude Lévi-Strauss, *Totemism,* trans. Rodney Needham (London: Penguin, 1973), 161–62; and most famously, Mary Douglas, *Natural Symbols* (London: Barrie and Jenkins, 1973), 98. "The human body is always treated as an image of society."

4. Peter Prosch

1. *Leben und Ereignisse des Peter Prosch, eines Tyrolers von Ried im Zillerthal, oder das wunderbare Schicksal, geschrieben in den Zeiten der Aufklärung,* ed. Karl Pörnbacher (1789; Munich: Kosel, 1964). Parenthetical page citations in the chapter text refer to this 1964 edition. Throughout, Prosch refers to visits to "Ellwang." I would like to thank H. C. Erik Midelfort for pointing out that this is in error for "Ellwangen."

2. First edition (Munich, 1789) bei Anton Franz, kurfürstl. Hof-Akademie- und Landschaftsbuchdrucker; 1865 (abbreviated), as *Peter Prosch, der kreuzfidele Tyrolabua, durchtriebene Spassvogel und lustige Hofnarr, erster Handschuhhändler aus Tirol. Eine durchaus wahre Geschichte voller Abenteuer aus der sogenannten guten alten Zeiten vor 100 Jahren* (Munich: Louis Finsterlin, 1865); new edition (Munich: Georg Muller, 1919); (abbreviated), ed. Heinrich Conrad, with original title; this text reprinted in its entirety (Stuttgart: Robert Lutz, 1922) as *Der freiwillige Hofnarr, Memoiren des Peter Prosch, Handschuhändlers aus Tirol.*

3. Felix Mitterer, *Das wunderbare Schicksal: Aus dem Leben des Hoftyrolers Peter Prosch. Ein Theaterstuck und sein historischer Hintergrund* (Innsbruck: Haymon, 1992).

4. Ralph-Reiner Wuthenow, *Das erinnerte Ich: Europäische Autobiographie im 18. Jahrhundert* (Munich: Beck, 1974), 157, 159, 161.

5. "Ein Autor bin ich wahrlich nicht, / Hab' weder Reime noch Gedicht / Mein Leben durch gekritzelt: / Und schrieb ich so mein Leben hin, / So war der Stil nach meinem Sinn / Tyrolisch geschnitzelt."

6. Günter Niggl, *Geschichte der deutschen Autobiographie im 18. Jahrhundert: Theoretische Grundlegung und literarische Entfaltung* (Stuttgart: Metzler, 1977) 65–72, 88.

7. Anne Richardot, *Le rire des lumières* (Paris: Honoré Champion, 2002); Antoine de Baecque, *Les éclats du rire: La culture des rieurs au dix-huitième siècle* (Paris: Calman-Levy, 2000), 23–56.

8. See also the discussion in Dickie, *Cruelty and Laughter*, 1–15.

9. Benjamin, *Gesammelte Schriften*, 5:575.

10. Christian Probst, *Fahrender Heiler und Heilmittelhändler: Medizin von Marktplatz und Landstrasse* (Rosenheim: Rosenheimer, 1992).

11. Explored in Dorinda Outram, "Before Objectivity: Wives, Patronage and Cultural Reproduction in Early Nineteenth-Century French Science," in *Uneasy Careers and Intimate Lives: Women in Science, 1789–1979*, ed. P. Abir-Am and Outram, 19–30 (New Brunswick, NJ: Rutgers University Press, 1987).

12. Burkard von Roda, *Adam Friedrich von Seinsheim, Auftraggeber zwischen Rokoko und Klassizismus: Zur Würzberger und Bamberger Hofkunst anhand der Privatkorrespondenz des Fürstbischofs (1755–1779)* (Neustadt/Aisch: Kommissionsverlag Degener, 1980). Prosch is mentioned beginning on page 48. See also Wilhelm Hoffmann, *Politik des Fürstbischofs von Würzburg und Bamberg, Adam Friedrich Greifen von Seinsheim während des Siebenjährigen Krieges* (Munich, 1903).

13. Samuel John Klingensmith, *The Utility of Splendor: Ceremony, Social Life, and Architecture at the Court of Bavaria, 1600–1800* (Chicago: University of Chicago Press, 1993), 159–69. Prosch is mentioned on page 283.

14. Frances A. Yates, *The Theatre of the World* (Chicago: Routledge and Kegan Paul, 1969).

15. J. van Horne Melton, *The Rise of the Public in Enlightenment Europe* (Cambridge: Cambridge University Press, 2001).

16. Arno Störkel, *Christian Friedrich Carl Alexander: Der letzte Markgraf von Ansbach-Bayreuth* (Ansbach: Weidfeld and Mehl, 1995).

17. Prosch almost certainly read Gleim and Haller in books given him by his patrons (*Leben und Ereignisse des Peter Prosch*, 125–26).

18. "Denn Kinder und die Narren sagen / Was wahr ist, immer net und fein / Und nun, die Wahrheit zu erholen / Will Peter redlich eingestehen / Ein Narr in folio zu sein."

19. Even the great were affected: Goethe, for example, held his house on the Frauenplan in Weimar at his sovereign's grace and favor (Peter J. Schwartz, *After Jena: Goethe's Elective Affinities and the End of the Old Regime* [Lewisburg, PA: Bucknell University Press, 2010], 49–51).

20. Derek Beales, *Joseph II: In the Shadow of Maria Theresa, 1741–1780* (Cambridge: Cambridge University Press, 1987), 319.

21. *Mèmoires d'Hippolyte Clairon, et réflexions sur l'art dramatique* (Paris: F. Buisson, 1799); Störkel, *Christian Friedrich Carl Alexander*.

22. On the significance of private rooms in the Residenz, see Klingensmith, *The Utility of Splendor*.

23. Klingensmith, *The Utility of Splendor*, 115–44.

24. Klingensmith, *The Utility of Splendor*, 159–68.

25. Jost Hermand, ed. *Von deutscher Republik (1775–1795): Texte radicaler Demokraten* (Frankfurt-am-Main: Suhrkamp, 1975), 261–75.

26. Schwartz, *After Jena*, 78–88.

27. *Allgemeine Deutscher Bibliothek* (1790): 295–97.

28. Johann Gottfried Seume, *Mein Leben*, ed. Jörg Drews (1813; Stuttgart, 1991).

29. Johann Gottfried Seume, *Mit der Stempel der Wahrheit* (Leipzig: Insel, 1982), 41.

30. Outram, *The Enlightenment*, 1–2.

31. "Wo der Fürst gnädig ist, ist er nie gerecht, und also immer ein schlechter Fürst. Gnade gehört nur für Verbrecher."

32. Johann Wolfgang von Goethe, *Dichtung und Wahrheit*, Frankfurter Ausgabe, 14:641; Schwartz, *After Jena*, 214–15.

5. Two Deaths

1. Otto G. Schindler, "Harlequin in Bohemia: Pantomime and Opéra Comique at Krumlov Castle under the Princes of Schwarzenberg," *New Theatre Quarterly* 19 (2003): 366–80.

2. Karen Jurs-Munby, "Hanswurst and Herr Ich: Subjection and Abjection in the Enlightenment Censorship of the Comic Figure," *New Theatre Quarterly* 23 (2007): 124–35.

3. Karl Friedrich Flögel, *Geschichte des Grotesk-Komischen: Ein Beitrag zur Geschichte der Menschheit* (Liegnitz: David Siegert, 1788), 38–39. "Chamaleon, der alle Farben annimmt, der in den Handen eines geistigen Mannes die Hauptrolle der Bühne wird. . . . Er ist . . . feig, treu, tätig, lasst sich aber aus Furcht oder Eigennutz in alle Arten von Schelmerei und Betrugereien ein."

4. Cited in Flögel, *Geschichte des Grotesk-Komischen*, 122.

5. Carlo Gozzi, *Useless Memoirs,* trans. John Addington Symonds; ed. Philip Horne (Oxford: Oxford University Press, 1962), 181–82.

6. Karl von Görner, *Der Hans Wurst-Streit in Wien und Joseph von Sonnenfels* (Vienna: Carl Konegen, 1884).

7. Friedrich Nicolai, *Beschreibung einer Reise durch Deutschland und der Schweiz im Jahre 1781,* 12 vols. (Berlin: Nicolai, 1783–96), 4:611, 571–74.

8. Jonathan B. Knudsen, *Justus Möser and the German Enlightenment* (Cambridge: Cambridge University Press, 1986), has no analysis of the *Verteidigung*. Paul M. Haberland, *The Development of Comic Theory in Germany during the Eighteenth Century* (Goppingen: Goppinger Arbeiten zur Germanistik, 1971), 75–80; Justus Möser, *Harlekin oder Verteidigung des Groteske-Komischen* (Bremen: Johann Heinrich Cramer, 1777).

9. Flögel, *Geschichte des Grotesk-Komischen:* "die so tief in der menschlichen Natur gegründet ist, als irgend eine andre; warum will man den der Despotismus einführen, wo sich die menschliche Natur ihm widersetzen kann, und sich widersetzen darf? Das Vergnügen an Grotesque-Komischen findet sich zwar in unaufgeklärten Zeiten sehr häufig, aber sein Dasein ist noch kein Beweis des Mangels der Aufklärung; den man trifft es eben sowohl bei aufgeklärten ganzen Nationen als bei einzelnen Menschen an, denen es gar nicht an Aufklärung fehlt."

10. James van Horn Melton, "From Enlightenment to Revolution: Hertzberg, Schlözer, and the Problem of Despotism in the Late Aufklärung," *Central European History* 12 (1979): 103–23.

11. Gotthold Ephraim Lessing, *Hamburgische Dramaturgie,* piece 18, 30 June 1767.

12. August Wilhelm Schlegel, *Vorlesungen über dramatische Kunst und Literatur* (1846; Heilbronn: Gebrüder Henniger, 1884), 404; Haberland, *The Development of Comic Theory in Germany,* 61–62.

13. Jacob Smith, "Laughing Machines," in *The Sound Studies Reader,* ed. Jonathan Sterne (London: Routledge, 2012).

14. James C. Scott, *Seeing Like a State* (New Haven: Yale University Press, 1998). Building on work by Max Weber, Gerhard Oestreich formulated the concept of social disciplining (see Winfried Schulze, "Gerhard Oestreichs Begriff 'Sozialdisziplinierung' in der Frühen Neuzeit," *Zeitschrift fur historische Forschung* 14 [1987]: 265–302; Peter N. Miller, "Nazis and Neo-Stoics: Otto Brunner and Gerhard Oestreich before and after the Second World War," *Past and Present* 76 [2002]: 144–86; and Gerhard Oestreich, *Geist und Gestalt des frühmodernen Staats: Ausgewählte Aufsätze* [Berlin: Duncker and Humblot, 1969], 179–97).

15. Ernest A. Zitzer, *The Transfigured Kingdom: Sacred Parody and Charismatic Authority at the Court of Peter the Great* (Ithaca, NY: Cornell University Press, 2004); Russell Zguta, "Peter I's 'Most Drunken Synod of Fools and Jesters,'" *Jahrbücher fur Geschichte Osteuropas* 211 (1973): 18–28.

16. Ludwig Tieck, *Der gestiefelte Kater,* ed. and trans. Gerald Gillespie (1795; Austin: University of Texas Press, 1974): "Ich bin ein armer verbannter Flüchtling, ein Mann der vor langer Zeit einmal witzig war, der jetzt dumm geworden ist, und in einem fremden Lande wieder in Dienste getreten, wo man ihn von neuem auf einige Zeit für witzig halt. . . . Meine Landsleute wurden um eine gewisse Zeit so klug, dass sie allen Spass ordentlich beistrafe verboten, wo man mich nur gewahr ward, gab man mir unausstehliche Ekelnamen, als: abgeschmackt, unanständig, bizarr—wer über mich lachte wurde eben so wie ich verfolgt, und so musst' ich in die Verbannung wandern."

17. Flögel, *Geschichte des Grotesk-Komischen,* 31–38.

18. For example, Jean-François Dreux du Radier, *Récréations historiques, critiques, morales et d'érudition: Avec l'histoire des fous en titre d'office,* 2 vols. (Paris: Robustel, 1767); Jean-Benigne-Lucotte du Tilliot, *Memoires pour server à l'histoire de la fête des fous qui se faisoit autrefois dans plusieurs églises* (Lausanne: Marc-Michel Bousquet, 1741). Du Tilliot's work formed the basis of the *Encyclopédie* article by the Chevalier de Jaucourt on the "fête des fous."

19. Rainer A. Müller, *Fürstenhof in der Frühen Neuzeit* (Munich: Oldenbourg, 1984).

20. Flögel, *Geschichte des Grotesk-Komischen,* 14. "Wir wollen das Amt, das ihm anvertraut war, ganzlich aufheben und abschaffen, damit das Andenken davon unter den Menschen ganzlich getilgt werde."

21. Clemens Amelunxen, *Zur Rechtsgeschichte der Hofnarren* (Berlin: De Gruyter, 1991).

22. Gerhardt Petrat, *Die letzten Narren und Zwerge bei Hofe: Reflexionen zu Herrschaft und Moral in der Frühen Neuzeit* (Bochum: Dieter Winkler, 1998).

23. R. O. Bucholz, *The Augustan Court: Queen Anne and the Decline of Court Culture* (Stanford: Stanford University Press, 1993).

24. Linda Colley, *Britons: Forging the Nation, 1707–1837* (New Haven: Yale University Press, 1992), 195–228.

25. Samuel John Klingensmith, *The Utility of Splendor: Ceremony, Social Life and Architecture at the Court of Bavaria, 1600–1800* (Chicago: University of Chicago Press, 1993), 165–66.

26. See the analysis by Flögel, *Geschichte des Grotesk-Komischen*, 26.

27. Flögel, *Geschichte des Grotesk-Komischen*, 5, 23.

28. Flögel, *Geschichte des Grotesk-Komischen*, 77.

29. Flögel, *Geschichte des Grotesk-Komischen*, 27–28.

30. For the cameralists, see André Wakefield, *The Disordered Police State: German Cameralism as Science and Practice* (Chicago: University of Chicago Press, 2009).

31. Flögel, *Geschichte des Grotesk-Komischen*, 29.

32. Flögel, *Geschichte des Grotesk-Komischen*, 27. For whole letter, see 27ff.

33. Prosch, *Leben und Ereignisse des Peter Prosch* (1964), 76.

34. This is a lively field of inquiry, and only a few works can be mentioned here: John Brewer, *The Pleasures of the Imagination: English Culture in the Eighteenth Century* (Chicago: University of Chicago Press, 1997); Dena Goodman, *The Republic of Letters: A Cultural History of the French Enlightenment* (Ithaca, NY: Cornell University Press, 1994); Louise E. Robbins, *Elephant Slaves and Pampered Parrots: Exotic Animals in Eighteenth-Century Paris* (Baltimore: Johns Hopkins University Press, 2002); Robert Darnton, *The Kiss of Lamourette: Reflections in Cultural History* (New York: Norton, 1990); Maxine Berg, *Luxury and Pleasure in Eighteenth-Century Britain* (Oxford: Oxford University Press, 2005); and John E. Crowley, *The Invention of Comfort: Sensibility and Design in Early Modern Britain and Early America* (Baltimore: Johns Hopkins University Press, 2001).

35. Henry Mackenzie, *The Man of Feeling* (London: T. Cadell, 1771); Samuel Richardson, *Sir Charles Grandison* (London: Samuel Richardson, 1753); Jean-Jacques Rousseau, *Julie, ou la nouvelle Héloïse* (Amsterdam: Marc Michel Rey, 1761); Johann Wolfgang von Goethe, *Die Leiden des jungen Werthers* (Leipzig: Weygandischen Buchhandlung, 1774).

36. Denis Diderot, *Supplément au voyage de Bougainville* (Paris: Chez Saillant et Nyon, 1796).

37. Pagden, *The Enlightenment and Why It Still Matters* (Oxford: Oxford University Press, 2013).

38. Pagden, *The Enlightenment and Why It Still Matters*, 74.

39. Pagden, *The Enlightenment and Why It Still Matters*, 151.

40. Pagden, *The Enlightenment and Why It Still Matters*, 268.

41. Pagden, *The Enlightenment and Why It Still Matters*, 300.

42. Pagden, *The Enlightenment and Why It Still Matters*, 302.

43. Pagden, *The Enlightenment and Why It Still Matters*, 313–14.

44. Pagden, *The Enlightenment and Why It Still Matters*, 328.

45. Pagden, *The Enlightenment and Why It Still Matters*, 336; Alisdair MacIntyre, *After Virtue: A Study in Moral Theory* (Notre Dame, IN: Notre Dame University Press, 1981).

46. Pagden, *The Enlightenment and Why It Still Matters*, 336.

47. Pagden, *The Enlightenment and Why It Still Matters*, 272.

48. Qtd. in Outram, *The Enlightenment*, 66.

49. Dorinda Outram, "The Enlightenment Our Contemporary," in *The Sciences in Enlightenment Europe*, ed. William Clark, Jan Golinski, and Simon Schaffer, 32–42 (Chicago: University of Chicago Press, 1999).

50. Dickie, *Cruelty and Laughter*.

51. Ernst Bloch, *Spüren* (Frankfurt-am-Main: Suhrkamp, 1959).

Conclusion

1. For another such attempt, see H. C. Erik Midelfort, *Exorcism and the Enlightenment: Johann Joseph Gassner and the Demons of Eighteenth-Century Germany* (New Haven: Yale University Press, 2005).

2. See Joachim Whaley, *Germany and the Holy Roman Empire: The Peace of Westphalia to the Dissolution of the Reich, 1648–1806* (Oxford: Oxford University Press, 2012).

3. Waltraud Müller, *Zum Wohlfahrt der gemeinen Wesens: Ein Beitrag zur Bevölkerungs- und Sozialpolitik Max III Josephs (1745–1777)* (Munich: Oldenbourg, 1984); Störkel, *Christian Friedrich Carl Alexander*; Eberhard Straub, *Representatio Maiestatis oder churbayerische Freudenfeste: Die hofischen Feste in der Münchner Residenz vom 16. bis zum Ende des 18. Jahrhunderts* (Munich: Stadtarchives München, 1969); Andrea Hofmeister-Hunger, " 'Provincial' Political Culture in the Holy Roman Empire: The Franconian Margravates of Ansbach-Bayreuth," in *The Transformation of Political Culture in England and Germany in the Later Eighteenth Century*, ed. Eckhart Hellmuth (Oxford: Oxford University Press, 1990), 149–64.

4. Outram, *The Enlightenment*, 2–3.

5. Jean Starobinski, *Jean-Jacques Rousseau: La transparence et l'obstacle* (Paris: Plon, 1957).

6. Frederick to Jourdan, 28 November 1740, in *Oeuvres de Frédéric le Grand*, 29 vols., ed. Johann David Erdmann Preuss (Berlin: Decker, 1846–57): 6:72: "C'est bien payer un fou; jamais bouffon de grand seigneur n'eût de pareils gages."

7. James Beattie, *Essays: On the Nature and Immutability of Truth, in Opposition to Sophistry and Scepticism; On Poetry and Music, as They Affect the Mind; on Laughter and Ludicrous Composition; On the Utility of Classical Learning* (Edinburgh: W. Creech, 1776).

8. Smith, "Laughing Machines."

Bibliography

Primary Sources

A Sancta Clara, Abraham. *Wunderlicher Traum von einem grossen Narrennest.* Salzburg: Melchior Haan, 1703.

Adelung, Johann Christoph. *Grammatisch-Kritisches Wörterbuch der Hochdeutschen Mundart mit beständiger Vergleichung der übrigen Mundarten besonders aber der Oberdeutschen.* 4 vols. Leipzig: A. Pichler, 1796.

Anonymous. Review of *Leben und Ereignisse des Peter Prosch,* by Peter Prosch. *Allgemeine Deutsche Bibliothek* 27 (1790): 295–97.

Beattie, James, *Essays: On the Nature and Immutability of Truth, in Opposition to Sophistry and Scepticism; On Poetry and Music, as They Affect the Mind; on Laughter and Ludicrous Composition; On the Utility of Classical Learning.* Edinburgh: W. Creech, 1776.

Dreux du Radier, Jean-François, *Récréations historiques, critiques, morales et d'érudition: Avec l'histoire des fous en titre d'office.* 2 vols. Paris: Robustel, 1767.

Ebeling, Friedrich Wilhelm. *Flögels Geschichte des Grotesk-Komischen, neu bearbeitet und erweitert.* Leipzig: Adolf Werl, 1862.

———. *Zur Geschichte der Hofnarren.* Leipzig: J. Lehmann, 1864.

Erasmus of Rotterdam. *Adages.* 1500. Edited by William Barker. Toronto: Toronto University Press, 2001.

———. *Praise of Folly and Letter to Martin Dorp.* 1511. London: Penguin, 1971.

Fassmann, David. *Das glorwürdigste Leben und Thaten Friedrich August des Grossen, Königs in Pohlen und Churfürstens zu Sachsen.* Hamburg and Frankfurt, 1733.

———. *Der gelehrte Narr, oder, Gantz natürliche Abbildung solcher Gelehrten, die da vermeynen alle Gelehrsamkeit und Wissenschaften verschlucket zu haben . . . nebst einer lustigen Dedication und sonderbaren Vorrede.* Freiburg: published by the author, 1729.

———. *Leben und Thaten des Allerdurchlauchtigsten und Großmächtigsten Königs von Preussen Friderici Wilhelmi, Biß auf gegenwärtige Zeit aufrichtig beschrieben.* 4 vols. Hamburg and Berlin, 1735.

Fielding, Henry. *The History of the Adventures of Joseph Andrews.* London: A. Millar, 1742.

———. *The History of Tom Jones, A Foundling.* London: A. Millar, 1749.

Flögel, Karl Friedrich. *Geschichte der Hofnarren.* Leipzig: David Siegert, 1789.

———. *Geschichte der komischen Literatur.* 2 vols. Liegnitz and Leipzig: David Siegert, 1784.

———. *Geschichte des Grotesk-Komischen: Ein Beitrag zur Geschichte der Menschheit.* Liegnitz and Leipzig: David Siegert, 1788.

———. *Geschichte des menschlichen Verstandes.* 3rd. ed. Liegnitz: David Siegert, 1776.

Friedrich II, King of Prussia. *Oeuvres.* 29 vols. Edited by Johann David Erdmann Preuß. Berlin: Decker, 1845–57.

Friedrich Wilhelm I, Der Soldatenkönig als Maler: Austellung 8. Juli bis 14. Oktober 1990: Turmgalerie der Orangerie in Sans Souci. Potsdam, Märkischer Verlag, 1990.

Gozzi, Carlo. *Useless Memoirs.* 1797. Translated by John Addington Symonds. Edited by Philip Horne. Oxford: Oxford University Press, 1962.

König, Anton Balthasar. *Biographisches Lexikon aller Helden und Militairpersonen: welche sich in Preussischen Diensten berühmt gemacht haben.* Berlin: A. Wever, 1788.

———. *Leben und Thaten Jakob Paul Freiherrn von Gundling, Königl. Preussischen Geheimen Krieges-Kammer-Ober-Appellations-und Kammergerichts-Raths, wie auch Zeremonienmeisters und Präsidenten bei der Königl. Societät der Wissenschaften etc., eines höchst seltsamen und abenteuerlichen Mannes. Aus bisher unbekannten Nachrichten, und seltenen gedruckten Schriften gezogen und anschaulich gemacht.* Berlin: Friedrich Francke, 1795.

Leibniz, Gottfried Wilhelm. *The Art of Controversies.* Edited by Marcelo Dascal et al. Dordrecht: Springer, 2006.

Morgenstern, Salomon Jacob. *Ius Publicum Imperii Russorum.* Halle, 1737.

———. *Neueste Staats-Geographie, wo jedes Landes natürlicher, politischer Kirchen-und Schulen-Staat genau abgeschildert.* Jena: Johann Adam Melchior, 1735.

———. *Ueber Friedrich Wilhelm I: Ein nachgelassenes Werk, vom Hofrath und Professor Morgenstern, Mitglied des Tabaks-Kollegii Friedrich Wilhelm I.* Braunschweig, 1793.

———. *Vorschlag wie die Zeitungen mit Nutzen zu erläutern. Wobey seine Winter-Arbeit zugleich bekannt machen wollen M. Salomon Jacob Morgenstern.* Halle, 1736.

Moser, Johann Jakob. *Lebens-Geschichte Johann Jacob Mosers, von ihm selbst beschrieben.* N.p., 1768.

Möser, Justus. *Harlekin oder Verteidigung des Groteske-Komischen.* Bremen: Johann Heinrich Cramer, 1777.

Nicolai, Friedrich. "Fortsetzung der Berlinische Nachlese." *Berlinische Monatschrift* 41 (1807): 257–97.

Prosch, Peter. *Leben und Ereignisse des Peter Prosch, eines Tyrolers von Ried im Zillerthal, oder das wunderbare Schicksal geschrieben in den Zeiten der Aufklärung.* 1789. Edited by Karl Pörnbacher. Munich: Kosel, 1964.

Schmidt, James, ed. *What Is Enlightenment? Eighteenth-Century Answers and Twentieth-Century Questions.* Berkeley: University of California Press, 1996.

Sieber, Siegfried, ed. *Johann Michael von Loen: Goethes Großoheim (1694–1776): Sein Leben, sein Wirken und eine Auswahl aus seinen Schriften.* Leipzig: Historia, 1922.

Sterne, Laurence. *The Life and Opinions of Tristram Shandy.* London: R. & J. Dodsley, 1759).

Thomasius, Christian, "Ob und wie weit Comödianten/Pickelheringe/item Scharfrichters Söhne ad Dignitates Academicus zuzulassen; item ob das Papiermachen denselben praejudiciere?" In *Ernsthaffte aber doch muntere und vernünfftige Thomasische Gedanken und Erinnerungen über allerhand außerlesene Juristische Händel,* by Thomasius. Halle: Zu finden in den Rengerischen Buchhandlung, 1721. HAB call number L242^b 4° Helmstedt.

Tieck, Johann Ludwig, *Der gestiefelte Kater.* 1795. Edited by Gerald Gillispie. Austin: University of Texas Press, 1974.

Tilliot, Jean-Bénigne Lucotte du. *Memoires pour servir à l'histoire de la fête des fous qui se faisoit autrefois dans plusieurs églises.* Lausanne and Geneva: Marc-Michel Bousquet, 1741.

Voltaire, François-Marie Arouet de. *Candide, ou de l'optimisme.* Geneva: Cramer, 1759.

von Loen, Michael. *Des Herrn von Loen gesammelte kleine Schriften.* Edited by Johann Caspar Schneider. Frankfurt: Philip Heinrich Huttern, 1751–52.

Weber, Friedrich Christian, *Das veränderte Ruszland . . . mit einem accuraten Land-Charte und Kupferstichen versehen.* 2 vols. Frankfurt and Leipzig: Nicolas Forster, 1739–44.

Zedler, Johann Heinrich. *Grosses vollständiges Universal-Lexikon aller Wissenschaften und Künste, Welche bißhero durch menschlichen Verstand und Witz erfunden und verbessert worden . . .* 64 vols. Halle and Leipzig: Zedler, 1732–50.

Secondary Sources

Aiton, E. J. *Leibniz: A Biography.* Boston: Adam Hilger, 1985.

Amelunxen, Clemens. *Zur Rechtsgeschichte der Hofnarren.* Berlin: De Gruyter, 1991.

Appiah, Kwame Anthony. *The Honor Code: How Moral Revolutions Happen.* New York: Norton, 2010.

Arden, Heather. *Fools' Plays: A Study of Satire and the Sottie.* Cambridge: Cambridge University Press, 1980.

———. "Le fou, la sottie, et Le Neveu de Rameau." *Dix-huitième siècle* 7 (1975): 209–23.

Ash, Eric H. "Expertise and Practical Knowledge in the Early Modern State." *Osiris* 25 (2010): 1–24.

Asper, Helmut G. *Hanswurst: Studien zum Lustigmacher auf der Berufsschauspielerbühne in Deutschland im 17. und 18. Jahrhundert.* Emsdetten: Lechte, 1980.

Baecque, Antoine de. *Les éclats du rire: La culture des rieurs au dix-huitième siècle.* Paris: Calman-Levy, 2000.

Baker, Steve. *Picturing the Beast: Animals, Identity and Representation.* Manchester: Manchester University Press, 1993.

Barenboim, Daniel, and Edward Said. *Parallels and Paradoxes: Explorations in Music and Society.* New York: Vintage, 2004.

Barnard, F. M., ed. *Herder on Social and Political Culture.* Cambridge: Cambridge University Press, 1969.

Basch, Sophie, and Pierre Chauvin, eds. *Pitres et pantins: Transformations du masque comique de l'Antiquité au théâtre d'ombres.* Paris: PUPS, 2007.

Baumgart, Peter. "Absolutismus, ein Mythos? Aufgeklärter Absolutismus ein Widerspruch? Reflexionen zu einem kontroversen Thema gegenwärtiger Frühneuzeit Forschung." *Zeitschrift für historische Forschung* 27 (2000): 573–91.

———. "Der Adel Brandenburg-Preußens im Urteil der Hohenzollern des 18. Jahrhunderts." In Endres, *Adel,* 141–61.

Beck, Friedrich, and Julius H. Schoeps, eds. *Der Soldatenkönig: Friedrich Wilhelm I in seiner Zeit.* Potsdam: Verlag für Berlin-Brandenburg, 2003.

Benjamin, Walter. *Gesammelte Schriften.* Edited by Rolf Tiedemann. 12 vols. Frankfurt-am-Main: Suhrkamp, 1980.

Berger, John, *About Looking.* London: Writers and Readers, 1980.

Bertrand, Dominique, *Dire le rire à l'âge classique: Représenter pour mieux controller.* Aix-en-Provence: Publications de l'Université de Provence, 1995.

Billington, Sandra. *The Social History of the Fool.* London: Harvester, 1984.

Blanning, Tim. *The Culture of Power and the Power of Culture: Old Regime Europe 1660–1789.* Oxford: Oxford University Press, 2002.

———. *Frederick the Great, King of Prussia.* New York: Random House, 2016.

Bluche, François. *Louis XIV.* Paris: Fayard, 1987.

Breger, Herbert, "Närrische Weisheit und weise Narrheit in Erfindung des Barocks." *Ästhetik und Kommunikation* 45–46 (1981): 114–22.

Brewer, Edward V. "Lessing and the Corrective Virtue in Comedy." *Journal of English and Germanic Philology* 26 (1927):1–23.

Brewer, John, and Eckhart Hellmuth, eds. *Rethinking Leviathan: The Eighteenth-Century State in Britain and Germany.* Oxford: Oxford University Press, 1999.

Bucholz, R. O. *The Augustan Court: Queen Anne and the Decline of Court Culture.* Stanford: Stanford University Press, 1993.

Burke, Peter. "The Demise of Royal Mythologies." In *Iconography, Propaganda and Legitimation,* edited by Allan Ellenius. Oxford: Oxford University Press, 1998.

Canel, A. *Recherches historiques sur les fous des rois de France et accessoirement sur l'emploi du fou en general.* Paris: Alphonse Lemarre, 1873.

Cassirer, Ernst. *The Myth of the State.* Hamburg: Felix Meiner, 2007.

Chew, Samuel C. *The Pilgrimage of Life.* New Haven: Yale University Press, 1962.

Clark, William. *Academic Charisma and the Origins of the Research University.* Chicago: University of Chicago Press, 2006.

Classen, Albrecht. "Laughter as the Ultimate Epistemological Vehicle in the Hands of Till Eulenspiegel." *Neophilologus* 92 (2008): 471–89.

Cleve, John Walter van. *Harlequin Besieged: The Reception of Comedy in Germany during the Early Enlightenment.* Berne: Lang, 1980.

Colie, Rosalie L. *Paradoxia Epidemica: The Renaissance Tradition of Paradox.* Princeton: Princeton University Press, 1966.

Colley, Linda. *Britons: Forging the Nation.* New Haven: Yale University Press, 1992.

Cox, Harvey. *The Feast of Fools: A Theological Essay on Festivity and Fantasy.* Cambridge: Harvard University Press, 1969.

Czernis-Ryl, Eva. "The Golden Years of Meissen Porcelain and Saxon Jesters: The Schmiedel Bust in Australia." *Mitteilungsblatt Keramik-Freunde der Schweiz* 104 (1989): 5–11.

Czok, Karl. "Der Adel in Kursachsen und August der Starke." In Rudolf Endres, ed., *Adel,* 119–40.

———. *August der Starke und seine Zeit: Kurfürst von Sachsen, König in Polen.* Munich: Piper, 2006.

———. "Zur Regierungspraxis Augusts des Starken." In Vogler, *Herrscher,* 186–201.

Darnton, Robert. *The Great Cat Massacre and Other Episodes in French Cultural History.* London: Penguin, 1985.

Dharendorf, Ralph. "The Intellectual and Society: The Social Function of the Fool in the Twentieth Century." In *On Intellectuals: Theoretical Studies, Case Studies,* edited by Philip Rieff. Garden City, NY: Doubleday, 1969.

Dickie, Simon. *Cruelty and Laughter: Forgotten Comic Literature and the Unsentimental Eighteenth Century.* Chicago: University of Chicago Press, 2011.

Diderot, Denis, *Le Neveu de Rameau.* 1761. London: Penguin, 1966.

Doran, John. *The History of Court Fools.* London: Bentley, 1858.

Dorwart, Reinhold August. *The Administrative Reforms of Frederick William I of Prussia.* Cambridge: Harvard University Press, 1953.

Douglas, Mary. Natural *Symbols.* London: Barrie and Jenkins, 1973.

Dreyfürst, Stephanie. *Stimmen aus dem Jenseits: David Fassmanns historisch-politisches Journal "Gespräche in dem Reiche der Todten."* Berlin: De Gruyter, 2014.

Duindam, Jeroen. "Early Modern Court Studies: An Overview and a Proposal." In Völkel and Strohmeyer, *Historiographie an europäischen Höfen,* 37–60.

———. *Myths of Power: Norbert Elias and the Early Modern Court.* Amsterdam: Amsterdam University Press, 1995.

———. *Vienna and Versailles: The Courts of Europe's Dynastic Rivals, 1550–1780.* Cambridge: Cambridge University Press, 2003.

Duncan-Jones, Elsie. "Enid Welsford (1892–1981)." In *Cambridge Women: Twelve Portraits,* edited by Edward Shils and Carmen Blacker, 203–19. Cambridge: Cambridge University Press, 1996.

Dutt, Carsten, and Reinhard Laube, eds. *Zwischen Sprache und Geschichte: Zum Werk Reinhart Kosellecks.* Göttingen: Wallstein, 2013.

Elias, Norbert. *The Court Society.* New York: Pantheon, 1983.

Empson, William. "The Praise of Folly." In *The Structure of Complex Words,* 105–24. London: Chatto and Windus, 1951.

Endres, Rudolf, ed. *Adel in der Frühneuzeit: Ein regionaler Vergleich.* Cologne: Bohlau, 1991.

Ernst, Eva-Maria. *Zwischen Lustigmacher und Spielmacher: Die komische Zentralfigur auf dem Wiener Volkstheater im 18. Jahrhundert.* Münster: Literatur Verlag, 2003.

Espagne, Michel, " '*L'histoire du grotesque et du comique*' de Karl Friedrich Flögel (1729–1788)." In Basch and Chauvin, *Pitres,* 153–68.

Evans, R. J. W. "The Court: A Protean Institution." In *Princes, Patronage and the Nobility: The Court at the Beginning of the Modern Age, ca. 1450–1650,* edited by Ronald G. Asch and Adolf M. Birke. Oxford: Oxford University Press, 1991.

Ferguson, George. *Signs and Symbols in Christian Art.* Oxford: Oxford University Press, 1974.

Fichtner, Fritz. "Darstellungen des kursächsischen Hofnarren J. Fröhlich." *Belvedere: Monatsschrift für Sammler und Kunstfreunde* 8 (1929): 1–24.

Firpo, Luigi. "Ancora a proposito di '*sapere aude.*' " *Rivista storica italiana* 72 (1962): 114–17.

Fors, Hjalmar. *The Limits of Matter: Chemistry, Mining and Enlightenment.* Chicago: University of Chicago Press, 2015.

Frevert, Ute. *Men of Honour: A Social and Cultural History of the Duel.* Cambridge: Polity, 1995.

Füssel, Marian. " 'Charlataneria Eruditorum': Zur sozialen Semantik des gelehrten Betrugs im 17. und 18. Jahrhundert." *Berichte zur Wissenschaftsgeschichte* 27 (2004): 119–35.

———. "Die Experten, die Verkehrten: Gelehrtensatire als Expertenkritik in der Frühen Neuzeit." In *Wissen, massgeschneidert: Experten und Expertenkulturen im Europa der Vormoderne,* edited by Björn Reich, Frank Rexroth, and Matthias Roick. Munich: Oldenbourg, 2012.

———. *Gelehrtenkultur als symbolische Praxis: Rang, Ritual und Konflikt an der Universität der Frühen Neuzeit.* Darmstadt: Wissenschaftliche Buchgesellschaft, 2006.

Gestrich, Andreas. *Absolutismus und Öffentlichkeit: Politische Kommunikation in Deutschland zu Beginn des 18. Jahrhunderts.* Göttingen: Vandenhoeck and Ruprecht, 1994.

———. "The Public Sphere and the Habermas Debate." *German History* 24 (2006): 413–29.

Glötzner, Johannes. *Die Lesegewohnheiten des sächsischen Hofnarren Joseph Fröhlich (1694–1757).* Munich: Edition Enhuber, 2007.

Goffman, Erving. "The Nature of Deference and Demeanor." *American Anthopologist* 58 (1956): 473–502.

Görner, Karl von. *Der Hans Wurst-Streit in Wien und Joseph von Sonnenfels.* Vienna: Carl Konegen, 1884.

Haas, A. "Hofnarren am pommerschen Herzogshof." *Archiv für Kulturgeschichte* 3 (1905): 32–50.

Haberland, Paul M. *The Development of Comic Theory in Germany during the Eighteenth Century.* Göppingen: Göppinger Arbeiten zur Germanistik, 1971.

Habermas, Jürgen. *The Structural Transformation of the Public Sphere: An Enquiry into a Category of Bourgeois Society.* 1960. Cambridge: MIT Press, 1989.

Hazard, Paul. *La crise de la conscience européenne (1680–1715).* Paris: Boivin, 1935. Translated by J. Lewis May as *The Crisis of the European Mind 1680–1715.* New York: New York Review Books, 2013.

Held, Wieland. *Der Adel und August der Starke: Konflikt und Konfliktaustrag zwischen 1694 und 1707 in Kursachsen.* Cologne: Böhlau, 1999.

Henshall, Nicholas. *The Myth of Absolutism: Change and Continuity in Early Modern European Monarchy.* London: Longman, 1992.

Hofmann, Wilhelm. *Politik des Fürstbischofs von Würzburg und Bamberg, Adam Friedrich Greifen von Seinsheim während des Siebenjährigen Krieges.* Munich, 1903.

Hofmeister-Hunger, Andrea. " 'Provincial' Political Culture in the Holy Roman Empire: The Franconian Margravates of Ansbach-Bayreuth." In *The Transformation of Political Culture in England and Germany in the Later Eighteenth-Century,* edited by Eckhart Hellmuth, 149–64. Oxford: Oxford University Press, 1990.

Jal, Augustin. "Fous en titre d'office." In *Dictionnaire critique de biographie et d'histoire,* 596–605. Paris: Plon, 1872.

Jones, Simon. "Flights of Fancy: Count Brühl and the Swan Service." *Antiques and Collecting Magazine* 105 (2000): 128–66.

Jost, Hermand, ed. *Von Deutscher Republik 1775–1795: Texte radikaler Demokraten.* Frankfurt-am-Main: Suhrkamp, 1968.

Jurs-Munby, Karen. "Hanswurst and Herr Ich: Subjection and Abjection in Enlightenment Censorship of the Comic Figure." *New Theatre Quarterly* 23 (2007): 124–35.

Kaiser, Michael, and Andreas Pecar, eds. *Der Zweite Mann im Staat: Oberste, Amtsträger und Favoriten im Umkreis der Reichsfürsten in der Frühen Neuzeit.* Berlin: Duncker and Humblot, 2003.

Kantorowicz, Ernst Hartwig. "Oriens Augusti: Lever du Roi." *Dumbarton Oaks Papers* 17 (1963): 117–77.

Klapp, Orin E. "The Fool as a Social Type." *American Journal of Sociology* 55 (1950): 157–62.

Klingensmith, Samuel John. *The Utility of Splendor: Ceremony, Social Life, and Architecture at the Court of Bavaria, 1600–1800.* Chicago: University of Chicago Press, 1993.

Kloosterhuis, Jürgen, and Lothar Lambacher. *Katte: Ordre und Kriegsartikel: Aktenanalytische und militärhistorische Aspekte einer "facheusen" Geschichte.* 2nd. ed. Berlin: Duncker and Humblot, 2011.

———. *Kriegsgericht in Köpenick! Anno 1730: Kronprinz-Katte-Königswort.* Berlin: Geheimes Staatsarchiv Preussischer Kulturbesitz, 2011.

Knudsen, Jonathan B. *Justus Möser and the German Enlightenment.* Cambridge: Cambridge University Press, 1986.

Koerner, Lisbet. *Linnaeus, Nature and Nation.* Cambridge: Harvard University Press, 1999.

Košenina, Alexander. *Der gelehrte Narr: Gelehrtensatire seit der Aufklärung.* Göttingen: Wallstein, 2003.

———. "Gelehrte Narren: Verteidigung des unverwalteten Denkens." *Zeitschrift für Ideengeschichte* 4 (2010): 32–36.

Kruedener, Jürgen von. *Die Rolle des Hofes im Absolutismus.* Stuttgart: Fischer, 1973.

Kühlmann, Wilhelm. *Gelehrtenrepublik und Fürstenstaat: Entwicklung und Kritik des deutschen Späthumanismus in der Literatur des Barockzeitalters.* Tübingen: M. Niemeyer, 1982.

Laden, Sonja. "Recuperating the Archive: Anecdotal Evidence and Questions of Historical Realism." *Poetics Today* 25 (2004): 1–28.

Lehmann, Hannelore, "Wurde Jacob Paul Freiherr von Gundling (1673–1731), in einem Sarg begraben, der die Gestalt eines Weinfasses hatte?" *Jahrbuch für Berlin-Brandenburgische Kirchengeschichte* 58 (1991): 199–217.

Leineweber, Richard Otto. *Salomon Jacob Morgenstern: Ein Biograph Friedrich Wilhelms I.* Leipzig: Duncker and Humblot, 1899.

Lever, Maurice. *Le sceptre et la marotte: Histoire des fous de cour.* Paris: Fayard, 1983.

Levi-Strauss, Claude. *Totemism.* Translated by Rodney Needham. London: Penguin, 1973.

Luebke, David Martin. "Serfdom and Honor in Eighteenth-Century Germany." *Social History* 18 (1993): 143–61.

Luh, Jürgen. "Vom Pagen zum Premierminister: Graf Heinrich von Brühl (1700–1763) und die Gunst der sächsisch-polnischen Kurfürsten und Könige August II und August III." In Kaiser and Pecar, *Der Zweite Mann im Staat,* 121–35.

Marschke, Benjamin. *Absolutely Pietist: Patronage, Factionalism and State-Building in the Early Eighteenth-Century Prussian Army Chaplaincy.* Tübingen: Max Niemeyer, 2005.

———. "The Crown Prince's Brothers and Sisters: Succession and Inheritance Problems and Solutions among the Hohenzollerns from the Great Elector to Frederick the Great." In *Sibling Relations and the Transformations of European Kinship, 1300–1900,* edited by Christopher H. Johnson and David Warren Sabean. New York: Berghahn, 2011.

———. "Princes' Power, Aristocratic Norms, and Personal Eccentricities: *Le caractère bizarre* of Frederick William I of Prussia (1713–1740)." In *The Holy Roman Empire, Reconsidered,* edited by Jason Philip Coy, Benjamin Marschke, and David Warren Sabean, 49–70. New York: Berghahn, 2010.

———. "Von dem am Königl. Preussischen Hofe abgeschafften *Ceremoniel*: Monarchical Representation and Court Ceremony in Frederick William I's Prussia." In *Orthodoxies and Heterodoxies in Early Modern Germany: Order and Creativity,*

1550–1750, edited by Randolph C. Head and Daniel Christensen, 227–52. Leiden: Brill Academic, 2007.

Martens, Wolfgang. *Die Botschaft der Tugend: Die Aufklärung im Spiegel der deutschen moralischen Wochenschriften.* Stuttgart: Metzler, 1968.

Marti, Hanspeter. "Grenzen der Denkfreiheit in Dissertationen des frühen 18. Jahrhunderts." In *Die Praktiken der Gelehrsamkeit in der Frühen Neuzeit,* edited by Helmut Zedelmaier and Martin Mulsow, 295–306. Tübingen: De Gruyter, 2001.

Meinecke, Friedrich. *Die Idee der Staatsräson in der neueren Geschichte.* 1923. Munich: R. Oldenbourg, 1960.

Melton, James van Horne. "From Enlightenment to Revolution: Hertzberg, Schlözer, and the Problem of Despotism in the Late Aufklärung." *Central European History* 12 (1979): 103–23.

———. *The Rise of the Public in Enlightenment Europe.* Cambridge: Cambridge University Press, 2001.

Mezger, Werner. *Narrenidee und Fastnachtsbrauch.* Konstanz: Universitätsverlag, 1991.

Middelton, W. E. Knowles. "What Did Charles II Call the Fellows of the Royal Society?" *Notes and Records of the Royal Society of London* 32 (1977–78): 13–16.

Midelfort, H. C. Erik. *Exorcism and Enlightenment: Johann Joseph Gassner and the Demons of Eighteenth-Century Germany.* New Haven: Yale University Press, 2014.

Miller, Peter N. "Nazis and Neo-Stoics: Otto Brunner and Gerhard Oestreich before and after the Second World War." *Past and Present* 76 (2002): 144–86.

Mitterer, Felix. *Das wunderbare Schicksal aus dem Leben des Hoftyrolers Peter Prosch: Ein Theaterstück und sein historischer Hintergrund.* Innsbruck: Haymon-Verlag, 1992.

Möller, Horst. *Vernunft und Kritik: Deutsche Aufklärung im 17. und 18. Jahrhundert.* Frankfurt-am-Main: Suhrkamp, 1986.

Moser, Dietz-Rüdiger. *Fastnacht-Fasching-Karneval: Das Fest der "Verkehrten Welt."* Graz: Styria, 1986.

———, ed. *Narren, Schellen und Marotten: Elf Beiträge zur Narrenidee.* Remscheid: Ute Kierdorf, 1984.

Moser-Rath, Elfriede, *Lustige Gesellschaft: Schwank und Witz des 17. und 18. Jahrhunderts in kultur- und sozialgeschichtlichem Kontext.* Stuttgart: Metzler, 1984.

Mulkay, Michael. *On Humor: Its Nature and Place in Modern Society.* Oxford: Basil Blackwell, 1988.

Müller, Rainer A. *Fürstenhof in der Frühen Neuzeit.* Munich: Oldenbourg, 1995.

Müller, Waltraud. *Zur Wohlfahrt des gemeinen Wesens: Ein Beitrag zur Bevölkerungs- und Sozialpolitik Max III Josephs (1745–1777).* Munich: Oldenbourg, 1984.

Mulsow, Martin, *Die unanständige Gelehrtenrepublik: Wissen, Libertinage und Kommunikation in der Frühen Neuzeit.* Stuttgart: Metzler, 2007.

———. *Prekäres Wissen: Eine andere Ideengeschichte der Frühen Neuzeit.* Berlin: Suhrkamp, 2012.

Neugebauer, Wolfgang. "Staatshistoriographen und Staatshistoriographie in Brandenburg und Preussen seit der Mitte des 17 Jahrhunderts." In *Historiographie an europäischen Höfen: Studien zum Hof als Produktionsort von Geschichtsschreibung und historischer Repräsentation,* edited by Markus Völkel and Arno Strohmeyer, 139–54. Berlin: Duncker and Humblot, 2009.

Nigg, Walter. *Der Christliche Narr.* Zürich: Artemis, 1956.

Niggl, Günter. *Die Autobiographie: Zu Form und Geschichte einer literarischen Gattung.* Darmstadt: Wissenschaftliche Buchgesellschaft, 1998.

———. *Geschichte der deutschen Autobiographie im 18. Jahrhundert: Theoretische Grundlegung und literarische Entfaltung.* Stuttgart: Metzler, 1977.

Oestreich, Gerhard. *Neo-Stoicism and the Early Modern State.* Cambridge: Cambridge University Press, 1982.

Ogilvie, Sheilagh C. "The State in Germany: A Non-Prussian View." In *Rethinking Leviathan: The Eighteenth-Century State in Britain and Germany,* ed. John Brewer and Hellmuth Eckhart, 167–202. Oxford: Oxford University Press, 1999.

Otto, Beatrice K. *Fools Are Everywhere.* Chicago: University of Chicago Press, 2001.

Outram, Dorinda. *The Enlightenment.* 3rd ed. Cambridge: Cambridge University Press, 2013.

———. "The Enlightenment Our Contemporary." In *The Sciences in Enlightenment Europe,* edited by William Clark, Jan Golinski and Simon Schaffer, 32–40. Cambridge: Cambridge University Press, 1999.

———. "The Work of the Fool: Enlightenment Encounters with Folly, Laughter and Truth." *Eighteenth-Century Thought* 1 (2003): 281–94.

Pagden, Anthony. *The Enlightenment and Why It Still Matters.* Oxford: Oxford University Press, 2013.

Peltonen, Markku. *The Duel in Early Modern England: Civility, Politeness and Honour.* Cambridge: Cambridge University Press, 2003.

Peppard, Murray. *"Narr" and "Narrheit" (1795–1855): A Study of the Conception and Its Echoes up to 1855.* New Haven: Yale University Press, 1948.

Peters, Edward. "The Desire to Know the Secrets of the World." *Journal of the History of Ideas* 62–63 (2001): 607–8.

Petrat, Gerhardt. *Die letzten Narren und Zwerge bei Höfe: Reflexionen zu Herrschaft und Moral in der Frühen Neuzeit.* Bochum: Dieter Winkler, 1998.

Pinson, Yona. *The Fool's Journey: A Myth of Obsession in Northern Renaissance Art.* Turnhout, Belgium: Brepolis, 2008.

Probst, Christian, *Fahrende Heiler und Heilmittelhändler: Medizin von Marktplatz und Landstrasse.* Rosenheim: Rosenheimer Verlagshaus, 1992.

Ramati, Ayval. "Harmony at a Distance: Leibniz' Scientific Academies." *Isis* 87 (1996): 430–52.

Richardot, Anne. *Le rire des lumières.* Paris: Honoré Champion, 2002.

Roda, Burkard von. *Adam Friedrich von Seinsheim: Auftraggeber zwischen Rokoko und Klassizismus: Zur Würzburger und Bamberger Hofkunst anhand der*

Privatkorrespondenz des Fürstbischofs (1755–1779). Neustadt-Aisch: Kommissions-verlag Degener, 1980.

Rospocher, Massimo, ed. *Beyond the Public Sphere: Opinions, Publics, Spaces in Early Modern Europe*. Bologna: Il Mulino, 2012.

Rückert, Rainer. *Der Hofnarr Joseph Fröhlich 1694–1757: Taschenspieler und Spass-macher am Hofe Augusts des Starken*. Offenbach-am-Main: Edition Volker Huber, 1998.

———. *Meissener Porzellan 1710–1810: Austellung im Bayerischen Nationalmuseum, München: Katalog*. Munich: Hirmer, 1966.

Rule, John C., and Ben S. Trotter. *A World of Paper: Louis XIV, Colbert de Torcy, and the Rise of the Information State*. Montreal: McGill-Queens University Press, 2014.

Rürup, Reinhard. *Johann Jacob Moser: Pietismus und Reform*. Wiesbaden: Franz Steiner, 1965.

Sabrow, Martin. *Herr und Hanswurst: Das tragische Schicksal des Hofgelehrten Jacob Paul von Gundling*. Stuttgart: Deutsche Verlag, 2001.

Sajda, Peter. "Abraham à Sancta Clara: An Aphoristic Encyclopedia of Christian Wisdom." In *Kierkegaard and the Renaissance and Modern Traditions*, 3 vols., edited by Jon Stewart, 2:1–20. Farnham, VT: Ashgate, 2009.

Schädlich, Hans Joachim. *Narrenleben: Roman*. Reinbeck bei Hamburg: Rowohlt, 2015.

Schaffer, Simon. "Wallification: Thomas Hobbes on School Divinity and Experi-mental Pneumatics." *Studies in the History and Philosophy of Science* 19 (1988): 275–98.

Schieder, Theodor. *Friedrich der Große: Ein Königtum der Widersprüche*. Berlin: Ullstein, 1998.

Schindler, Otto G. "Harlequin in Bohemia: Pantomime and Opéra Comique at Krumlov Castle under the Princes of Schwarzenberg." *New Theater Quarterly* 19 (2003): 366–80.

Schneiders, Werner. *Die wahre Aufklärung: Zum Selbstverständnis der deutschen Aufklärung*. Freiburg: Karl Alber, 1974.

Schörle, Eckhart. *Die Verhöflichung des Lachens: Lachgeschichte im 18. Jahrhundert*. Bielefeld: Aisthesis, 2007.

Schulze, Winfried. "Gerhard Oestreichs Begriff 'Sozialdisziplinierung' in der Frühen Neuzeit." *Zeitschrift für historische Forschung* 14 (1987): 265–302.

Schwartz, Peter J. *After Jena: Goethe's Elective Affinities and the End of the Old Re-gime*. Lewisburg, PA: Bucknell University Press, 2010.

Scruton, Roger, and Peter Jones. "Laughter." *Proceedings of the Aristotelian Society. Supplementary Volumes* 56 (1982): 197–228.

Selwyn, Pamela E. *Everyday Life in the German Book Trade: Friedrich Nicolai as Bookseller and Publisher in the Age of Enlightenment, 1750–1810*. University Park: Pennsylvania State University Press, 2000.

Shahar, Galil. *Verkleidungen der Aufklärung: Narrenspiele und Weltanschauung in der Goethezeit*. Göttingen: Wallstein, 2006.

Sheehan, Jonathan, and Dror Wahrman. *Invisible Hands: Self-Organization and the Eighteenth Century.* Chicago: University of Chicago Press, 2015.

Smith, Jacob. "Laughing Machines." In *The Sound Studies Reader,* edited by Jonathan Sterne, chap. 44. London: Routledge, 2012.

Sorkin, David. *The Religious Enlightenment: Protestants, Jews, and Catholics from London to Vienna.* Princeton: Princeton University Press, 2008.

Stagl, Justin. "Die Ehre des Wissenschaftlers." In *Ehre: Archaïsche Momente in der Moderne,* edited by Ludgera Vogt and Arnold Zingerle. Frankfurt-am-Main: Suhrkamp, 1994.

Stefanovska, Malina. "Exemplary or Singular? The Anecdote in Historical Narrative." *SubStance* 38 (2009): 16–30.

Steussy, Frederic. *Eighteenth-Century German Autobiography: The Emergence of Individuality.* New York: Peter Lang, 1996.

Stewart, Frank Henderson. *Honor.* Chicago: University of Chicago Press, 1994.

Störkel, Arno. *Christian Friedrich Carl Alexander: Der letzte Markgraf von Ansbach-Bayreuth* Ansbach: Weidfeld and Mehl, 1995.

Straub, Eberhard. *Representatio Maiestatis oder churbayerische Freudenfeste: Die höfischen Feste in der Münchner Residenz vom 16. bis zum Ende des 18. Jahrhunderts.* Munich: Stadtarchiv München, 1969.

Stuart, Kathy. *Defiled Trades and Social Outcasts: Honor and Ritual Pollution in Early Modern Germany.* Cambridge: Cambridge University Press, 1999.

Tietze-Conrat, Erika. *Dwarfs and Jesters in Art.* New York: Phaidon, 1957.

Trepp, Anne-Charlotte. "The Emotional Side of Men in Late Eighteenth-Century Germany: Theory and Example." *Central European History* 27 (1994): 127–52.

Venturi, Franco. "Contributi ad un dizionario storico: I: Was ist Aufklärung? 'Sapere aude.'" *Rivista storica italiana* 71 (1959): 119–28.

Vierhaus, Rudolf. 'The Prussian Bureaucracy Reconsidered." In *Rethinking Leviathan: The Eighteenth-Century State in Britain and Germany,* edited by John Brewer and Hellmuth Eckhart, 149–65. Oxford: Oxford University Press, 1999.

Vogler, Günther, ed. *Europäischer Herrscher: Ihre Rolle bei der Gestaltung von Politik und Gesellschaft vom 16. bis zum 18. Jahrhundert.* Weimar: Hermann Bohlaus Nachfolger, 1988.

———. "Herrscherpersönlichkeit und Übergangsepoche." In *Europäischer Herrscher: Ihre Rolle bei der Gestaltung von Politik und Gesellschaft vom 16. bis zum 18. Jahrhundert,* by Vogler, 7–17. Weimar: Hermann Bohlaus Nachfolger, 1988.

Völkel, Markus, and Arno Strohmeyer, eds. *Historiographie an europäischen Höfen: Studien zum Hof als Produktionsort von Geschichtsschreibung und historischer Repräsentation.* Berlin: Duncker and Humblot, 2009.

Wahrman, Dror. *The Making of the Modern Self: Identity and Culture in Eighteenth-Century England.* New Haven: Yale University Press, 2004.

Wakefield, André. *The Disordered Police State: German Cameralism as Science and Practice.* Chicago: University of Chicago Press, 2009.

Walker, Mack. *Johann Jakob Moser and the Holy Roman Empire of the German Nation.* Chapel Hill: University of North Carolina Press, 1981.

Walther, Gerrit. "Das Lächeln der Klio." In *Valenzen des Lachens in der Vormoderne (1250–1750)*, edited by Christian Kuhn and Stefan Bießenecker. Bamberg: University of Bamberg Press, 2012.

Wardroper, John. *Jest upon Jest: A Selection from the Jestbooks and Collections of Merry Tales Published from the Reign of Richard III to George III.* London: Routledge and Kegan Paul, 1970.

Watanabe-O'Kelly, Helen. *Court Culture in Dresden from Renaissance to Baroque.* Basingstoke: Palgrave, 2002.

——. "Religion and the Consort: Two Electresses of Saxony and Queens of Poland (1697–1757)." In *Queenship in Europe 1660–1815: The Role of the Consort*, edited by Clarissa Campbell-Orr, 252–75. Cambridge: Cambridge University Press, 2004.

Welsh, Alexander. *What Is Honor? A Question of Moral Imperatives.* New Haven: Yale University Press, 2008.

Welsford, Enid. *The Court Masque: A Study in the Relationship between Poetry and the Revels.* Cambridge: Cambridge University Press, 1927.

——. *The Fool: His Social and Literary History.* London: Faber and Faber, 1935.

Whaley, Joachim, *Germany and the Holy Roman Empire: The Peace of Westphalia to the Dissolution of the Reich, 1648–1806.* Oxford: Oxford University Press, 2012.

Whitfield, Peter. "The Fool's Cap World Map, ca. 1590." In *The Image of the World*, by Whitfield, 78–79. London: British Library, 1994.

Willeford, William. *The Fool and His Sceptre: A Study in Clowns and Jesters and Their Audience.* London: Edward Arnold, 1969.

Williams, Paul V. A., ed. *The Fool and the Trickster: Studies in Honor of Enid Welsford.* Cambridge: Rowman and Littlefield, 1979.

Wilson, John. *Court Wits of the Restoration.* Princeton: Princeton University Press, 1948.

Winterling, Aloys. *Der Hof der Kurfürsten von Köln (1688–1794): Eine Fallstudie zur Bedeutung "absolutistischer" Hofhaltung.* Bonn: Ludwig Rohrscheid, 1986.

Wuthenow, Ralph-Rainer. *Das erinnerte Ich: Europäische Autobiographie im 18. Jahrhundert.* Munich: Beck, 1974.

Yates, Frances A. *The Theatre of the World.* London: Routledge and Kegan Paul, 1969.

Zguta, Russell. "Peter I's 'Most Drunken Synod of Fools and Jesters.'" *Jahrbücher für Geschichte Osteuropas* 211 (1973): 18–28.

Zijderveld, Anton. *Reality in a Looking-Glass: Rationality through an Analysis of Traditional Folly.* London: Routledge and Kegan Paul, 1982.

Zitzer, Ernest A. *The Transfigured Kingdom: Sacred Parody and Charismatic Authority at the Court of Peter the Great.* Ithaca, NY: Cornell University Press, 2004.

Zunkel, Friedrich, "Ehre, Reputation." In *Geschichtliche Grundbegriffe: Historisches Lexikon zur politisch-sozialen Sprache in Deutschland,* 8 vols., edited by Otto Brunner, Werner Conze, and Reinhart Koselleck, 2:1–64. Stuttgart: Klett-Cotta, 1972–97.

Index

Mendelssohn, Moses, 15–16
Merck, Johann Gottfried, 103
middle class: antagonism toward aristocracy of, 103–4; Enlightenment and, 84; rise and self-definition of, 112, 118–19
Migazzi, Christoph Bartholomäus Anton, 92
Mitterer, Felix, 88
Montagu, Mary Wortley, 107–8
Montesquieu, Charles-Louis de Secondat, 35
"moral economy," 35, 38
Morgenstern, Salomon Jacob, 1, 23, 31–32, 41, 46–64, 76; background of, 46–47, 49; costume forced on, 57, 64, 66, 80; debate on reason and folly and, 46, 50, 52–64, 108, 128; on Gundling, 41, 42; historians on, 47; publications by, 46, 47–48, 49, 50; roles of, 47; theses of, 58–59, 61, 63, 96; *Ueber Friedrich Wilhelm I,* 50–52
Moser, Johann Jakob, 54, 55–57, 60, 61
Möser, Justus, 109
Müller, Rainer, 114
multiculturalism, 11
Munich, court of, 18, 90, 97, 115

Narrenfreiheit ("fool's freedom"), 60, 69–70, 127
Neuber, Frederike, 108
New Historicism, 3–4
newspapers: Morgenstern on, 49–50; royal use of, 30–31, 49, 63. See also *Zeitungs-Referent* post
Newton, Isaac, 35
Nicolai, Friedrich, 104, 109
Niggl, Günter, 88

Oestreich, Gerhard, 137n59
Otto, Beatrice, 11–12
owl symbol, 33, 65, 68, 72, 77, 80, 81–82, 84

Pagden, Anthony, 119–23
paradox: anecdotes and, 12; Christian, 10; Enlightenment and, 14, 15–17; fool and, 17–19

patronage system, 90–91, 92, 94
Peter the Great, 8, 113
Petrat, Gerhardt, 114
Polignac, Jules, Duc de, 99
Pöllnitz, Karl Ludwig von, 114
porcelain, 67, 71–72, 75, 84, 96
Potsdam, court of, 18, 43
Procopius, 12
Prosch, Maria Fiechtlein, 91–95, 100–102, 122–23
Prosch, Peter, 1, 5, 19, 47, 86–105, 113, 115–16, 117–20, 122–23, 126–27; background of, 91; children of, 97; as Hanswurst, 106; historians on, 86, 88; *Leben und Ereignisse,* 13, 86, 88–90, 96, 100–102, 104–5, 115; library of, 101; as "other," 101; on his peculiarity (*Seltenheit*), 16, 90; suicide attempt of, 93, 96, 100–101
Pufendorf, Samuel von, 38
public debates, 54, 60, 61–63
public sphere, 62–63, 80, 84–85
Pussman (Frederick I's fool), 60–61
Regensburg, court of, 90, 98
Reinhold, Karl Leonhard, 14, 16
relativism, 11
Richards, I. A., 9
Rousseau, Jean-Jacques, 92, 119, 122, 128
Rückert, Rainer, 67
Rule, John C., 49

Sabrow, Martin, 25, 26–27, 28, 30, 37–39, 43, 47, 126
Saxony, courts of, 18, 19, 20, 62, 65, 68–69, 71, 77, 113, 114, 115, 117
Scheider, Theodor, 24, 29
Schiller, Friedrich, 53
Schlegel, August Wilhelm, 110–12
Schmidt, Jacob, 76
Schmiedl, Gottfried, 68, 71–72
scholar-fool. *See* learned fool topos
sentimental novels, 119
Seume, Johann Gottfried, 103, 104
Shakespeare, William, 3, 9–10, 129
Sheehan, Jonathan, 17

Silenus (and *sileni*), 28, 55, 56, 59, 64, 128
slavery, 17, 119
Socrates, 55, 128
Sonnenfels, Joseph von, 111
Sophia Dorothea of Hanover, 39, 43
state building, 19, 29–30, 63, 120, 127
statists, 48–49
Stein, "Baron" von, 39
Stranitsky, Josef Anton, 111

Tabakskollegium (advisory group):
    Gundling and, 24, 28, 30, 31, 41–42,
    44, 45, 53; Morgenstern and, 47, 49,
    50, 52
table (*Tafel*), 69, 78, 95–96, 103, 115, 127
Tannenburg, Ignaz von, 91, 98
Taxis, Alexander von, 91
taxonomy, 17–18, 82, 128
theater, debates on, 18, 108–11
Thomasius, Christian, 136n26
Tieck, Ludwig, 113, 118
Trotter, Benjamin S., 49

universalism, 11–12, 13, 16, 58
universities, growth of German, 53–54

Vienna, court of, 18, 90, 92, 98, 103
Vierhaus, Rudolf, 20
Voltaire, 128; *Candide,* 34
von Loen, Johann Michael, 25, 35–36, 68

Wahrman, Dror, 17, 27
Walker, Mack, 138
Weber, Friedrich Christian, 8
Weidemann, Georg Moritz, 76
Welsford, Enid, 1, 8–11, 12, 116
Wolff, Christian, 6, 40, 47, 128
Würzburg, court of, 18, 90, 94–95, 97, 101,
    117
Wuthenow, Ralph-Rainer, 88

Zedler, Johann Heinrich, 6, 34
Zeitungs-Referent post, 7, 23, 27, 30, 31, 41,
    42, 43, 46, 49, 50, 75–76
Zöblerin, Eva Christina, 77
Zöllner, Johann Friedrich, 14

Studies in Early Modern German History